Pass Notes

Pass Notes

Edited by Stephen Moss

FOURTH ESTATE · *London*

First published in Great Britain in 1994 by
Fourth Estate Limited
289 Westbourne Grove
London W11 2QA

A catalogue record for this book is available from the British
Library.

ISBN 1–85702–267–X

Typeset by York House Typographic Ltd
Printed in Great Britain by Cox & Wyman Ltd

CONTENTS

Bernard Ingham
Eddie Izzard
Michael Jackson
Jesus Christ
James Joyce
Radovan Karadzic
Paul Keating
Harvey Keitel
Graham Kelly
Charles Kennedy
Kim Il Sung
Hanif Kureishi
Norman Lamont
k d lang
Tim Laurence
Mike Leigh
Jean-Marie le Pen
Bernard-Henri Lévy
Lennox Lewis
Martyn Lewis
Peter Lilley
Viscount Linley
Loch Ness Monster
Louis XVI
Joanna Lumley
Lord Mackay
Madonna
Nigel Mansell
Diego Maradona
Rik Mayall
Sir Patrick Mayhew
Peter Mayle
Paul McCartney
Victor Meldrew
Carlos Menem
Paul Merton
George Michael
Milk Tray Man
General Ratko Mladic
President Moi
John Monks
David Montgomery
Sir Alastair Morton
Kate Moss

Mr Motivator
Mo Mowlam
James Naughtie
Steven Norris
John Osborne
Camille Paglia
Ian Paisley
Andrew Parker-Bowles
Camilla Parker-Bowles
John Patten
Jeremy Paxman
Pablo Picasso
Mary Pierce
Harold Pinter
Raymond Plant
David Platt
Pontius Pilate
Pooh
Michael Portillo
Marjorie Proops
Paul Raymond
John Redwood
Oliver Reed
Lord Rees-Mogg
Sir Bob Reid
Albert Reynolds
Sophie Rhys-Jones
Stella Rimington
Tim Robbins
Katie Roiphe
Salman Rushdie
Ken Russell
Jimmy Savile
Arthur Scargill
Arnold Schwarzenegger
Selina Scott
Will Self
Vikram Seth
Brian Sewell
Nigel Short
Nicholas Soames
George Soros
Ronald Spark
Sir Maxton Spencer MP

Raine Spencer
Serena Stanhope
Evan Steadman
Gloria Steinem
Jocelyn Stevens
Rod Stewart
Sting
Oliver Stone
Sharon Stone
Barbara Streisand
Alan Sugar
The Sultan of Brunei
John Tavener
Graham Taylor
Norman Tebbit
Mark Thatcher
D. M. Thomas
Emma Thompson
Torvill and Dean
Anthony Trollope
Joanna Trollope
Mike Tyson
Gore Vidal
The Virgin Mary
William Waldegrave
Murray Walker
The Warlords
The Duke of
     Westminster
Edith Wharton
James Whitaker
Jimmy White
Doctor Who
William of Orange
Barbara Windsor
Michael Winner
Terry Wogan
Woodrow Wyatt
Boris Yeltsin
Tim Yeo
The Duke of York
Vladimir Zhirinovsky

INTRODUCTION

Pass Notes is a curious phenomenon. It occupies a modest space on page 3 of the *Guardian*'s second section, dealing each day with a person, institution or object in the news. Yet from the start, in October 1992, its impact has been remarkable and it has spawned a host of imitators. Readers seem either to love it or loathe it; happily they seldom ignore it.

Take Jonathan Miller, the well-known director and savant. In an article in the London *Evening Standard* discussing Andrew Neil's contribution (*sic*) to British journalism, he suddenly launched into a tirade against the awfulness of Pass Notes. 'There is no culture in this country any more,' he thundered, lumping it together with other journalistic 'pollutants'. Pass Notes has not yet had an opportunity to return fire, but we await Dr Miller's next opera production – a version of *The Flying Dutchman* set on a nuclear submarine, or some such conceit – with eager anticipation.

Pass Notes was originally billed as 'a daily briefing on contemporary people and events which may be of use to those whose commitments do not permit them to immerse themselves as fully as they might wish'. In other words, a short cut through the lookalike profiles and portentous analytical pieces that fill the grander newspapers. At their best, Pass Notes inform, amuse and, sometimes obliquely, express an opinion – usually, it must be said, derogatory. And like all good satire, the bigger the target the better it works.

This collection of almost 250 Pass Notes draws together the best columns from the past two years. Most of the subjects are as current as when they were written. Others – Peter Brooke, Brian Clough, Torvill and Dean – will soon be distant memories. Two – Pablo Escobar and Kim Il Sung – are dead, though we can claim no credit in either case.

The columns have been left substantially unaltered, misjudgements and all. For example, Pass Notes admired Matthew Bannister's reshaping of Radio 1; recent indicators suggest we were in a minority. The age of the subject quoted is in each case that at the time the column was written. The date of publication is given at the foot of the page, along with a brief note updating the story where that is necessary.

If Pass Notes can claim to be contemporary history with attitude, the characteristic subjects of the past two years cast an interesting, and at times alarming, light on our age. African dictators, Eastern European madmen, shrill American feminists, even shriller American anti-feminists, incomprehensible novelists, minor royals and their identikit consorts, fading pop stars, and Conservative ministers called Norman. Truly, funny old world.

Pass Notes is a collective effort and many people have contributed to its success (or notoriety, depending on your point of view). Thanks to all of them, but especially to Catherine Bennett, John Cunningham, John Dugdale, John Duncan, Dan Glaister, Ian Katz, David McKie, Alan Rusbridger and Adam Sweeting. I am also grateful to Nick Richmond, Helen Stallion and Karen Tucker for tracking down photographs, the *Guardian*'s library and information unit for checking those slippery things called facts, and Pat Blackett for fending off the more persistent critics.

Stephen Moss
August 1994

Gerry Adams

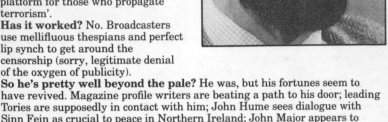

Age: 45.

Appearance: Sociology lecturer (specialising in violent crime).

How to recognise him: Well-trimmed beard, stylish specs, collar and tie, bulletproof vest. Often surrounded by men in balaclavas.

Status: President of Sinn Fein and voice of the Irish Republican movement.

And what does that voice sound like? Difficult to remember, as it has been banned from TV and radio since 1988.

Why? Then Home Secretary Douglas Hurd said it was time to deny 'a platform for those who propagate terrorism'.

Has it worked? No. Broadcasters use mellifluous thespians and perfect lip synch to get around the censorship (sorry, legitimate denial of the oxygen of publicity).

So he's pretty well beyond the pale? He was, but his fortunes seem to have revived. Magazine profile writers are beating a path to his door; leading Tories are supposedly in contact with him; John Hume sees dialogue with Sinn Fein as crucial to peace in Northern Ireland; John Major appears to think he could do business with him.

Any dissenters? Victims of IRA violence; the Democratic Unionist Party, who see government overtures to Adams as a surrender to the IRA; and the *Sun*, which recently headlined its front page 'Gerry Adams: The two most disgusting words in the English language'.

Is blood thicker than water for Gerry? Sure is. Father and mother were leading Republicans. In 1971 he, his father, his brother, two cousins and an uncle were all in the same internment camp.

Bullets and ballots: Educated at St Mary's Grammar School, Belfast. Allegedly joined the IRA in 1965, rising to adjutant of Belfast brigade. Spent much of the seventies interned in Long Kesh. Released in 1977. Stood for West Belfast in 1983 and defeated veteran SDLP MP Gerry Fitt despite being arrested during campaign. Held seat until 1992 but refused to attend a 'fo. ˙ign' parliament.

Social life: Apart from frequent funerals, very limited because of security – he was shot in 1984 and grenades are routinely thrown at his home. Drives around in an armour-plated taxi. Married with an 18-year-old son but family rarely stay with him.

What does he do to cheer himself up? Told *Esquire* he was fond of listening to Leonard Cohen.

Not to be confused with: A resting actor from Belfast's Lyric Theatre; the Addams family.

Least likely to say: 'Another half of Guinness, Mr Paisley?'

Andre Agassi

Born: Las Vegas, 1970.
Born again: Las Vegas, 1986.
Lookalikes: Peter Stringfellow, Nigel Kennedy, Pat Cash, at least two of the Chippendales, most *Kerrang!* readers.

Background: The youngest of four children, he learned hand-eye coordination in the highchair, hitting a tethered balloon with a table-tennis bat. His father strung the rackets of the famous pros who came into town for exhibition matches, and Connors, Nastase and Borg were persuaded to hit a ball around with young Andre. By the age of 12, he'd won a handful of junior titles. He turned professional in 1986.

Current form: Since winning Wimbledon in 1992 he has played in just 13 events and been beaten 10 times in 40 matches.

Style, clothes: Ridiculous. Famous for wearing two pairs of shorts where one would do. Fond of day-glo trim and ludicrous T-shirts that billow flirtatiously to expose the most lusted-after navel since Madonna's.

Style, tennis: Great talent but erratic application. Hard-hitting baseline player who lacks the killer instinct.

Style, religion: His commitment to the Lord is such that while on tour last year he insisted that Wendy Stewart, his girlfriend of 13 years, was booked into a separate single room. Much given to falling to his knees on court, making the sign of the cross and ostentatiously praying.

Reputation: Outrageous, charismatic, a 'rock'n'roll tennis rebel'.

So he spits on the lawn and shouts at linesmen? No, he smiles a lot, has blond streaks and a novelty earring.

Sexy? You bet. Those big, damp, Disney eyes and that orphaned puppy demeanour appeal to women of all ages, among them Barbra Streisand, with whom he was romantically linked. Not one of the women queueing up to tickle his tummy is long-suffering Wendy, the childhood sweetheart who has reportedly dumped him.

Can we blame her? No. Despite continually protesting that he is a 'one-girl kinda guy', he seems to have strayed at least twice.

Other distinctly un-Christian behaviour: Made gratuituously offensive remarks about fellow American Pete Sampras's appearance, suggesting he had recently swung down from a tree.

What the critics and jealous, hairless men say: Sweet but stupid, cheap hustler, 'Scumbagassi', showboating nincompoop, infantile twerp.

Likes: Barry Manilow, God, Wella home perms, being nice to umpires.

Least likely to say: 'You bald, blind bastard. That ball was in.'

Princess Alice

Age: 92.
Appearance: The small figure at the end of the balcony in a hat.
Position: Second oldest royal. Least-known royal.
Full maiden name: Alice Christabel Montagu Douglas Scott.
Pay: Received £87,000 a year under Civil List. Now receives an unspecified 'allowance' from the Queen.
Duties: 51 engagements last year. This works out at £1,700 an engagement.
Other jobs: A little light air chief-marshalling; occasional colonelling duties; a fair amount of patroning. Attending memorial services.
Background: Descended from Charles II. Daughter of the 7th Duke of Buccleuch and Queensberry, who spent childhood aiming cricket balls

at ancestral statues. Vaguely related to almost everyone. Early childhood spent at Montagu House, Whitehall, London, where the Foreign Office stands today. Household numbered 68 permanent residents during the London season. Educated in Malvern and in Paris. Spent much of youth in Kenya as a 'kind of pre-beatnik'.
Marriage: Was the Diana of her day. Married the Duke of Gloucester, third in line to throne, in highly publicised wedding in 1934. He died in 1974. She is mother of present Duke of Gloucester.
Home: Barnwell Manor, Peterborough, where she has lived for 53 years. It boasts a ruined castle in the garden, inside which there is a tennis court.
Fashion notes: Not one of the great patrons of the British fashion industry. Wears shoes made by Mr Anderson of Edinburgh *circa* 1930. And a kilt made in 1914.
Outlook: Group Captain Peter Townsend wrote of her: 'She was painfully shy, so that conversation with her was sometimes halting and unrewarding, for you felt that she had so much more to say, but could not bring herself to say it.' The Queen Mother – 17 months her senior – says of her: 'She has the courage of a lion.'
Motto: 'One gets on with it.'
Alice on Mrs Simpson: 'She was a very good hostess. She was all right as Mrs Simpson. Less so as the Duchess of Windsor, or whatever she became.'
Alice on the Empire: 'One always seemed to be giving places away, which was sad. They have been at war since, in most cases.'
Could she be Queen one day? Very unlikely. She is not even in the top 150 in line – way behind such contenders as Princess Maria of Romania, Prince Albrecht of Hohenlohe-Langenburg or Baroness Irina von Plotho.
Least likely to say: 'I've told you never to ring me on my mobile phone.'

Curtly Ambrose

Age: 30.
Appearance: Nemesis.
Job: Humiliating English batsmen.
Is he good at it? You have
obviously been asleep. Ambrose is
the world's best fast bowler and
produced an inspired spell which
turned England's winning position
in the Trinidad Test into a national
nightmare.

Give me the grisly statistics: 7.5
overs, 1 maiden, 22 runs, 6 wickets.
Which means? He reduced
England's best batsmen to a bunch of
quivering wrecks.
And the maiden? Not bothered in
the slightest.
I take it we lost? The West Indies
squeezed home by 147 runs, to take a
series-winning 3–0 lead. Another
blackwash beckons.
What's a blackwash? A politically
correct version of whitewash.
Are there any crumbs of comfort for England? They scored 46 in their
ill-fated second innings.
Hardly comforting: It was one more than they managed in their worst-ever
Test score – 45 all out against Australia in Sydney in 1887.
So tell me about Curtly. Funny sort of name: Best not to say that to his
face. In any case, it goes well with his middle names.
Which are? Elconn Lynwall.
Any distinguishing features? He's extremely tall.
How tall? About 6ft 7in, though the more he terrorises England the bigger
he seems to get and the *Telegraph* now says 6ft 9in.
Pretty fearsome! As a bowler, yes. As a person, no. He's an intensely private
man who likes to bury himself in calypso music on his Walkman.
He loves his cricket presumably? No. He thought cricket was boring and
intended to be a basketball player, but was press-ganged into playing for his
local side in Antigua at 17. He was considering retiring from international
cricket but the current series seems to have rejuvenated him. He recently
took his 200th Test wicket and is now talking confidently of aiming for 300.
How long will that take? If he carries on playing against England, probably
about a month.
He must be a hero in Antigua? Much loved, especially by his mother Hillie,
who rushes into the street and rings a handbell when he takes a wicket.
What did she say after Tuesday's epic? She was too exhausted to speak.
Not to be confused with: Courtney Walsh.
Do say: 'Hey man, I love the calypso by King Obstinate.'
Don't say: 'Come on Curtly, try and bowl a fast one.'

31 March 1994. England's disaster in Trinidad was followed by a glorious victory in
Barbados and an honourable draw in Antigua, though they still lost the series 3–1.

Clive Anderson

Age: 40.

Appearance: Frequent, usually on television, sometimes in court.

No, stupid, what does he look like? Self-satisfied stockbroker who hasn't been told the eighties are over.

Is he something in the City? No, that was a joke. He presents himself as a barrister who dabbles in television; in reality he's a TV 'personality' who dabbles in the law.

So he's a reluctant star? That's what he says: 'I'm a barrister first; I can't imagine being a TV person for very long.'

Why should we doubt his word? Because he is introducing the eighth series of *Clive Anderson Talks Back* on Channel 4.

The chat show that debunks existing formats and affectionately mocks the assorted pluggers who are prepared to appear? That was the original rationale and it worked splendidly for a while. The problem is that with Aspel and Wogan having abandoned their comfy chairs, there is nothing left to debunk. Anderson has become the *éminence balde* of the chat show.

What does he have that his rivals didn't? A receding hairline, wit and remarkable rudeness.

An example of this rudeness please: To Jeffrey Archer: 'Is there no beginning to your talent?' The legendary novelist turned puce with rage and threatened to sue.

Does he use such techniques in court? The law is, of course, a branch of showbiz but only judges are allowed to be rude; the more senior you are, the ruder you can be.

Any previous? Nothing to detain us long: childhood in Stanmore; father a bank manager; went to Harrow (no, not that one – the grammar school), then Cambridge; president of Footlights (natch); toured in a comedy revue while studying for the Bar.

Yet beneath that bemused exterior lurks . . . That's right, a remarkably well-connected chap: schoolmate of Michael Portillo, and Cambridge contemporaries included Douglas 'Hitchhiker' Adams, John 'Mr Comedy' Lloyd, Griff 'Rhys' Jones. And then there are the judges . . .

Master of the roles: Renowned as the 'funniest man on campus' at Cambridge. His stand-up routine included such examples of suave sophistication as: 'My wife's very musical – oh, how the old bag pipes.'

The sexiest man on TV? Only when Ian McCaskill's under the weather.

But he is the most hard-working? Sorry, far too busy to answer that.

Passions: Work, stripey shirts, tasteful ties, his wife Jane (a publicity-shy hospital doctor) and Arsenal (a publicity-shy north London football team).

Most likely to say: 'Afunnythinghappenedonthewaytocourtthismorning . . .'

Least likely to say: Nothing.

Yasser Arafat

Real name: Mohammed Abed Ar'ouf Arafat.

Age: 64.

Appearance: Confusing. Below the neck, immaculate – tailored uniform, polished buttons and holster. Above the neck, grunge – stubble and raggedy headwear.

What is that thing on his bonce? A *keffiyeh*. Adopted as a revolutionary totem in 1955, it now serves to hide the fact that Yasser is the Bobby Charlton of Arab politics.

First job: Junior site engineer, road-building and sewage section, Kuwait public works department.

Current job: Mr Palestine.

He's a body builder? No, he's the self-appointed president of Palestine – although the country doesn't actually exist yet. Best to keep referring to him as the leader of the Palestine Liberation Organisation (PLO).

Marital status: Pre-1992, married to the cause. Post-1992, married to Suha Tawil, a 29-year-old Christian.

Odd habit: For breakfast, he pours tea on his cornflakes.

Why's he in the news? Israel and the Palestinians are signing their first-ever peace agreement.

Is this good news for Yasser? It's a gamble. If all goes well and Palestine gets self-rule eventually, he'll be a hero. If things go wrong, he'll be accused of sacrificing long-term objectives for short-term gains – basically, the Gaza Strip and the town of Jericho.

So this is the high point of his career? No, that's probably his address to the UN in 1974, which marked his transformation in the public eye from stubbly terrorist thug to international power-broker.

That's 20 years ago . . . Yes, in recent years he's been increasingly sidelined by telegenic talking heads like Hanan Ashrawi. Siding with Saddam during the Gulf War did him no favours at all.

An expensive mistake? You could say that – it cut him off from his sources of funding in Saudi Arabia and Kuwait. The PLO is vying with John Major's Conservative Party for the title of the world's most financially unsound political organisation.

Is Yasser worried? Yes, but not half as worried as he is about death threats from hardline Palestinian guerrilla leader Ahmed Jibril, who thinks Arafat has let the side down by agreeing to an initial compromise. 'We remind Arafat of the fate of Sadat and Sartawi and others . . . '

What did happen to Sadat and Sartawi? Put it this way: RIP.

Not to be confused with: Yosser Hughes; a chessboard.

Least likely to say: 'Oh, all right then, have the bloody place.'

31 August 1993. Arafat returned to Gaza on 1 July 1994 after a gap of 26 years; under the terms of the peace accord the Palestinians gained limited self-rule in Gaza and Jericho.

Paddy Ashdown

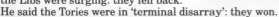

Age: 52.
Appearance: Action man – but more plastic.
Temperament: Determined, outgoing, optimistic, impetuous.
Role: Lib Dem leader since 1988 (after only five years in Parliament).
Would you place him in the direct tradition of Gladstone? Not entirely. Paddy's hardly an intellectual, though he speaks Chinese. Gladstone, so far as we know, never served in the SBS or got exposed in the tabloids for having a mistress.
Lowest point in his leadership: Probably 1989, when the Liberals were pushed into fourth place by the Greens in the Euro-elections and in the opinion polls. The 1992 election was a bit of a downer too. He said the Libs were surging: they fell back. He said the Tories were in 'terminal disarray': they won.

Highest point in his leadership? Could be this week, as the party acclaims him at its conference in Torquay after its Newbury and Christchurch by-election victories.
Will he be fêted wherever he goes? Not entirely. It's a Liberal tradition not to trust your leaders too much. Some worry about his faith in markets. Others complain he foists policies on them with inadequate consultation.
How did he get into politics? He was Labour in his youth, even while in the Marines. Joined the party in 1975. A year later, abandoned a Foreign Office career to go into politics. Worked in factories to sustain himself and his family: for a time was out of work, so he knows how it feels.
How does he play in Parliament? He says he hates it; quite a lot of it hates him. They complain, with some justice, that he's sanctimonious. Tories tend to think a man with his military record should be siding with them.
Name other leading figures in the Liberal Democrat Party: That fellow with the glasses that talks about the economy. The one with the red hair who's always on the telly. Er . . . that's about it.
List his main political causes: Europe – it's a federalist party. Bosnia – he's repeatedly visited former Yugoslavia and called for intervention. Alienation – he's been touring the country and says people are cheesed off with politics.
And distinguishing traits? When asked an awkward question on TV, tends to say (apparently kindly): 'Let me see if I can explain that for you / help you with that.' This is designed to suggest that it is the interviewer who is in difficulties with the question, rather than Paddy with the answer.
Why is he called Paddy? It was a nickname (his real name's Jeremy) acquired at Bedford School and refers to Northern Ireland, where he grew up.
Other nicknames: Paddy Backdown/Climbdown/Pantsdown.
Least likely to say: 'Go back to your constituencies and prepare for government.'

John Aspinall

Age: 67.

Appearance: Dyspeptic retired brigadier.

Occupation: Gambler and zookeeper.

Doesn't he own Port Lympne, the zoo in Kent where a chimp ripped off a woman's hand over the weekend? You exaggerate. It bit off her finger and thumb.

All the same, pretty nasty. And wasn't it the same animal that tore off a 2-year-old's arm? Bustah does, it must be said, have a mean streak.

Presumably the latest incident is the end of the road for the crazy chimp? Absolutely not. His latest victim, zoology student Angelique Todd, has forgiven him and he is being sent to a retirement home in South Africa.

Don't Mr Aspinall's zoos have a history of accidents? There have been one or two, er, problems.

Gory details please: A woman was savaged by wolves at Port Lympne in 1977; a keeper was crushed to death there by an elephant in 1984; and at Aspinall's other zoo, Howletts, a Siberian tigress killed two keepers in 1980.

What does he do when he isn't running zoos? He gambles, prodigiously apparently. 'I have always been a gambler. I owed everyone in London as a young man.'

But he doesn't owe everyone any more? No, everyone owes him. In 1962 he opened his own casino, the Clermont, and has never looked back.

You mean he's rich? Worth about £35 million.

What does he spend his money on? Lavish entertaining and the zoos, which are reckoned to cost about £3 million a year. He likes to provide lamb with rosemary, courgettes and passion fruit.

For his guests? No, for his gorillas.

Wasn't he a pal of Lord Lucan's? Lucan was a leading member of the Clermont set. When asked: 'What would you do if he walked into the room now?' Aspinall famously replied: 'I would embrace him.'

Any other pals? King Goodwill Zwelithini, who has christened him a 'white Zulu' and made him an honorary adviser.

Is the King a keen gambler? You misunderstand the connection. Aspinall is a supporter of the Zulus and their campaign for an independent state.

Heroes: Zulu chief Shaka the Great and the Hoarusib bull elephant.

Villains: The human race. He thinks the world is overpopulated, we are ruining the environment, and that on balance the odd plague would be rather handy.

Most likely to say: 'Down, Bustah!'

Least likely to say: 'Put down Bustah!'

The Ven. George Austin

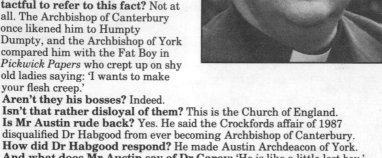

Age: 62.
Appearance: Bunteresque.
Job: Archdeacon of York and general Rentacassock.
What? He is the Anthony Beaumont-Dark of the Church, always obliging with a quote, no occasion too small.
Today's quote? 'Charles is not fit to govern.'
Nickname: The Fatboy.
I take it he is circumferencially challenged? He is. He refers to himself as 'comfortably covered'.
I suppose his colleagues are too tactful to refer to this fact? Not at all. The Archbishop of Canterbury once likened him to Humpty Dumpty, and the Archbishop of York compared him with the Fat Boy in *Pickwick Papers* who crept up on shy old ladies saying: 'I wants to make your flesh creep.'
Aren't they his bosses? Indeed.
Isn't that rather disloyal of them? This is the Church of England.
Is Mr Austin rude back? Yes. He said the Crockfords affair of 1987 disqualified Dr Habgood from ever becoming Archbishop of Canterbury.
How did Dr Habgood respond? He made Austin Archdeacon of York.
And what does Mr Austin say of Dr Carey: 'He is like a little lost boy.'
They don't like each other then? They don't. Austin regards Carey and Habgood as weak-kneed liberals who have betrayed the Church. They regard him as a slightly clownish figure with verbal incontinence.
What's the main cause of disagreement? Women.
You don't mean . . . I certainly don't. Mr Austin is happily married to a woman called Bobbie and is the father of one son. But he is fervently against women becoming priests.
Where does he see women's position in the Church? Seated in the congregation with Sunday frocks and frilly bonnets.
Sounds like a bit of an obsession. It is. He launched a jihad against the liberals within the Church from the pulpit of York Minster in 1991.
He must be a very eminent churchman to be quoted so much in the media? Er, no. An archdeacon is actually pretty low down in the cathedral hierarchy. He is seen as a sort of clergy shop steward and is only entitled to preach once a year in York Minster. But he is very quotable.
Hobbies: Cooking and eating. When in London he breakfasts at his club, the Athenaeum, and lunches at Simpson's.
Dress sense: Awful. Favourite mufti is a T-shirt with a corpulent sheep on it. The front reads: 'Ewe's not fat.' The back reads: 'Ewe's just cuddly.'
Least likely to say: 'I, of course, could not possibly comment.'

Nicholson Baker

Age: 36.

Nickname: Onan the Barbarian.

Appearance: Quintessence of geek, complete with bristly beard, sheeny pate, wire specs, earplugs and a skin complaint.

Occupation: Pornographer.

So what's he doing in all the literary pages? Well, once upon a time Nicholson Baker was a very talented fellow. He wrote three remarkably original novels – *The Mezzanine, Room Temperature* and *U and I* – which examined previously unexplored areas of existence.

Such as? Milk cartons, shoelaces and escalators. This inspired scores of mostly male imitators. Features pages buzzed with self-conscious digressions on mobile phones, computers and microscopic trends in industrial gadgetry.

And the fourth? That was *Vox*, a book about telephone sex, which is to say, a book about masturbation, or as Baker puts it, 'strumming'. Loyal critics were slightly shaken, but polite. After all, the next novel would come along soon. And here it is: *The Fermata*. Trouble is, it's all about strumming.

Nothing wrong with that is there? Exactly what Baker thinks. 'What else is there in the world besides masturbation? Nothing,' says his hero. Nice!

So what's it about? The hero, Arno Strine, has a knack of making the world stand still. While it stands still, Arno runs about undressing women and masturbating over them. When it doesn't, he masturbates anyway.

Is that it? Well, not quite. Creepy Arno writes porn for a hobby. He tricks women into reading it, and masturbates at the thought of their arousal.

But it's tastefully done, right? *Au contraire.* If Boffiny Baker has proved anything, it's that porn's porn, from Berwick Street to Berkeley, Cal.

Pricey though? No, at £14.99 for over 300 pages of unflagging sexual fantasy, *The Fermata* compares very favourably with specialist magazines.

His publishers say: 'Sad', 'unsettling', 'how horny is it?'

Female readers say: 'Put it away, you pervert!'

Every flasher's dream: Just like mucky Arno's, Baker's hand gets all twitchy at the idea that women might be excited by *his* home-made filth. 'For me, that's the pinnacle of sexuality,' he's told one respectful male interviewer. 'The idea of women masturbating. I like watching women read, I like to think of them reading my books.' He likes it so much, he strums as he writes: 'I mean, everybody does.'

Well, do they? Ask Anita Brookner? Catherine Cookson? V. S. Naipaul?

Most likely to say: 'It's what your right hand's for.'

Least likely to say: 'That's disgusting!'

Matthew Bannister

Age: 36.
Appearance: Ad executive.
Job: Controller of Radio 1.
Ah, you mean the hatchet man who has single-handedly reduced Radio 1's audience to three students in Sheffield with an inexplicable passion for Smashing Pumpkins? That is the conventional wisdom.

... the brute who deprived us of the wit and wisdom of Dave Lee Travis, the sensitivity of Simon Bates, the vitality of Whispering Bob Harris? That's what the *Daily Mail* leader writers tell us.

... the Birtian dalek who has destroyed the station we grew up with and introduced science, more live music, earnest discussion and *poetry*? Oh, for God's sake be quiet and let me get a word in. Yes, he did get rid of the Hairy Monster, Simes and his execrable Our Tune, and all manner of other detritus. Yes, there was a wave of controversy, with dispossessed DJs resigning on air and sounding off about the death of radio as we knew it. And, yes, listeners were lost. But the latest leaked figures suggest that the slump has been reversed, with February's audience 300,000 up on the previous month.

That's still about 3 million people down on the audience when he took over last October: There's no accounting for tastes.

All right, all right, we're obviously not going to see ear to ear on this. But you can't deny that Bannister is a Birtian super-bureaucrat and, by definition, a Bad Thing: He is unquestionably a man in a suit; he spent almost two years working on 'Extending Choice', Birt's blueprint for the Beeb; even his friends admit he is ruthlessly ambitious; and he stands accused of liking opera and collecting P. G. Wodehouse first editions. But behind the Birtian Bright Young Thing lurks an experienced radio man.

And where was this experience gained? He moved swiftly from dogsbody at Radio Nottingham in the late seventies to head of news and talks at Capital in the mid-eighties. He then became managing editor of the BBC's London station, GLR, introducing Danny Baker to an eager public.

Didn't he dream up 'zoo' radio? Indeed. And critics of Radio 1's Night of the Long Mikes would say he was responsible for abattoir radio as well.

Has anyone ever said anything nice about him? Tony Blackburn said he was the best thing that ever happened to commercial radio.

When he was at Capital? No, when he took over at Radio 1.

Does he have any other plans to alienate Radio 1 listeners – sorry, extend the station's creative frontiers? Possibly a soap opera.

An everyday story of bloodletting among media folk? It has potential.

Not to be confused with: Matthew 5:9 – 'Blessed are the peacemakers, for they shall be called the children of God.'

Most likely to say: 'The old guard acknowledged it was time to move on.'
Least likely to say: 'Simon/Dave/Bob/Fluff, great to see you again.'

30 March 1994. The encouraging February figures proved a blip, and Radio 1 audiences have continued to fall.

The Marquess of Bath

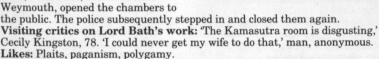

Name: Alexander Thynne.
A.k.a.: The Loins of Longleat.
Age: 60.
Appearance: Psychedelic Oliver Reed.
Position: Marquess of Bath, proud owner of Longleat ancestral pile including lions, etc. (full-time). Mural painter (part-time).
Attention-grabbing antics: Opening up private quarters to public and media, including the 'Kamasutra Bedroom' with mirrored ceiling, the 'Heaven and Hell Corridor' and depictions of various other fantasies from his life's work. The 'easily shocked' are warned to stay away from the more sexually graphic work.
Is this the first viewing? No. In 1969, Lord Bath, then Viscount Weymouth, opened the chambers to the public. The police subsequently stepped in and closed them again.
Visiting critics on Lord Bath's work: 'The Kamasutra room is disgusting,' Cecily Kingston, 78. 'I could never get my wife to do that,' man, anonymous.
Likes: Plaits, paganism, polygamy.
Dislikes: Prudes; discussing relationship with brother Lord Christopher (sacked as Longleat comptroller within a week of father's death).
Marital status: One wife – Anna Gael, Lady Bath, an accomplished writer. Long history of 'wifelets'.
Is the term 'wifelet' not a little patronising? ' . . . as a polygamist what other word do you use? It is much less patronising than mistress. And, anyway, they call me their hublet.'
Unlikely to win: Approval of Prince Charles for conservation of English heritage.
Carbuncles (existing): Huge murals depicting detailed erotica and 'glimpses of the painter's psyche'.
Carbuncles (planned): Centre Parcs recreation village; 'love maze' with romantic and titillating topiary; life-size Stonehenge replica to be titled 'Thynnhenge'.
Notable literary works: *Pillars of the Establishment*, narrating the fortunes of a marquess and his three sons who all contract an unfortunate disease from the same woman.
Chances of Booker Prize: Slim.
Not to be confused with: The Marquess of Blandford; the Marquis de Sade.
Least likely to appear on: *Through the Keyhole*: 'Whooze explicit erawtic paintings are theeze?'
Most likely to appear on: *The Word*.
Most likely to say: 'Anglo-Disney for Longleat.'
Least likely to say: 'Enough is enough.'

Presiley Baxendale

Age: 42.
Appearance: Firm but friendly head girl.
Occupation: Lord Justice Scott's hit-woman as chief inquisitor of ministers and mandarins at the arms-for-Iraq inquiry: feared Whitehall figure.
Any other claim to fame? Once chosen by her colleagues as having the most mellifluous name at the Bar. Her middle name is Lamorna.
Is that why she got the job? Actually, no. Although she became a QC only in 1992, she has a long record in civil cases representing government.
Did Whitehall assume she'd be a soft touch? Possibly, but wrongly. Lord Lester QC, a senior member of her chambers, warned: 'She gives the impression of being a pushover. In fact, she is very strong personally. You could be deceived by her.'

Does she appear deceptive to witnesses? Well, she does have an unsettling idiosyncrasy – laughing before putting the boot in.
For example? When she asked FO mandarin David Gore-Booth: 'So [the policy] was [to] say nothing until you were asked a question about it?' To William Waldegrave, minister for open government: 'I didn't think you meant what you were saying.'
Other examples of her inquisitorial style? 'I have seen no document which supports what you're saying' (to Waldegrave). 'You don't need to say any more' (to former FO minister David Mellor).
Arms dealing and the Bar are pretty much men's worlds? Yes. After suggestions from witnesses that she was not bowling a straight ball, she told Waldegrave: 'I am so bad at cricketing terms, but this is not a googly.'
Other official jobs outside the courtroom: Counsel to the 1985 inquiry into the Jasmine Beckford child abuse case. Member of phoneline watchdog ICSTIS where she rejected a plea to ban Dial Dr Dark. 'I find it extremely boring. It makes no reference to chopping up one's mother.'
Family: Mother to Felicity and Charlie. Describes herself in *Who's Who* as Mrs R. K. FitzGerald. Richard FitzGerald is a tax barrister.
Particular hate: Pomposity.
Particular love: Reading Whitehall documents.
Not to be confused with: Priscilla Presley; Leo Baxendale.
Most likely to say: 'Are you sure you meant what you said?'
Least likely to say: 'Politicians never lie.'

Samuel Beckett

Age: Died aged 83 in 1989.

Appearance: Rock face.

Occupation: 'Left-handed batsman, left-arm medium-pace bowler . . . winner of the Nobel Prize for Literature' – *Who's Who of Cricketers*.

Why is he in the news? His 1975 short play *Footfalls* has just had its West End debut at the Garrick Theatre.

Just how short is it? Twenty minutes.

That is short! By Shakespeare's standards, perhaps, but not by Beckett's. His shortest is the 35-second *Breath*, in which faint light shines on a rubbish-strewn stage, followed by a brief cry during which the light brightens for 10 seconds, followed by silence for 5 seconds, followed by a slow decrease in the light for 10 seconds, followed by a repeat of the cry. Followed, perhaps, by audience applause.

Not to be confused with: The interval.

Does anything actually happen in *Footfalls*? Yes. A woman paces up and down a narrow strip of stage communing with her dead mother.

Didn't Beckett make a thing of theatrical oddities? Characters in dustbins, funeral urns, buried up to their necks in sand.

Sounds absurd: The Theatre of the Absurd was indeed ridiculed as absurd by some critics.

But what exactly was it? It offered a vision of humanity struggling vainly to control its fate in a world bent on destruction. While the French accepted it as a philosophical doctrine expressed in art, the British took it literally.

What have the French got to do with it? Beckett was born in Foxrock, near Dublin, but lived for most of his life in Paris, teaching English at the Ecole Normale Supérieure, and writing many of his best-known works in French.

Such as? *En Attendant Godot*, *Malone Meurt*, *L'Innommable*, *Le Dépeupler*, *Fin de Partie*.

Ça suffit! **Didn't writing in a foreign language limit him?** That was the idea. Beckett, ever the minimalist, didn't want to be distracted by the 'embellishments of style'.

What were those titles again? *Waiting for Godot*, *Malone Dies*, *The Unnameable*, *The Lost Ones*, *Endgame*.

Trademarks: Existential optimism – 'Ever tried. Ever failed. No matter. Try again. Fail again. Fail better' (*Worstward Ho*); insanity – 'We are all born mad. Some remain so' (*Waiting for Godot*); mortality – 'Personally I have no bone to pick with graveyards' (*First Love*).

Hobbies? Spent much of his last years playing golf.

Ah, the celebrity circuit, Tarby, Brucie . . . Beckett's game was cerebral. He played by himself, two balls, competing against each other.

Most likely to say: 'Habit is the ballast that keeps the dog chained to his vomit' (Beckett's book on Proust).

Least likely to say: 'Godot, good to see you, where have you been?'

16 March 1994

Sister Wendy Beckett

Age: 64.

Appearance: George Formby cameo in *Nuns on the Run*.

Nickname: 'One-Take Wendy'.

Occupation: Bride of Christ, living in spartan Portakabin in grounds of Carmelite convent in Norfolk; part-time art critic and TV presenter.

Has she been seduced again into roving all-expenses-paid from art gallery to art gallery, staying in plush hotels and lunching journalists at the Ritz? Only with great reluctance. Her BBC2 series *Sister Wendy's Grand Tour* has just started.

Why is she in demand? She says it's just 'novelty value', and the BBC loves eccentric presenters. But she does have a knack for the sound-bite, praising a Stanley Spencer nude's 'lovely and fluffy' pubic hair, observing of Botticelli's Venus that 'you can't imagine her doing the washing up'.

How is she rated by other art critics? Views are mixed. The late Peter Fuller encouraged her to write for his magazine *Modern Painters*; others see her approach as setting criticism back 150 years. Germaine Greer scoffed at the spectacle of a virgin discussing sexuality in art.

What does Wendy say? 'You don't have to experience things to understand them. Look at Jane Austen – she was a virgin!'

Is she a feminist? Consider the evidence. She went out and got a job because she was finding life wholly devoted to her somewhat distant 'husband' less than fulfilling. She favours women priests. Her debut book was *Contemporary Women Painters*. She insists on being called 'Sister'. Looks like she qualifies.

Unfruitful conversational ice-breakers: 'Liam Neeson – is he a hunk or what?' 'Where would *you* play Le Tissier?' '*Absolutely Fabulous* has really gone off the boil, hasn't it?'

Fruitful conversational ice-breakers: 'You must identify closely with Juliana of Norwich?' 'Is Cindy Sherman's work narcissistic, or a satire on narcissism?' 'Another kir, Wendy?'

Parallels with *The Word* presenter Huffty: Shaved head; doesn't sleep with men; not wild about Guns n' Roses.

Merchandising opportunities overlooked by BBC: Bendy Wendy dolls; Sindy's New Look micro-habits; Jasper Conran wimples; robot Sister Wendy gallery guides; Carmelite Culture Key-Notes.

Not to be confused with: Samuel Beckett; Margaret Beckett; Thomas à Becket; Trevor Nunn; Julie Andrews; Whoopi Goldberg.

Least likely to say: 'Yo, dudes, poker in my trailer after we wrap?'

Most likely to say: 'Now, Damien Hirst's *Dead Moose with Gangrene 43* – here I must confess to being just a *tiny* bit disappointed.'

Jeffrey Bernard

Age: 60.

Appearance: Exhumed corpse.

Background: Son of opera singer (mother) and architect. Disappointed early by making his own bombs and discovering drink aged 14. At 16 fled from Pangbourne Nautical College to Soho and 'never looked forward'.

Past occupations: Gigolo, dishwasher, actor, coal miner, builder, boxer, scrounger, philanderer, drunk, wastrel.

Current occupations: Columnist, scrounger, philanderer, drunk, wastrel.

The making of Jeffrey: After 15 years at *Sporting Life*, *Daily Express* and *Private Eye*, his 'Low Life' column in the *Spectator* developed cult following. Promoted to household namehood when Peter O'Toole played him in the Keith Waterhouse play *Jeffrey Bernard Is Unwell*. Since painted for the National Portrait Gallery and now the subject of a biography by Graham Lord.

Usual subjects of his column: The appalling state of his health/relationships/psyche brought about by his heavy drinking and generally self-destructive lifestyle.

Alcohol consumption: 30 units a day.

Recommended alcohol consumption for adult male: 21 units per week.

Cigarette consumption: 50 per day.

Number of marriages: Four.

Number of liaisons: 500.

Income: £190 a week, plus £50,000 royalties from play.

Habitual haunts: Coach and Horses, Groucho Club, Middlesex Hospital.

Jeffrey on Jeffrey: 'I know I look as if I am dead but I am still alive.' 'I actually think drunks are bores.' 'Without a drink I'm like a teabag without hot water.' 'Starting tomorrow, it's all going to be different.'

Graham Lord on Jeffrey: 'I told him when I decided to write it: You are a shit and I am going to show you are a shit.'

Jeffrey on Graham Lord: 'After a little less than 100 pages, my fears that it had been a mistake to allow Graham Lord to write it [the biography] were confirmed.'

Don't say: 'Isn't it a bit early for a snifter?' 'Can I help you across the street?' 'I liked you in *Lawrence of Arabia*.'

Least likely to say: 'Sorry, I can't make it, I've got an aquaerobics class.'

Benazir Bhutto

Age: 39.

Appearance: Dazzling, with dress to match. Otherwise hardened hacks known to whimper and burble in her presence. Nice line in red-rimmed fashion specs.

Nickname: Bibi.

Background: Feudal landowning family in Sind province, of secular disposition. Fitted in well at Oxford.

First job: Prime Minister of Pakistan, 1988–90.

Qualifications: Being the daughter of Zulfiqar Ali Bhutto, Prime Minister of Pakistan, 1971–7.

Wants to be: Prime Minister of Pakistan for ever and ever, or until son Bilawel grows up.

Why? Believes passionately in family's destiny to rule. Hero-worships father, who was hanged (judicially murdered, most would

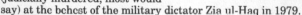

say) at the behest of the military dictator Zia ul-Haq in 1979.

Loathes: The memory of Zia ul-Haq, who died in a military plane crash (assassinated, most believe) in 1988.

Slightly milder dislikes: Nawaz Sharif, who took her job; anyone who dares criticise her.

Former dislikes: President Ghulam Ishaq Khan, for sacking her.

What she probably thinks of Khan now: Wise elder statesman; really ought to have another term.

Married: Asif Zardari, modestly well-off businessman in 1988; fabulously successful businessman in 1990. Period of good fortune curiously coincided with wife's prime ministership. Period of imprisonment commenced after wife was kicked out.

Campaigning style: Raucous motorcades, huge rallies, lots of chanting. Likes to arrive hours late.

Proudest moment: Returning in triumph from exile in 1986 to re-establish PPP as mass movement in the teeth of Zia oppression.

Least proud moment: Leaving supporters in the lurch by failing to sustain even a teeny-weeny march in November 1992.

Excuse: She was expecting third child, by imprisoned Asif.

Come again? He was let out to attend National Assembly sessions.

Ideology: Well concealed. As Prime Minister, abandoned father's demagogic socialism, vaguely talked of market economy, failed to flog anything off. Launched People's Programme for poverty alleviation with much fanfare, and not much result.

Job creation good news: An estimated 64,000 people got government jobs while she was Prime Minister.

And the bad news: All of them were members of the PPP.

Not to be confused with: Bibi Netanyahu, leader of the Israeli opposition; Bebe Daniels; B. B. King; Biba.

Never ask: 'What's in a name?'

John Birt Ltd

Age: Approximately 20 tax years.
Appearance: Outrageous tax dodge.
Stated principal activity:
'Providing consultancy services in
the field of theatre and television.'
Corporate headquarters:
Victorian house near Wandsworth
Common.
Principal shareholder: John Birt.
**But isn't he Director-General of
the BBC?** Indeed.
Surely that's a full-time job? Not
according to Mr Birt's accountant.
**Doesn't a John Birt live in a
Victorian house near
Wandsworth Common?** Funny you
should mention that.
Other shareholders: Jane Birt.
**You mean John's wife and
daughter of the noted
Washington, DC, road lobbyist?**
The same.
Company's annual turnover: £163,141.
Company's major expenses: Entertainment, theatre visits, clothes.
Did you say clothes? The company's latest tax return listed 'wardrobe'
expenses at £3,666.
That's rather a lot, isn't it? Armani suits don't come cheap.
Did John always have such an expensive wardrobe? No, during the
seventies at *World in Action* he was known for his Jesus Creepers.
**Is sartorial extravagance a necessary qualification for high office
within the BBC?** Alan Yentob is a major client of Paul Smith, but does not
file returns at Companies House.
What do John's BBC colleagues call him? Stalin, Hitler, Cromwell.
What will they call him now? Lester.
Favourite words: Erm . . . and ERM.
What is meant by the word Birtist? Someone who knows which way their
bread is buttered.
Is it not frequently used as an expletive? Some people do not know which
way their bread is buttered.
What admirers say: Hidden passion and intensity, formidable intellect
fortuitously conjoined with insatiable curiosity. Who is his accountant?
What enemies say: Grey, worthy, autocratic, repressed, soulless, ruthless,
cold, blank, 'almost Martian'. 'How long do I have to clear my stuff?'
Mr Birt on how enormous success has not changed him: 'I still look at
Time Out to see if the Everly Brothers are in town.'
Has Mr Birt ever said anything enigmatic? He once said that life is 'a bit
like a novel, isn't it?' He did not explain.
Least likely to say: 'Don't bother with a receipt.'

Sir Harrison Birtwistle

Age: 59.
Appearance: Absent-minded professor.
Occupation: Composer.
Why is he in the news? Group of anti-avant-garde 'musical terrorists' called the Hecklers plan to ambush his opera, *Gawain*, at Covent Garden.
What do they object to, the fact that the Green Knight's head is chopped off and he lurches about the stage carrying it? No, they have no objection to gore; it's the lack of good tunes they hate.
So they want to revert to the swirling arias of Verdi and Puccini? Dangerous radicals in the eyes of the Hecklers. Their preference is for Handel, Bach and Mozart.

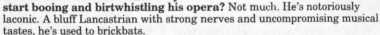

Will Sir Harrison care when they start booing and birtwhistling his opera? Not much. He's notoriously laconic. A bluff Lancastrian with strong nerves and uncompromising musical tastes, he's used to brickbats.
From whom? Benjamin Britten and Peter Pears, for a start. They walked out of the première of Birtwistle's *Punch and Judy* at Aldeburgh in 1968.
Wrong kind of child abuse? Rather. Not seaside frolics but musical sadism, with dodecaphonic screaming until you could bear it no longer.
Any other setbacks? The BBC commissioned the music drama *Yan Tan Tethera* but then rejected it. And his opera *The Mask of Orpheus* was shuffled back and forth between Covent Garden, Glyndebourne and the English National Opera, before the latter at last agreed to put it on.
And how was it received? I think the phrase is *succès d'estime*. It was hailed as a masterpiece but ran for just eight performances and has never been revived.
So what is it about his music that people find so provocative? In the argot of the critics, it's angular, rugged, with strong colours – woodwind timbres to the fore, abrasive, lots of determined brass. A bit too much like Rugby League to have in your living room.
Works to mention: *Tragoedia*; *The Mask of Orpheus*; *Yan Tan Tethera*; *Bow Down*; *Ring a Dumb Carillon*; *Verses for Ensemble*; *Down by the Greenwood Side*; *For O, for O, the Hobbyhorse Is Forgot*.
Does the critical establishment agree with the Hecklers? Far from it. To many of the cognoscenti Birtwistle is Britain's greatest musical talent; the *FT*'s critic called *Gawain* 'a towering masterpiece', and Birtwistle has been commissioned to write an opera for the new Glyndebourne.
Something suitably summery, I hope? Hardly. It's called *The Second Mrs King* and deals with the rebirth of King Kong.
Not to be confused with: Harrison Ford; Sir Andrew Lloyd Webber.
Most likely to say: 'Methera, lethera, severa, hovera, dovera, dik.'
Least likely to say: 'Any chance of a transfer to the Palladium?'

14 April 1994. Twenty or so fearsomely fogeyish Hecklers duly stood up and booed *Gawain*, but were drowned out by Birtwistle's supporters led by Arts Council chairman Lord Gowrie.

Conrad Black

Age: 49.
Vaguely amusing middle name?
Moffat.
Appearance: Retired wrestler.
Occupation: Press baron, military
historian, ideologue.
What papers does he own? The
Daily and *Sunday Telegraph* and
more than 200 others in Canada, the
USA, the Middle East and Australia.
Any other famous titles? He does
own the *Waikiki Pennysaver* and the
Punxsutawny Spirit.
**Not the *Independent* of London
then?** No, though he tried to buy a
40 per cent stake in Newspaper
Publishing.
**But isn't he well known for his
right-wing views?** He did write
that he intended to buy some
English papers to rid them of leftish
journalists like Christopher
Hitchens.
Doesn't sound very independent: Not terribly, no.
Still, he might be a hands-off proprietor, I suppose? He once said: 'A
newspaper that is run by the journalists tends, in my experience, to be
sanctimonious and tendentious.'
Doesn't care much for journalists then? He has called them 'a swarming,
grunting mass of jackals'.
All of them? Presumably not his wife, columnist Barbara Amiel.
Background: Son of a Toronto businessman, he bought his first shares aged
8. After studying history and law, built up a chain of small Canadian
newspapers. In 1978 he won control of the giant Argus corporation. Took
control of the *Telegraph* group in 1986 and rapidly steered it to profitability.
Bit of a breeze really? Not quite: he was twice expelled from school (once for
stealing and reselling exam papers) and failed his law exams.
That business with Hitchens? The two have feuded since Black wrote to
the *Spectator*, attacking a Hitchens piece on Ronald Reagan's colonic cancer.
He likes writing letters to the papers then? As long as they belong to him.
He frequently takes issue with his journalists on the letters pages of his
titles. One recent salvo was in defence of Mangosuthu Buthelezi – 'an
advocate of racial tolerance and the free market economy'.
At least he doesn't commandeer the editorial columns: He does that too.
He once lambasted a new trend towards long skirts: 'Long has its place, but
for most women it is a banal, humdrum and reactionary style.'
What people say about Black: 'A genuinely civilised man when most
proprietors are brutes' (Max Hastings). 'Certainly the most charming and
intelligent of the proprietors' (Charles Moore).
Aren't they the editors of the *Daily* and *Sunday Telegraph?* So they are.
Hobbies: Napoleon, naval history, croquet, chess, letter writing.

The Marquess of Blandford

Full name: Charles James Spencer-Churchill, Marquess of Blandford.
Age: 37.
Appearance: Overweight toff with heavy cold.
Position: Heir to Duke of Marlborough and 11,500-acre Blenheim Palace estate valued in excess of £100 million. Great-nephew of Sir Winston Churchill.
Family motto: Faithful, though Unfortunate.
Background: Duke divorced James's mother when he was 4. Educated at Harrow and Royal Agricultural College at Cirencester.
Career: Decided to forgo conventional career in favour of a life of crime. He has been convicted of drugs offences and burglary and has notched up 12 motoring convictions. Has also assaulted a policeman and burned down a potting shed. Served two gaol sentences.
Who does he blame? His father, for refusing to kiss him, aged 8, when dropping him at prep school for the first time; the burdens of high birth.
Nickname in prison: Jimmy the Weasel.
Family: Married Becky Mary Few Brown, former girlfriend of Paddy McNally, former boyfriend of Fergie, in 1990. They had baby son, George, in July 1992. By then Becky had walked out after Jamie was linked with old flame Arabella Tait.
What Becky says about him: 'When James is nice he's lovely. When he's nasty, he's horrible.'
Jamie on Becky: 'Unfortunately she is not possessed with too many brains.'
Becky on Becky: 'I can't spell or anything clever, so I knew I couldn't be a secretary.'
Perks of owning Blenheim: Free tickets to pop concerts, use of bouncy castle, garden centre and gift shoppe. No need for driving licence in grounds.
Why is Jamie cross with Becky? Because she has sold her story to the *Daily Mail*. She says she needs the money to look after George – and 'because Daddy has had a bad Lloyd's bash'.
Main storyline in *Mail* serialisation: Becky claims father-in-law is demanding a blood test to establish whether George is really Jamie's son.
Can Jamie be stopped from inheriting Blenheim? Only if Duke can get Jamie certified as insane.
Least likely to say: 'Oh dear, someone's spilled some baking powder.'

23 February 1993. On the minus side, the Marquess was convicted on fraud and deception charges in June 1994 and the Duke has taken further steps to stop him inheriting; on the plus side he did a stint as motoring correspondence for *Voila!* magazine.

Mr Blobby

Age: One.

Appearance: Seven foot tall, pink with yellow spots, three stubby fingers on each hand, almost spherical.

But anything distinctive? Multicoloured bow tie.

Status: TV personality and now pop superstar. His record, imaginatively titled 'Mr Blobby', has just reached number one in the charts.

You don't mean he's going to follow in the hallowed footsteps of Cliff Richard and bestride the charts at Christmas? Yip. And he's had nearly as many marriage offers.

What is the secret of his musical success? According to one retailer: 'At Christmas time everyone's taste goes out of the window.'

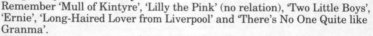

Any other evidence of this temporary mass insanity?
Remember 'Mull of Kintyre', 'Lilly the Pink' (no relation), 'Two Little Boys', 'Ernie', 'Long-Haired Lover from Liverpool' and 'There's No One Quite like Granma'.

OK, you've made your point, but how did he become a cultural icon? Had a waddle-on part in *Noel's House Party* on BBC1, annoying celebrity guests. Graduated to starring role as Blobby-mania took hold.

Blobby-mania? There's no other word for it. Blobby artefacts are being sold by the million.

Such as? Blobbycakes, Blobbyduvets, Blobbycopters, Blobbymobiles . . . oh, and a Blobbumentary called *A Day in the Life of Mr Blobby*.

Somebody must be making a packet. *House Party* host Noel Edmonds is doing very nicely, thank you, out of a marketing deal with the BBC.

So Mr Edmonds dreamt up Mr Blobby, did he? Apparently not, he was created by the programme's producer, Michael Leggo. But, as a member of the BBC staff, he is not allowed to share the profits.

Mr Leggo must be a brick: Do you mind, I do the jokes.

Anyone else involved? A Shakespearian actor, Barry Killerby, wears the pink latex suit, bringing *gravitas* and classical intonation to the role.

And what is Mr Killerby's most famous line? To blobby or not to blobby?

Is Mr Blobby universally loved? Just two groups of dissenters – Radio 1 DJs, who think the record is crap and refuse to play it, and bookies, who stand to lose a fortune if it is number one on Christmas Day.

Where does Mr Blobby go from here? Obvious next step is a duet with Frank Sinatra – *Blobby and Frank Sing the Blues*. Topped a poll to choose next England football manager (the new Blobby Robson?) and tipped to be next chairman of the Arts Council.

Not to be confused with: Meat Loaf; Leigh Bowery; something washed up near Sellafield.

Most likely to say: 'Blobby, Blobby, Blobby . . . etc.'

Least likely to say: 'My record company is cramping my creative style and I want to terminate my contract.'

6 December 1993. The bookies lost: Mr Blobby was indeed number one on Christmas Day.

Helena Bonham Carter

Age: 27.

Appearance before: Denis Healey crossed with Little Nell.

Appearance after: Ditto, but daubed with make-up by Yardley, which has just launched H.B.C. as its New Face. Barry Norman called her 'a role model for British women'.

Message to British women: Grow your eyebrows, wear your nightie in the street, shrink.

Profession: Actress.

Specialities: Englishness. Poshness. Innocence. Sexual awakening. Usually a combination of the above: cf. Lucy Honeychurch, Lady Jane Grey, Helen Schlegel, Ophelia.

Unique selling point: Genuine double barrelled.

Lloyd George knew my father: Great-grandfather was Herbert Asquith; grandmother was Lady Violet Bonham Carter; uncle is Lord Bonham Carter, former Liberal MP.

Career: Aged 13 sent her photograph to an agent, later abandoned Oxbridge to act Lady Jane Grey in Trevor Nunn's dreadful film. Adopted by Merchant–Ivory as all-purpose Edwardian *ingénue*.

Little-known achievement: Perfected grunge at least five years early.

Any flaws? No neck.

The Blighty spirit: Grew it two inches with posture exercises.

Praise for H.B.C.: 'Good value for money' (Yardley executive); 'London's Sexiest Celebrity' (listeners to Capital FM).

Typical line: 'I can't marry you, Wilfrid, I can't. I'm going to Poggibonsi with the Yardleys. Don't follow me, Wilfrid, only connect!' (drops teacake and runs sobbing into glorious English garden).

The price of fame: Recently took out injunction against a spook called Farquharson who'd stalked her for five years.

Luvvie rating: Too intelligent and articulate to score highly. She's said to have rejected advances by Warren Beatty, called Mickey Rourke 'one of the rudest men I've ever met' and described Mel Gibson as a wimp with short legs. So, three out of twenty.

What's the three for? 'Nude scenes are probably like childbirth: you forget about the pain until you do it again'; 'Acting is constant therapy'; 'There's nowhere to go in the evenings, just to the Groucho Club . . . '

A Passage to Mauritius: Recently took the *Hello!* shilling, accepting holiday in exchange for innumerable shots of H.B.C. in her bodice.

Does she ever take her clothes off? Recently crushed rumours that her corsets were stuffed with top-quality sawdust by playing a strippagram. 'I would certainly like to show my strength and maturity,' she says.

Has she? If she had, she wouldn't be wearing that Yardley mascara.

Advice: Diversify. Pose nude for *Vanity Fair*. Adopt a baby. Invent an abused childhood. Leave home.

The Booker Prize

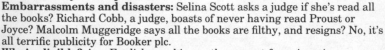

Born: 1958.

Declared purpose: 'To reward merit, raise the stature of the author in the eyes of the public and increase the sale of the books'.

Real purpose: To publicise a gigantic company specialising in food distribution, agribusiness, fish farming and ready meals.

Products that would benefit more from the Booker Prize than the novel: Alternatives to the condom; cures for snoring.

Value: Has gone up from £5,000 to £20,000, but is no longer the most valuable British book prize.

What's it got over other literary prizes? Goes out live on TV.

A few writers who haven't won: Muriel Spark, Julian Barnes, Martin Amis, J. G. Ballard, Anthony Burgess.

The authority of the prize: Nil.

Embarrassments and disasters: Selina Scott asks a judge if she's read all the books? Richard Cobb, a judge, boasts of never having read Proust or Joyce? Malcolm Muggeridge says all the books are filthy, and resigns? No, it's all terrific publicity for Booker plc.

Who's eligible? Any English-speaking author except from America.

Why no Americans? Because they'd always win, dummy.

Where does the money go? The Black Panthers (John Berger); curtains (Kingsley Amis); swimming pool in *résidence secondaire* (A. S. Byatt); sex tour to Bangkok (Anita Brookner – just kidding, Anita!).

Most obscure Booker winners: P. H. Newby (1969); Keri Hulme (1985).

Least bookish judge: A tie between Joanna Lumley, Mary Wilson and Trevor McDonald.

What single act would make you believe that the judges had any standards? If they said that none of the books were good enough this year.

Judging system: Chaotic compromise. The five judges all get their own book on, with one for luck. 'I'll vote for yours if you vote for mine.'

Result of this system: Anita Brookner wins.

What not to say to a winning author: 'It's all luck, isn't it?'

What not to say to a losing author: 'Well, it is a very sophisticated judging system, isn't it?'

What the literary editors say to cover their shame: 'I wasn't going to come but my editor said I had to.'

Other ways of getting £20,000 for literary composition: Kiss and tell with famous fat old man.

Meaning of the words 'Booker Prize' when stamped on novel's cover: Almost impossible to read; ideal present for somebody else.

13 October 1992. Michael Ondaatje and Barry Unsworth shared the prize in 1992; Roddy Doyle won in 1993; and to mark the 25th anniversary of the award Salman Rushdie's *Midnight's Children* was named Booker of Bookers.

Betty Boothroyd

Age: 63.
Vocation: Speaker of the Commons.
What job might you guess she'd been doing before? Rugby League referee.

And what did she really do before? She was once a member of a high-kicking dance group, the Tiller Girls. Tabloids have tried to reassemble the group she Tilled with, but have always failed. But the *Mail* did trace her fellow-musicians in a forties group called the Swing Stars (they tootled, she tapped).
Is there a parallel here with the early lives of great Speakers like Lenthall and Arthur Onslow? Not at first sight. But she was also into politics early, in the Labour League of Youth, and as secretary at Westminster to various party bigwigs, including Barbara Castle and Geoffrey de Freitas. She was elected to Parliament at her fifth attempt (the West Bromwich by-election of 1973).
What does being Speaker involve? Dressing up. Keeping order. Deciding what gets discussed. Sending people off. Loneliness.
Is she popular? Very – though not at the moment (see below) with the government. She got the Speakership because Tory MPs backed her against the advice of their whips, who wanted somebody safer. Some MPs say she is bossy; but most of them like that really.
Name her characteristic cries: 'Order, order!' (inherited from her predecessors). 'Call me Madam!' (when asked how a woman deputy speaker should be addressed). 'Time's up!' (invented by herself for use at the end of Questions).
Who was her first sending off? Someone or other from Bolsover.
And was that her greatest ordeal? No, that came recently when she had to rule on whether the Commons could vote on Amendment 2 (né amendment 27) of the Maastricht Bill. The issue was this: many MPs wanted to vote on whether or not Britain ought to opt out of the social chapter provisions of the Maastricht Agreement, and Betty had to decide whether to let them. The press described it as her toughest-ever decision.
What's so tough about that? Isn't voting on issues like that the essence of parliamentary democracy? Indeed. But the Deputy Speaker had earlier ruled against a vote, and the House had defended him in a censure debate. So it might have looked as though Betty was overruling him. Also government sources were saying she should forbid it because the effect of the amendment was unclear, and because some of those backing it had 'ulterior motives'.
Does that not amount to a monstrous edifice of chicanery and cant? Of course. But if Betty thought so, she couldn't say that. Speakers never give reasons for their decisions.
Not to be confused with: Betty Boop; Betty Boo; Ethel Merman.
Least likely to say: 'Do as you please, it's Liberty Hall round here.'

Ian Botham

Age: 37.
Nicknames: Both, Beefy, Guy the Gorilla, Mr Iron Bottom (India only).
Reputation: The Greatest All-Rounder English Cricket Has Ever Seen (by common agreement). Britain's Biggest Hero since Nelson (his former agent, Tim Hudson). The Last Working-Class Hero (*New Socialist*).
Politics: Often described as slightly to the right of Attila the Hun, although, unlike Botham, Attila the Hun would have had no compunction in joining the rebel English cricket tours to South Africa.
Intimations of mortality: A growing vulnerability to injury which he says will force him to retire at the end of his two-year contract with Durham.
Plans for a happy retirement: Huntin', shootin' and fishin'; more charity walks (he has raised more than £2 million for leukaemia research); appearances in pantomime; buying woollies for another series of *A Question of Sport*.
Friends call him: Loyal, generous, courageous, roguish, patriotic.
Critics call him: Bullying, boorish, insolent, intimidating, stubborn.
Worst advice he ever received: 'You should have stuck to soccer, lad,' proffered by coach Len Muncer during his time on the Lord's ground staff.
Heroes and heroines: Mike Brearley, a fatherly England captain; Viv Richards, West Indian batsman and Somerset soulmate; Margaret Thatcher, the daughter of a Grantham shopkeeper.
Great escape: Headingley '81, where Botham's 149 not out transformed the third Test against Australia and enabled England, 500–1 outsiders at one stage, to triumph by 18 runs.
Greatest scrape: Banned by the Test and County Cricket Board in the mid-eighties for 'bringing the game into disrepute' by admitting in a Sunday newspaper that he had smoked pot.
Opinions on Pakistan: Not somewhere he would send his mother-in-law.
Opinions on Pakistani cricketers: Not players he would share a joint with.
Cattiest remark received: 'In no way inhibited by any capacity to over-intellectualise' – Frances Edmonds.
Most besotted admirer: 'If you made him Prime Minister tomorrow, he'd pick this country up in 10 minutes' – Bill Alley, former umpire and Somerset cricketer.
Not to be confused with: P. W. Botha.
Opinion on England under Graham Gooch: 'I'm probably best out of it. Nobody seems to smile any more on tour.'
Most likely retirement speech: 'We're only here for a short time, so let's bloody well enjoy ourselves.'
Least likely retirement speech: 'Anyone fancy a quiet game of Scrabble?'

21 April 1993. Botham retired at the end of the season.

Virginia Bottomley

Appearance: Joan Hunter Dunn, played by Joyce Grenfell. Tory backbenchers turn to jelly at the mere thought of her.

Family: Father was John Garnett, ex-director of Industrial Society. Mother, Barbara, took part in Jarrow marches as a child. Her aunt, Peggy Jay, was 'devastated' when she became a Tory. Cousin of Peter Jay. Three children.

Background: Putney High School. May well have been the only Conservative at Essex University in mid-sixties. Originally good Tory wife to Peter Bottomley, the slightly loopy MP for Eltham. Worked as a researcher for the Child Poverty Action Group, then as vice-chair of National Council of Carers (*sic*). Fought Isle of Wight under slogan 'Turn Wight Blue' in 1983. Lost, and cried on the boat all the way back to mainland. Won South West Surrey in by-election shortly afterwards. Joined the cabinet as Health Secretary in 1992.

Ideology: Fabian managerialism.

Relationship with Peter: Her rise has precisely mirrored his fall. He was turfed out of office just as Virginia finally made it. He is said not to be bitter about this.

Useful adjectives to use when writing about Virginia: 'Attractive' (*Sunday Times*); 'attractive' (Kenneth Clarke, *Telegraph*); 'extremely attractive' (*Evening Standard*); 'staggeringly sexy' (anonymous Labour MP, *Independent*); 'incredibly good-looking' (Frank Field).

Useful sobriquets: Nurse Bossyboots, Nurse Matilda, Fragrant Ginny, Lady Bountiful, Goody-Two-Shoes, Mary Poppins, Lady with the Lamp.

Skeletons: Had first baby three months before marrying Peter. This was not uncommon behaviour for sociology students at Essex in 1967, but appeared to embarrass Virginia when revealed in 1992 at height of her campaign against teenage pregnancies.

Faults: Tends to bossiness. Desperately uncertain of herself; hopeless without a brief and pre-scripted sound-bites; civil servants under strict orders to keep her away from Walden, Paxman and any moderately taxing live interviews. Hated by the Right, who regard her as the Shirley Williams of the Tory Party.

Strengths: Staggeringly sexy, etc., etc. Tremendously caring. Organised. Capable of ruthlessness. Down to earth. Entirely unlike Kenneth Clarke.

Most precocious act as a child: Ejecting the au pair from the kitchen for not cooking the breakfast right and taking over herself.

Ideal weekend away: Rowing 26 miles down the Thames.

Least likely joke to make: How many Essex girls does it take to call for an ambulance?

Least likely to say: 'Dunno, really, I leave all that to me husband.'

Boudicca

Name: Boudicca; a.k.a. Boadicea, Bonduca.
Age: Died AD 62, when 35 years old.
Appearance: Raging queen.
CV: Trashed London, Colchester and St Albans and sparked a slaughter of colonists and collaborators after the Roman Raj annexed Norfolk, previously ruled as client king by her late husband Prasutagus. But her 200,000 ill-disciplined East Anglians were wiped out at Towcester by an imperial army of 10,000.
Why's she in the headlines? Anything to do with D-Day? No, no, we won that one. The Duchess of York has turned down an invitation to play Boady in a £14 million British biopic. Ken Russell is slated to direct.

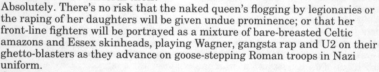

So bound to be tasteful then? Absolutely. There's no risk that the naked queen's flogging by legionaries or the raping of her daughters will be given undue prominence; or that her front-line fighters will be portrayed as a mixture of bare-breasted Celtic amazons and Essex skinheads, playing Wagner, gangsta rap and U2 on their ghetto-blasters as they advance on goose-stepping Roman troops in Nazi uniform.

Any scope in the film for a financial adviser? Definitely. John Fletcher's 1619 smash hit *Bonduca* centres on Caractacus, the queen's sagacious counsellor. The play depicts their relationship as platonic, but . . . she's widowed, she's lonely, it's wartime . . . and massacring 70,000 people is a powerful aphrodisiac. They hit the sack in the third reel.

So why approach Fergie? Any form there as a performer? Not unless you count her demanding roles as dedicated professional author and committed charity worker. The generous view is that Russell saw analogies between two spirited single women responding to crises by taking control of their lives, whether by dieting and aromatherapy or by staging a pogrom. And the spin-off potential for *Chubby the Cheerful Chariot* books was clearly massive.

And the cynical view? Irked by accusations of over-employing his thesp wife Hetty Baines, Ken feels obliged to make *pro-forma* approaches to other actresses, preferably completely unsuitable. Armed with their refusals, he can then cast Baines. On recent form, he is also likely to appear himself in love scenes with his missus, playing the Chief Druid and Emperor Nero.

Not to be confused with: Elizabeth I; Joan of Arc; Graham Taylor.
Most likely to say: 'Obviously, losing when you outnumber the opposition 20 to 1 is disappointing, but I thought Towcester was a good result for us, with lots of positive performances . . . '
Least likely to say: 'So that's a complimentary first-class return galley to Anglesey for two, baggage limit waived, if I guarantee publicity in *Ave! . . .* '

Boutros Boutros-Ghali

Age: 72.

Appearance: Egyptian customs official.

Club: The United Nations.

Occupation: Secretary-General of above.

Which means? Heading a whacking great overblown monster organisation stuffed with time-servers and the cousins of cabinet ministers, all waiting for fat pensions while they devote themselves to perfecting the finest red tape in the world.

Really? No wonder he's in the news: *Au contraire*, all that's perfectly normal.

Get on with it then, he's in the news because . . . Because he's told NATO stop dithering and authorise air strikes 'against artillery positions in or around Sarajevo, which are responsible for attacks on civilian targets'. Namely, the 68 who died in the mortar bombing of a Sarajevo market.

But didn't the UN say it couldn't prove who was responsible? Draw your own conclusions.

Does NATO take orders from the head of the UN? Er, rather the reverse actually.

So what was his point? Career damage limitation. Boutros is tired of carrying the can when the UN's leading members opt for inertia and point the finger at UNHQ, whacking great monster organisation stuffed with . . . etc., etc.

Fair enough, but isn't he the chap who often says . . . ? Quite: 'Our mandate is to maintain peace, not to impose peace.'

So it's all a bit of a muddle? All too often, and the problem is . . .

Yes? That the Secretary-General seems better at rowing with members and employees than he is at international diplomacy or UN reform.

Not everyone is keen on him then? Where have you *been*? Adjectives include vain, aloof, arrogant, abrasive, bossy, high-handed. I could go on.

In that case, wherever can he have served his apprenticeship? In the Egyptian government, surprise surprise, with some early modesty training at the Sorbonne where he earned his PhD in law in 1949. Served as Egyptian Foreign Minister 1977–91, then Deputy Prime Minister.

Any other worrying qualities? Yes, as a matter of fact. He wants his own UN army, volunteers who 'would have to be more heavily armed than peacekeeping forces'.

Future prospects? Limited, if many members have anything to do with it, after his term ends in 1996.

Favourite self-image? 'I personify the UN.'

Wife's view: 'An ass living is better than a dead lion.'

Favourite sound: His own voice.

Most likely to say: 'Just call me Your Highness.'

Least likely to say: 'Honestly, I've made a ghastly mistake and really I am most dreadfully sorry.'

9 February 1994

Emma Bovary

Née: Roualt.
Born: 1857.
Brief life: Passionate country girl marries dull husband, regrets it almost at once, takes a lover, and another, gets heavily into debt with the local draper, existence becomes a tissue of lies, fears disgrace, swallows arsenic, dies writhingly.
In the news because: (1) Claude Chabrol's film, starring Isabelle Huppert, has just been released – to an almost universal panning; (2) it's a set book for A-level sitters everywhere.
Wife of: Charles Bovary, an anxious-to-please, easy-to-deceive provincial doctor.
Mistress of: (1) Rodolphe; (2) Leon.
Mother of: Berthe, a daughter in whom she took no interest whatsoever.

Famous for? First, piety: as a spotless convent girl, she used to invent sins so she could stay longer in the confessional; then as one of the first fictional heroines to make an art form out of boredom; thirdly, adultery.
Was Bovary a feminist? A question on which women are divided. To the extent that she followed her own instincts (spend, spend, spend; shop, shop, shop; screw, screw, screw) and tried to remap her destiny, yes. Insofar as she fell victim to her own passions and to manipulative men, no.
A role model for other women? Well, only for a line of fictional heroines: Anna Karenina, Hedda Gabler, Molly Bloom, Ursula Brangwen *et al*.
Any interesting theories about what made Emma tick? The book's latest translator (Geoffrey Wall, in Penguin Classics) points out that the four men in Emma's life have an image of her which is 'decidedly fetishistic'. Emma appears to have had more slippers, shoes, clogs and boots than Imelda Marcos. The novel has more references to footwear than a Clarks catalogue.
What, in the film, is Emma most likely to be glad didn't happen? The fact that Gérard Depardieu wasn't cast by Chabrol as Hippolyte with the club foot, or else the plot might have been changed so that they could go to bed together.
Not to be confused with: Emma Woodhouse; Emma Thompson; Emma Soames; Flaubert's Parrot; Edna Flaubert, as the subtitles on Chabrol's movie put it at one point.
How would Barbara Cartland have treated the story? Cut out the arsenic and added more old lace.
How would Jilly Cooper have treated it? Cut the guilt and the arsenic; added more open-air pursuits: horse riding and bonking.
Least likely to say: (1) To her husband: 'I'm feeling fine tonight – the headache's gone and the pain in my back's vanished.' (2) To Neil Lyndon: 'Lick my boots, toerag.'

1 June 1993

David Bowie

Age: 46, though the boyish grin, svelte cheekbones and elfin figure dare you to believe it.

Appearance: High-class pickpocket attempting to pass himself off as international fine-art dealer.

Early life: Born David Jones in Brixton, 8 January 1947. Wanted to be a jazz saxophonist, probably because there can be no cooler prop for a born poseur. Honked eagerly if inexpertly throughout future career, and does so again on the album *Black Tie White Noise*. Changed name to Bowie to avoid confusion with Davey Jones of the Monkees. Lured into theatre and mime by Lindsay Kemp, and was never sure whether to be rock'n'roll star, actor or mime artist. Sceptics say he has always been a mime artist.

Main claim to fame: Became best-known manipulator of image, style, sound and sexuality in the music industry. Having decided that there was more to showbiz than cloning the celebrated philosopher and songwriter Anthony Newley with 1967's 'Laughing Gnome', Bowie became famous for 'reinventing himself' at frequent intervals, firstly and most fabulously with 1972's *Ziggy Stardust* album. Declared himself bisexual to a *Melody Maker* interviewer. Thereafter showed a great deal of thigh, bottom and chest.

Bowie's Greatest Hits: *The Man Who Sold the World* (the Lauren Bacall period), *Ziggy Stardust*, *Aladdin Sane*, *Pinups*, *Young Americans*, *Station to Station*, *Low*, *Heroes*, *Scary Monsters* and er . . . Philip Glass's *Low Symphony*?

Bowie's Lowest Moments (apart from *Low*): Punitive settlement with ex-manager Tony Defries in 1975. Notorious 'fascist salute' episode at Victoria Station in May 1976 (denied, futilely, by Bowie entourage). Despite glimmers of hope on *Let's Dance*, practically everything since 1980 has suggested pathetic attempt to appear current by frantic name-dropping and frequenting flash designers.

Finest achievement in the nineties: Marriage to erstwhile supermodel Iman, commemorated in recent song 'The Wedding'. Dream lifestyle in the USA, Switzerland and picturesque Mustique, where Mr & Mrs Bowie can retreat to their agreeable dwelling designed by Swedish architect Arne Hasselqvist.

Most risible moment in the nineties (apart from Tin Machine tour): The hitherto agnostic star's blush-tastic appeal to worldwide TV audience to join him in the Lord's Prayer at Freddie Mercury Memorial Concert.

What hope for former Thin White Duke? Unlike most pop stars, Bowie is on safer ground acting than singing. Excelled in Nic Roeg's *Man Who Fell to Earth* (1976) and Julien Temple's short, *Jazzin' for Blue Jean* (1984). Urgently needs sympathetic roles/friendly directors. Would undoubtedly find warm welcome and feel thoroughly at home in Luvvy-land. Dave's Oscar acceptance speech would be all-time classic.

Richard Branson

Appearance: Super-enthusiastic, slightly clumsy youth-club organiser.
Background: Public-school educated (Stowe); left at 16 after headmaster turned down request for business telephone in his study.
First business premises: A telephone box, from which he ran mail-order operation.
Became famous for: Selling cheap imported records in the sixties.
Stayed famous for: Signing the very boring Mike Oldfield.
But also: Signed the Sex Pistols when no one else would.
Consolidated fame in eighties by: Opening very large record shops; being the owner of Heaven; floating his company on the Stock Exchange (1987); unfloating it again at the end of the decade; assorted dangerous balloon 'n' boat stunts.

Was infamous in eighties for: Being Minister of Litter (1986).
And also for: Setting up the world's first charity to supply French letters.
Is now famous for: Tireless crusade against British (that's right, British, not French or German) Airways; his allegations against BA involve minutiae of landing slots and airline routes, details which everyone other than he and six aviation journalists find stunningly tedious.
Also quite well known for: Giving up smoking (giving up buying cigarettes, anyway); never carrying any money on him; once having lived on a houseboat even when a millionaire.
Things he has never been famous for but which have made him money: Publishing; video games; T-shirts and other teen-ery.
Best business decision: Steering well clear of involvement in British Satellite Broadcasting (he was horrified by the extravagance of what was supposed to be a start-up operation).
Worst business decision: *Event*, the *Time Out* copy launched in 1981 that sank without trace.
He is no longer connected with: The Virgin record company, which made him famous. He sold it to EMI in 1991.
Admirers say about him: Buccaneer, swashbuckler, old-fashioned merchant adventurer, hippy businessman, caring capitalist, if we had a few more like him there wouldn't be a trade deficit, etc., etc.
Detractors say about him: Dilettante eighties hero who couldn't stand the heat in the City; self-publicising promoter of candyfloss industries; grasshopper mind incapable of sticking with one thing, etc., etc.
Don't say to him: Love your sweet pickle.
And he won't say: BA takes more care of you.

The Brontës

Born: Charlotte 1816; Branwell 1817; Emily 1818; Anne 1820.
Died: Branwell and Emily 1848; Anne 1849; Charlotte 1855.
Home address: From 1820 until their deaths, Haworth Parsonage, Haworth, West Yorkshire.
Admission: £3.50.
Number of visitors: 180,000 per year.
Annual number when the Brontës were alive: 10 (not counting the postman).
Rival attractions: Catherine Cookson country, Emmerdale Farm.
Who were they? Three brilliant novelists, one male sot, the four longest-lived children of Patrick Brontë, a parson.
What did they do? Girls: housework, read romantic literature, wrote eight novels, volumes of poetry. Boy: drank himself to death.
Social life: Bleak (father quarrelled with all local gentry).
Feminist interpretation: Subordinate women obliged to publish their work under male pseudonyms.
Postmodern interpretation: If only Branwell had been banged up a bit more he might have picked up a pen, not the bottle.
Contemporary exploitation: As governesses. 'Be a governess! Better be a slave at once!' Charlotte wrote.
Posthumous exploitation: By the manufacturers of tea towels, jams and films, by tour operators, by jobbing biographers and sequel merchants.
Products the Brontë name might not enhance: Training shoes, vitamin pills, new crisp variety.
Spot the Brontë theme: The struggle between duty and passion, the struggle between rebellious governesses and patriarchal oppressors, the struggle between proto-Marxist rebels and their imperialist masters, the struggle between good weather and bad.
Famous fans: Matthew Arnold, Pat Phoenix, Kate Bush, Queen Victoria.
Kate Bush rewrites *Wuthering Heights*: 'Heathcliff! It's mee, your Catheee, I'm come home . . . '
Hollywood's interpretation of *Wuthering Heights*: Pretty Woman meets Ghost.
Commonest misconception: The Brontës baked exceedingly good biscuits.

Peter Brooke

Age: 58.

Appearance: Country gent straight from the pages of Buchan. Astonishing eyebrows.

Family: Second wife, Lindsay Allison, 47, is a Conservative agent. Three sons from first wife, who died in 1985 during routine surgery.

Family motto: Ex fonte perenni (From a perpetual spring).

Background: Son of Henry 'Babbling' Brooke, hanging and flogging Home Secretary much satirised by *TW3*, and Baroness Brooke, vice-president of the Tory Party. Educated at Marlborough and Oxford, where he was president of the Union. Fascinated with minutiae of the Brooke family dating back almost as far as Windsor Castle.

Career: Delayed becoming an MP until he was in his forties and his father had retired. Survived the Thatcher years without anyone quite knowing whether he was wet or dry. Played decent innings as party chairman with brief to soothe abrasions left behind by Tebbit. Astonished everyone by actually enjoying time in Northern Ireland – and not just for the opportunities it offered for beagling. Displayed remarkable patience in coaxing truculent rival politicians to sit around same table, even if it came to very little in the end. Good show on a sticky wicket.

Strengths: Affable old bufferish manner conceals a shrewd and decisive mind honed at Harvard Business School. Well-developed talent for listening. Legendary courtesy. Photographic memory. Bowls line and length.

Weaknesses: Can be a very dull speaker when the occasion demands it – and sometimes when it doesn't. Slightly gaffe-prone if bowled googlies by the reptiles. More interested in heritage than contemporary arts. Bit of a closet Quiller-Couch fancier.

Golden ducks: Lowest number of Tory votes ever polled in Bedwelty. Broke into song on Irish chat show – considered tactless on the evening of IRA murder of seven civilians in County Down.

Friends: Lord Justice Bingham, Nicholas Goodison, Jeremy Isaacs.

Hobbies: Cricket – once dreamed of being a cricket correspondent and can recite from *Wisden* until the early hours. Collects pictures (never pays more than £50) and books. Claims to have the biggest collection of wood engravings in the country. Speaks fluent Latin and Greek.

Personal slice of heritage: Owns 80 per cent of Wordsworth's manuscripts.

Opening gambits to be avoided: 'I loved your *Midsummer Night's Dream*.' 'Are you by any chance related to Rupert?' 'Give us a few bars of "Danny Boy".'

Least likely to say: 'Just wait while I change into my Chelsea strip.'

26 November 1992. Brooke replaced David Mellor at the Department of National Heritage after revelations of the latter's affair with Antonia Da Sancha. He left the Cabinet in the July 1994 reshuffle.

Bienvenida Buck

Age: Somewhere between 32 and 38-ish. Or thereabouts.

Appearance: Bottle-blonde Feydeau soubrette.

You can do better than that, surely? OK: body of a young girl, enchanting mouth, elegant neck, satin skin, petite breasts, legs of a gazelle (© Ministry of Defence).

Father: A respected Spanish lawyer.

Really? Oh all right. An alcoholic bricklayer who deserted his penniless wife while pregnant.

Mother: Remarried a retired naval officer.

Really? No, not really. She is a retired hospital cleaner named Garvin who lived with a greengrocer.

This is too confusing. Can we start at the beginning? Name: How much time have you got?

You mean it's not Bienvenida? Not necessarily. Could be Bernadette. There again, could be Francisca.

What about the surname? Appears to have started out as Ms (or possibly Señorita) Pérez-Blanco. Later became Lady Buck.

As in the well-known limerick? Just so.

And now? Is now Mrs Nicholas Sokolow.

Not the 32-year-old former Sotheby's dealer now working as a Mayfair art consultant? The very same.

How did she get to be Lady Buck? She married former Navy Minister Sir Antony Buck, after a whirlwind romance in 1990. Divorced three years later.

Sir Antony is nearly twice her age. What was in it for her? 'Friends' of Sir Antony claim she got through half a million quid on his Amex during the marriage.

Why did the marriage break down? Sir Antony's theory is that she became bored after he stepped down as MP for Colchester North.

Is that all? His action for divorce did claim adultery by Bienvenida.

With whom? Oh come, come.

OK, when did she first meet the Chief of the Defence Staff? They met at the Indian High Commission in 1991 and began a passionate affair within weeks.

Sir Peter is nearly twice her age. What was in it for her? She pocketed a fat cheque from the *News of the World* for spilling the beans about him.

How fat? Estimates range between £90,000 and £175,000.

Have we heard the last of Bienvenida? By no means. She's now a client of Max Clifford, the man who gave the world Freddie Starr's hamster and David Mellor's Chelsea strip. *NoW* promises more on her 'love romps' with Sir Peter. This will be followed by the book, the film starring Joanne Whalley-Kilmer, the perfume and the exotic lingerie range.

Least likely to say: 'Come and say hello to Mum.'

17 March 1994. Sir Peter Harding resigned over his affair with Lady Buck; in June 1994 she served divorce papers on Nicholas Sokolow.

Budgie the Helicopter

Age: 4.

Appearance: Anthropomorphic. The *ne plus ultra* of cuteness.

Also known as: 'The bravest, cheekiest, friendliest little helicopter Harefield Airfield's ever known'.

Occupation: Money-spinner.

For whom? Well, the Duchess of York wrote the books. She got £80,000 for American serialisation rights. And, though charities have benefited, she has also taken a fair amount of the royalties.

Has she written a new one? Even better. The cartoon series has just started on ITV.

Lucrative, eh? Co-producers Sleepy Kids plc announced a rights issue last year to raise £1.2 million to 'take a direct financial involvement' in the production.

What kind of talent does that sort of money buy? Er, scriptwriter Brian Trueman writes the scripts for *Dangermouse!* and *Count Duckula*. The narrator, Jeff Rawle, plays George on *Drop the Dead Donkey*.

And? Um, Budgie's voice is provided by Richard Pearce. He does voice-overs for *Crimewatch* and *The Cook Report*.

You're getting desperate: I haven't even mentioned the fact that Pippa the Plane has the voice of Bristol schoolgirl Abigail MacVean yet.

Is there any reason for being interested in Budgie? Psychologist David Lewis thinks the books reveal the secret stresses of the royal family. 'It is very common for people under stress to write about their feelings, often in a disguised way. D. H. Lawrence wrote about his love for his mother in *Sons and Lovers*, and Ernest Hemingway wrote about bullfighting, an obvious metaphor for his own conflicts. Most first novels are autobiographical, full of sexual desires, unfulfilled wishes and fears. Fergie is following a typical pattern.'

That must make him the first man to compare Budgie to some of the great works of world literature? And the last, probably.

If he's right, what titles can we expect in the future then? *Budgie Gets Some Financial Advice. Budgie Talks Exclusively to the 'Daily Mail'*.

Fergie's not one of the world's great thinkers, is she? No. But she did once paraphrase Coleridge's *Biographia Literaria* for the *Mail on Sunday*: 'I believe imagination is the starting point of all creativity.'

Is it? Well, cynics suggest an old children's book called *Hector the Helicopter*, by Arthur Baldwin, was actually the starting point of Fergie's creativity.

That's tantamount to treason! Not any more it's not. Fergie has had to drop 'Her Royal Highness' from the covers of the reprinted Budgie books.

Budgie not to be confused with: Any of the helicopters in *Apocalypse Now*.

Fergie not to be confused with: That other guffawing, prank-fond, limelight-hogging, helicopter-piloting hate figure, Noel Edmonds.

Budgie least likely to say: 'Show us yer undercarriage, Pippa.'

Fergie least likely to say: 'I've got an idea! How about a new character, an American . . . called Bryan the Big Bald Boeing?'

Naomi Campbell

Age: 22.
Size: 34-23-34, 5ft 10in in her (size seven) stockinged feet.
Born: Streatham, south London.
Job: Supermodel.
What does that mean? Like a supergun is a gun only longer, she's a model only taller.
What it doesn't mean: That she wears her underpants on the outside.
Biggest payday: Her model agency's lips are sealed. Rumoured to have been paid £100,000 for her appearance in Madonna's book *Sex*; said last year to have earned 'somewhere in the region of £1 million'.
Biggest regret: Being photographed having her toe sucked by Madonna in *Sex* ('My mum was upset').

She's been called the queen of the catwalk. Does this mean she has a royal background? Not exactly – though she was brought up by one parent, as was the Princess of Wales.
So what is her background then? She was born to Valerie, the 19-year-old daughter of Jamaican immigrants, who brought her up while touring the world with a dance troupe. Her father 'wasn't anything special' in Valerie's life. Naomi also trained as a dancer before doing bread-and-butter modelling jobs for fashion magazines, including several dodgy spreads involving being dressed in headscarves, floral pinnies and white gloves.
Love interest: Mike Tyson, Robert De Niro.
Mike Tyson? What did her mum have to say about that? 'He is so sweet, so shy . . . He really is a lovely young man.' This was before the rape case.
What she learnt from Mike Tyson: That actions speak louder than words. Reported to have KO-ed her relationship with De Niro by scrapping in the street with another woman. One witness said, 'Naomi grabbed her hair, slammed her against the car and started slugging her.'
Likes: Giggling; other models; Amanda de Cadenet.
Things they say about her: 'No Einstein' (fashion photographer Michael Roberts); 'What she needs is a relationship with someone who is nice' (Grace Coddington, fashion director of American *Vogue*); 'The Black Bardot' (Karl Lagerfeld).
Things she says about herself: 'I'm a Gemini, so I get bored with looking the same way for too long'; 'I'd rather be a rock singer than a movie star.'
Pretensions picked up in New York: American accent with a south London twang; a taste for flea-market grunge; a recording contract; aspirations to acting career; boring pat response to questions ('I don't talk about my private life').
Not to be confused with: Naomi Wolf; Bea Campbell; Valerie Campbell (Naomi's mother has, at 42, launched her own catwalk career).
Least likely mate: Bernard Manning.
Least likely to say: 'Did you see that piece in *Guardian* Women?'

9 March 1993. Ms Campbell published her first novel, *Swan*, in September 1994.

Albert Camus

Age: Born 1913. Died 1960.
Appearance: Fifties film star.
Status: Novelist and philosopher.
Why is he in the news? His latest
novel, *Le Premier Homme*, has just
appeared.
**Haven't the publishers been a
little tardy?** His family objected to
parts of the highly autobiographical
book, and there were problems
deciphering the text.
Some autobiography please: Born
into a poor settler family in Algeria,
his father was killed in the First
World War, and he was brought up
by his grandmother, who used to belt
him with a dried ligament of bull's
neck. Was variously an actor,
teacher, journalist and playwright.
Fought for the French resistance.
Died in a car crash. *Le Premier
Homme* was found in his briefcase at
the scene of the crash.

Wasn't he Sartre's mate? They met in Paris in 1943 and set up a left-wing
magazine, *Combat*. Joined the café-going existentialist group, but in 1952 he
and Sartre fell out.
Over unpaid bills at Les Deux Magots? Don't be absurd. Sartre hated
Camus's *L'Homme Revolté*, which rejected communism, while Jean Paul was
trying to arrange a marriage between existentialism and Marxism.
What was Camus's view? The revolutionary can never be absolutely right
and the fatal dialectic of power idealism leads to murder and oppression.
Could you sum up his philosophy in two words? Nihilism and absurdity.
Was he unreadable? Not at all. His novels *L'Etranger* and *La Peste* won him
the Nobel Prize for Literature in 1957 and produced a generation of angst-
ridden students.
What inspired Camus's philosophy? His impoverished upbringing, life in
a settler community but perhaps most of all football.
You're joking? No. He once said: 'All that I know most surely about
morality and the obligations of a man, I know from football.'
What was he? Dignified centre-half; cultivated outside left . . . ? A
goalkeeper, actually, like all literary greats.
Now I know you're joking: The evidence is irrefutable. Yevtushenko was a
very fine goalkeeper; Nabokov was a rather shakier custodian ('I was less the
keeper of a soccer goal than the keeper of a secret'); and Roy Hattersley was
no mean performer.
But did keeping goal really contribute to Camus's art? You bet. 'I
quickly learned that the ball never came to you where you expected it,' he
explained. 'This helped me in life.' His *Myth of Sisyphus*, about a man
condemned for ever to roll a large football like stone up a hill, could be seen
as a paean to the goalkeeper's lot.
Most likely to say: 'Je crois la justice mais je défendrais ma mère avant la
justice.'
Least likely to say: 'Eh, Jean Paul, où est Cantona?'

Eric Cantona

Age: 26.
Pronounced: Contonah.
A.k.a.: Le Brat, the Frog, Mad Eric.
Position: Number 7 for Manchester United (as worn by George Best).
Background: At Montpellier, fought with team-mates; at Auxerre, fined for striking the French international goalkeeper; at Marseilles, suspended for throwing his shirt at the referee; at Nîmes, suspended for throwing the ball at the referee. As sentence was passed by French FA committee, Cantona muttered: 'Idiots.' Asked to repeat the point, he walked up to each of them in turn and bellowed: 'Idiot.' Ban of one month was doubled, and he promptly retired. In 1988 he was suspended for one year from the national team for describing Henri Michel, the manager, as a bag of *merde*. Joined Leeds United instead. Transferred to Manchester after a year.
Hobbies: Shooting. Painting. Playing the piano and violin. Ideas. Poetry. Yoga.
Command of English: Not total.
Heroes: Rimbaud, Jim Morrison and Antoine de St Exupéry, the French novelist and airman.
Home: Leeds. Commutes to Manchester, or stays in hotel.
Cantona on the British press: 'When I give an interview the quotes that are used aren't the ones I would like them to use.'
Cantona the philosopher: Life is like a woman. You weary of some women, but some always find something new – every day, every evening in their dress, their conversation, the way they behave.
Cantona the football philosopher: Leaving a club is like leaving a woman. When you have nothing left to say you go.
Cantona on Rimbaud: 'He had the spontaneity of a child, and I believe in that.'
Platini on Cantona: 'I have the impression that if he cannot score a beautiful goal he'd rather not score.'
Howard Wilkinson on Cantona: 'Eric likes to do what he likes, when he likes, because he likes it – and then eff off. We'd all want a bit of that.'
Marriage: To Isabelle. She works at Leeds University as a foreign language assistant. One 4-year-old son.
Not to be confused with: Vinnie Jones and his hero, Rambo.
Singing career: After Leeds's title win told crowd: 'I don't know why I love you, but I do.'
Do not say: 'Ooh-là-là, Can-to-na!'
Least likely to say: 'Je suis malade comme un perroquet.'

George Carey

Age: 53 going on 75.
Appearance: Balding unemployed undertaker with tooth-gap emphasising penury.
Job: Archbishop of Canterbury.
Real job: Keeping the Church of England's warring factions together, criticising the government, proving critics wrong when they say he isn't up to the job.
Famous for: Gaffes. Such as calling opponents of women priests heretics, defending Muslims over the *fatwa* and criticising Roman doctrine just before his first official visit to Rome.
Why is he in the news? He isn't. Criticising the government for leaving a 'trail of chaos and bewilderment' in the coal industry isn't new. The Bishop of Durham has been saying it forcefully for years. And Carey softened his attack, as he always does, by admitting that all industries have to adapt to circumstances – and wrapping up his point in a long sermon to miners on the text: May the God of Hope Fill You All with Joy.
When was he in the news then? When he politely criticised the government for urban aid cuts. Before that he mildly attacked inordinate pay rises for top executives and suggested there could be a link between urban riots and social deprivation.
Did anyone listen? Not the government, which blamed the Church for not teaching people to be good.
Why was he appointed? He was thought to be a pious, happy-clappy evangelical and Mrs Thatcher hoped he would leave politics to her.
Was he and did he? Catchy tunes took only 10 minutes in his enthronement service. He says he isn't now an evangelical or anything else like that. And by the time he took office Thatcher had gone.
Who is his hero? John Major. The ex-hospital porter has said he identifies with the failed bus conductor.
What else have he and Major in common? Nuff said.
Is there any difference at all? Carey has 12 more years in office.
What does he want to achieve in all that time? He has said he wants the Church to be more businesslike, vicars to have regular performance checks and sermons to be less boring.
Has he done anything to make it all happen? Nothing visible.
Least likely to say: Anything memorable.

George Carman QC

Age: 64.

Appearance: In mufti, silvery-haired family doctor with artistic leanings.

Occupation: Barrister. Favourite brief of tabloid editors and the cast of *Hello!* magazine. Latest triumph is his successful defence of the *Sun* in a libel case brought by *EastEnders* star Gillian Taylforth.

How was his performance in court? A1.

No soft soaping? You have clearly never been cross-examined by him.

Is he well paid for his pains? £500,000 a year, at a conservative estimate.

Reputation: 'Vinny Jones in a horsehair wig.'

Speciality: Georgy Porgy, pudding and pie, quizzed the girls and made them cry. Taylforth, Sonia Sutcliffe, Jani Allen and Mona Bauwens all underwent elegant character assassination. Assisted by mysteriously acquired private diaries and videos, he fixes one tellingly sordid image in the jury's mind: Taylforth drunkenly brandishing a sausage and bragging 'I give very good head', Allen having sex with a porcine neo-fascist in torn green underpants.

A bit of a bastard then? Steady on; he has also pulled off some near-miraculous acquittals of pilloried personalities – Jeremy Thorpe (conspiracy to murder), paediatrician Dr Leonard Arthur (attempted murder), *Coronation Street* actor Peter Adamson (indecent assault), Ken Dodd (tax fiddling).

All blokes? Curious, isn't it?

100-per-cent record? Not quite. Appearing for the *Observer*, he lost a libel case brought by Edwina Currie over a comparison between her and a murderous Tory Euro MP in a David Hare film.

Have the tabs ever turned him over? Yup. The *Mail* revealed a third, earlier dissolved marriage, besides the two recorded in *Who's Who*.

Sound-bite highlights: '[David Mellor] behaved like an ostrich and put his head in the sand, thereby exposing his thinking parts'; '[Sutcliffe] danced on the graves of her husband's victims'; 'We learn, do we not, that idols sometimes have feet of clay' (Thorpe case); 'Some accountants are comedians, but comedians are never accountants' (Dodd case).

Examples of Carmanspeak: 'In drink' (pissed); 'animadverting' (giving a bollocking); 'discharging his vomit' (throwing up).

The most boring castaway ever on *Desert Island Discs*? Possibly – piqued at being unable to extract a single revealing answer, Sue Lawley said she felt as if she'd been on the witness stand. But competition for the title is pretty fierce.

Not to be confused with: George Graham; Lord Scarman; Carmen Callil; Carmen Miranda.

Least likely to say: 'The *Sun*? No way, José.'

Most likely to say: 'Shall we say the usual £40,000 retainer and £2,000 daily refreshers? See you at the Savoy.'

Bill Cash

Appearance: Extremely tall (6ft 4in) and equally earnest; serious grey hair; motivated glasses.
Other notable features: Gabby.
Likes: European integration: strongly supported the Bill which endorsed the Single European Act. Small print. Drafting things. Cricket (often listed as a former Staffordshire fast bowler, though does not appear in the Minor Counties averages). The Riot Act: believes its provisions on the dispersal of mobs ought to be reinstated. Jazz.
Dislikes: European integration: earnestly opposed to the Maastricht Bill and the Maastricht Treaty. Delors. Abortion. The designs of Baroness Warnock: he once begged the Commons to consider 'the long-term prospect of a super-race served by super-proles'. Fluoridation.
Chief claim on the nation's attention: The busiest bee in the whole buzzing apiary of Euro-scepticism. At the centre of most of its plots. Runs its office in Great College Street in a house owned by Lord McAlpine.
What exactly is Euro-scepticism? It's a form of atheism. Cash is sceptical about the EC in the sense that Savonarola was sceptical about sin.
What does he tend to see when he looks out of the window? Garden paths, down which most of his colleagues are being led by the government. Trojan horses, Pandora's boxes. Cads and bounders. Collusive understandings. Bludgeons.
Where did he spring from? From the family that gave us Cash's name-tapes, which explains why his presence may give you an itchy feeling at the back of your neck. Direct descendant of the William Cash who, with his cousin John Bright, played a decisive part in the founding of Abbey National. Entered Commons at Stafford by-election in '84. Before that, a solicitor and nifty drafter of parliamentary bills, wrecking amendments, etc.
Who are his heroes? John Bright; Disraeli ('I have always been a great devotee of Disraelian politics').
Which does he most resemble? Hard to say. Lacks Bright's power to move an audience to rapture and tears. Lacks Disraeli's adaptability and talent for chatting people up.
What are his greatest assets? Diligence; pertinacity; straightness; one of Westminster's most admired and dashing wives (Biddy); a mouthwatering 16th-century manor house in Shropshire; gabled gatehouse with two polygonal turrets; 'deserves more intensive study' – Pevsner.
Is it true he made the longest speech in recent Commons history? No, he was expected to, but sat down quite suddenly after a mere three hours. Brougham once spoke for six.
What is he likely to call his autobiography? On present trends, *The Impotence of Being Earnest*.
Least likely to say? 'Can't make the rally, I'm off for a jar with Ted Heath.'

Lady Chatterley

Age: First published privately in Italy in 1928.

Background: Lawrence's last novel, and banned in 1928, prosecuted in 1960, published by Penguin same year, vilified (by feminist movement) in 1970s.

In the news because of: BBC dramatisation starring Joely Richardson as Lady Chatterley and Sean Bean as Mellors, the gamekeeper.

Best thing about the BBC version: It is only a four-part series (there'll be plenty of other parts around).

Worst thing: It is directed by Ken Russell, perpetrator of the film adaptation of *Women in Love*.

What the tabloids say: 'A drastically toned-down final version' (two f-words, no c-words); 'Joely in saucy new TV role'; 'Sean Bean as randy gamekeeper Mellors'.

Lawrence on Lady Chatterley: 'A soft, ruddy, country-looking girl, inclined to freckles, with big blue eyes, and curling brown hair, and rather strong, female loins.'

Lawrence on Mellors: 'He had a native breeding which was really much nicer than the cut-to-pattern class thing . . . and the strange weight of the balls between his legs!'

LC's literary status: Dismissed as last spasm of the dying Lawrence, and justly ignored until the 1960 Old Bailey trial, when defence witnesses – including E. M. Forster, Richard Hoggart and the Bishop of Woolwich – claimed it as a classic of compassion and 'reverence' (Hoggart's favourite word).

Current reputation: Most readers probably concur with the prosecuting council: 'Reverence? Reverence? For the weight of a man's balls?'

Most significant page of the book: The copyright page, which runs – 'Reprinted 1960, 1961, 1965, 1966, 1967, 1969 (twice), 1970, 1971, 1972, 1975 (twice), 1976, 1977, 1978 (twice), 1979 (twice), 1980 (twice), 1981 (twice), 1982 (twice) . . . ' and so on.

Its appropriateness for 1993: Combines sex and coal mines, the country's twin obsessions. Features randy character called Mellor(s).

Mervyn Griffith-Jones QC on *Lady Chatterley*: 'Is it a book you would wish your wife or your servants to read?'

Worst writing in novel: 'And he stuck flowers in the hair of his own body, and wound a bit of creeping-jenny round his penis, and stuck a single bell of hyacinth in his navel and she pushed a campion flower in his moustache where it stuck, dangling under his nose . . . '

Alternative titles (Lawrence's own): *Tenderness*; *John Thomas and Lady Jane*.

Not to be confused with: Any other, better book by Lawrence.

The Chelsea Flower Show

Age: First held 1913.
Vital statistics: 170,000 visitors over four days (riff-raff admitted only on last two); 25 theme gardens; central Great Marquee covers two and a half acres.
Function: Wimbledon of horticulture; holiday camp for middle England; prologue to the Season.
Dress code: Viyella shirt (men); M&S beige mac (women). No admission without *Daily Telegraph.*
Attractions: First sighting of new floral varieties; chance of glimpse of Queen Mum or even Alan Titchmarsh; outstanding pick-up opportunities.
You are joking? No, it's been going on for years. Already in a frisky away-day mood on arrival, gardeners from the sticks are further excited by jostling erotic demigods like Geoff Hamilton and Anne Swithinbank in the congested walkways; and by conversations devoted to reliable bushy growths and vigorous stems.
But leaving sex aside, it's an English Eden? No question. Albeit marred a little this year by a big rumpus involving a veteran lily grower who confessed to purchasing his prize-winning blooms. The practice of nurserymen buying in plants 'has long been an open secret', a show spokesman admitted.
Lumme. But everything else is fragrant and harmonious? Definitely. Although the bitter feud between Radio 4's *Gardeners' Question Time* team and Classic FM's ex-BBC panel has spread to Chelsea, with the latter upstaging their rivals by broadcasting from the show. And then there's the brouhaha over Paul Cooper's garden 'to accommodate sexual needs'.
Gracious, not that again. Fill me in, if you must: Supposedly a thirties 'constructivist' concept, Cooper's display incorporates a floral four-poster bed with *in flagrante* couple and a hidden fan to lift skirts à la Marilyn Monroe. He conned us, says the show's spokesman sniffly: 'His brief gives no indication that bedroom furniture, air blowers or sexual activity are to be included . . . '
Otherwise, though, Chelsea is a tranquil, timeless idyll where art and nature embrace? Absolutely. Except that it's hideously crowded and it invariably rains.
Newcomers not to be missed: The pink rose Trevor Griffiths; the sweet pea Kiri Te Kanawa: the rhododendron Seb Coe: and *Country Life* recommends the latest lupins, the salmon-pink Gloria Hunniford and 'the lovely, lemon-yellow Stefan Buczacki'.
Not to be confused with: The Festival of Mind/Body/Spirit, a hippy rally mischievously staged one Tube stop away at the Royal Horticultural Halls.
Don't say: 'That Geoffrey Smith's a pompous dickhead, isn't he?'
Do say: 'You show me your *Aquilegia vulgaris*, and I'll show you my *Buxus sempervirens.*'

Linford Christie

Born: Jamaica, came to London at 7.
Pastimes: Dominoes, crosswords.
Appearance: On track, a psychopathic body-builder being chased by herd of elephants. Off track, pleasant, ordinary sort of bloke.
Previous jobs: Tax collector, social worker, bank clerk. Now runs agency for sports people with athletes Colin Jackson and Mark McKoy called Nuff Respect.
Why in the news? Won world championship 100m in Stuttgart in 9.87sec, a piddling 0.01sec outside the world record, to complete grand slam of Commonwealth, European, Olympic and world gold medals.
But not the world record? No, but Carl Lewis's 9.86 was on a downhill bouncy track in Tokyo in 1991, so that doesn't count – except in the record books. Christie won a new Mercedes for winning in Stuttgart.

That'll be fun to drive around Shepherds Bush: Perhaps not. Christie's one run-in with the police came in July 1988 when they arrested him at West London Stadium for 'stealing' a car which had been loaned to him by a sponsor. Successfully sued the police for £30,000 for wrongful arrest.
His body is a temple, right? More of a liberal synagogue. Didn't train at all until he was 20, and as young athlete stayed out late and trained sporadically. Taken under the wing of coach Ron Roddan, who sorted him out.
Other achievements? Brought the word 'lunchbox' out of the mad bad world of Tupperware and into the tabloids.
Lunchbox? Don't ask me. Something to do with genital endowment and lycra shorts, not unconnected with tiresome racial sterotype about black men having big willies.
But you know what they say about big feet: Christie is size 13.
Does he get on with other athletes? Not really. Christie got into trouble in 1992 for criticising world champion 400m relay team. 'I don't like their attitude.'
What he says: 'All the bad stuff has proved my mental strength.'
What they say: 'He's a well-balanced athlete. He's got a chip on both shoulders' – 400m runner Derek Redmond.
Drugs and Christie: Vociferous campaigner against drug abuse.
But? At the Seoul Olympics he tested positive for pseudoephedrine, a stimulant found in cough linctus and other medicines. Christie's explanation that he had taken ginseng on the advice of the team doctor was accepted.
Christie and children: Loves 'em. But got into trouble over comments that single mothers should accept more responsibility.
Why should he care? He has just been ordered to fork out £60 a week maintenance for two 8-year-old twins he fathered.

Alan Clark

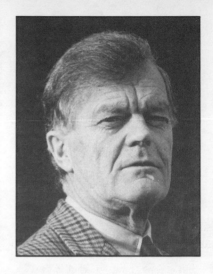

Age: 65. But not expected to draw his bus pass.

Politics: Romantic radical reactionary British nationalist. Mainly an English nationalist, but also embraces Scotland, perhaps because he owns such a lot of it.

Family background: Father was Lord Clark of *Civilisation*. ('Just after the war he took us to Holland to see art and all I wanted was to get to the nearest Buick dealer.') Family money came from threadmaking business in Paisley.

Homes: Too many to mention. Main one is Saltwood Castle in Kent, where he lives with his wife Jane whom he married in 1958 (he 30, Jane 16). He sold a Turner to meet a bill for capital transfer tax; now has to make do with the odd Degas, Gainsborough, Reynolds, Cézanne, etc., etc.

Past ambition: To get out of the House of Commons before he began to dodder: 'I wish to leave in my prime.' Stood down at the 1992 election.

Present ambition: To get into the House of Commons, preferably at the Newbury by-election. One of 400 brave/foolhardy souls who sought the Conservative nomination.

Why this abrupt change of mind? Perhaps he's stopped ageing. Or else it's because the threat of prosecution over Matrix Churchill has lifted. Or else he expected to go to the Lords, but hasn't been asked. He says he'd expected politics to get pedestrian after the last election: he now finds they haven't.

Where would you place him in the context of the modern Conservative Party? In a very expensive anteroom. Once said: 'When I consider my own outlook' (e.g. soft on unions, in favour of protectionism and industrial intervention) 'I sometimes marvel that I should continue to be accepted within the party at all.'

Dislikes: The royal family (except the Queen and Di) for their 'vulgarity, brutishness and maladroitness'. America: 'a barbarian civilisation with its Chesterfields and chewing gum'. NATO. Hunting.

Likes: Fast cars (two convictions for over-enthusiastic propulsion of his Porsche). Gossip. Margaret Thatcher ('Sexually, I have never come across any other woman in politics so attractive'). Admires Dennis Skinner.

What phrases has he given to the language? 'Bongo Bongo Land' (reference to the Third World in a ministerial memo which some cad later leaked). 'Economical with the *actualité*': his courtroom description of how he told Matrix Churchill to emphasise the pacific uses of machine tools rather than their potential military use to Iraq.

Clarks with whom he has no connection: Petula Clark. The Society of Town Clerks. The Dave Clark Five.

Least likely to say: 'Call me Nobby.'

10 March 1993. Clark's gossipy *Diaries* were published three months later and delighted critics and public alike. But two of his former lovers, Valerie Harkess and her daughter Josephine, claiming they were enraged by hints in the book, gave detailed accounts of the affairs to the press. Clark preserved his customary detachment: 'Sex is an agreeable activity and people like to read about it.'

Ken Clarke

Age: 52.
Appearance: Ringmaster in a small provincial circus, puffing on a cigar while pondering how to discipline the elephant for acting stroppy.
Employment: Home Secretary; hammer of the police; sometime hammer of the doctors, the ambulance crews and the teachers. Prime Minister in waiting.
Name some previous Prime Ministers in waiting: Francis Pym. John Moore. Kenneth Baker.
And what became of them? Exactly.
Political characteristics: Blokishness. Good cheer. Zest for a scrap. Candour, or its simulacrum. Persistent insouciance.
Give examples of this insouciance: Wearing Hush Puppies in Parliament. Shameless

smoking and drinking as Minister of Health: he used to light up to annoy the atmospherically correct. Refusing to be fazed by interviewers or events. Asked what he thought of one particularly venomous attack on John Major, he said he hadn't really thought about it: he had better things to do with his Saturday (i.e. watching the Cup Final).
But wasn't the Cup Final a wretched, boring game? Exactly.
Doesn't this kind of casual behaviour sometimes put people's backs up? You bet. Clarke sometimes infuriates colleagues by telling the truth where sleeker men would dissemble: e.g. his admission at the height of his party's Maastricht turmoil that he hadn't read the treaty. He's also accused of not listening. Police leaders complained that while they were lecturing him on the error of his ways, he began to read the *Daily Telegraph*.
Which bit of the *Daily Telegraph*? The football, probably. He's a Forest supporter. Possibly the jazz reviews. Or something about Group 4.
Where would you locate him on the political spectrum? Originally on the left of the party; Tory Clarkeophiles believe his heart is there still. Anti-hanging. Anti-Thatcher in the battle for the leadership in 1975 (and was the first cabinet minister in 1990 to tell her to her face that she'd have to go). Suspected on the right as being wet and wildly pro-European.
Could that stop him becoming leader of his party? Possibly. But the Right like his pugnacity and directness. And he's playing the Europhilia down. Defined his vision of Europe thus: 'Britain as an independent nation state in a European community of nations'; which should be good for most of the party, if not for Ted Heath.
Not to be confused with: Alan Clark, whose diaries describe Ken as 'a pudgy puffball'. Kenneth (never Ken) Clark, father of the aforementioned. Frank Clark, manager of Nottingham Forest. A pudgy puffball.
Least likely to say: 'Doesn't Wittgenstein make much the same point somewhere in his *Tractatus*?'

Max Clifford

Age: 92.
But that can't be true! So what?
Current profession: Peddler of
gossip, smut and outright fantasy.
Can you prove it? Who cares?
Appearance: Lubricious badger.
He totally denies that: Just
kidding, Max!
Career: Started as reporter on local
paper, where he learned how to
advance his own interests in the
guise of news, then became a PR in
the music business, where he
discovered that people will believe
anything. He put the two together
and emerged as Max Clifford PR,
specialist in selling scandals and
promoting tabloid names.
Significance: He embodies all that
is worst about British tabloid excess
and public prurience.
Achievement: Has single-handedly
done more than anyone else, including Murdoch and Maxwell, to encourage
censorship of the press.
How so? Two of his greatest scoops, the Mellor/de Sancha story and Princess
Diana in the gym, relied on amateur spying: respectively, surreptitious tapes
and sneaked photographs.
Max's redeeming features: None.
C'mon, there must be something: OK, he's devoted to his wife, disabled
daughter and his dog. And, of course, his clients.
How do we know? Max appeared with them in a TV programme.
The wages of sin: Between £2,000 and £5,000 per client, payable monthly.
Life of Riley, eh? If that's what you call a semi in Raynes Park. 'I know
stars who live in vast houses,' says Max, 'and they're very unhappy.'
Most commonly inspired adjectives: Smarmy, sleazy, simian.
Can't help liking the chap, what? Absolutely. His numerous friends
include the Harkess family, Antonia de Sancha, Degsy Hatton, Freddie Starr,
Bryce Taylor, Katie Baring, Simone Hyams, Bienvenida Buck and, oh, a
whole host of lovely guys, gals and the occasional hard-up adulterer.
Eminent enemies: Max is working his way through *Who's Who*. So far he's
nobbled Alan Clarke, Michael Winner, David Mellor, Sir Anthony Buck, Sir
Peter Harding and the Princess of Wales.
He deserves a medal! They don't yet give one for profiting from stories
based on entrapment, phone tapping, deceit, spite, adultery and revenge.
Tacky, or what? Well, not tacky at all according to the big-hearted badger:
'Tacky people throw coins from the terraces at football matches.'
How to talk to Max: Repeat after me: 'Sweetheart, fabulous, lovely girl,
attractive young ladies, harmless fun, you're talking out of your arse!'
Not to be confused with: Beta-max; Max Factor; Maxpax; Pacamacs;
Tampax.
Most likely to say: 'Princess Diana Ate My Toes.'
Least likely to say: 'Shsssshh! Mum's the word!'

Chelsea Clinton

Age: 12½.

Appearance: All-American 12½-year-old, right down to the mouthful of ironmongery. Five feet two, long curly brown hair. Size five feet.

Has she anything in common with David Mellor? No. She is named after the Judy Collins song 'Chelsea Morning', rather than the football club.

Position: Daughter of 42nd President of the USA.

Hobbies: Ballet (recent appearance in the *Nutcracker* resulted in stress fracture). Plays in softball league run by local dentists (the Molar Rollers). Does a bit of volleyball.

Does she do interviews? Never.

What does she want to be when she grows up? A scientist.

Dress sense: Preferred mode is T-shirt, jeans and trainers, but will dress up in floor-length purple gowns if occasion really demands it.

How does she keep in touch with Bill? Faxed her maths homework to him while he was on campaign trail.

What Bill says: 'If I win, she loses.'

What sympathisers say of her: 'Imagine going through puberty, with hormones pouring out of your skin like hyperactive geysers, in front of the whole world, especially Sam Donaldson [Jeremy Paxman without the shyness].'

What the comedy scriptwriters say of her: 'We have half the staff trying to rewrite Quayle jokes for Chelsea, but it ain't easy.'

IQ: Unknown. But she can spell 'potato'.

Other White House adolescents: Kermit Roosevelt (12); Louisa Adams (14). Amy Carter was only 9 when her father was made President.

Role models to avoid: Tricia and Julie Nixon; Luci Baines and Lynda Bird Johnson; Mark Thatcher.

Parental discipline: Bill and Hillary refuse to let her even talk about having her ears pierced before she's 13.

Subjects Bill would do well never to discuss with Chelsea: Nuclear proliferation, GATT, Bosnia, the budget deficit.

Brian Clough

Age: 58.
Appearance: Young Leonid Brezhnev.
Nickname: Old Big 'Ead.
Status: Newly created freeman of the city of Nottingham, for services to Nottingham Forest FC.
But does he deserve it? On past record, yes – took Forest into the First Division, won the League Championship and the European Cup. But this season has been dismal and Forest are rooted to the foot of the table, with relegation looming.
Other freemen of Nottingham: Torvill and Dean; William Booth, founder of the Salvation Army. Not thought to share Booth's views on temperance (local joke: he's getting the freedom of the city but not the keys to the drinks cabinet).
Managing to survive: In management for 27 years, at Hartlepool, Derby, Brighton, Leeds (for 44 days) and since 1974 Forest. Had a brief but electrifying career as a player, scoring freely for Middlesbrough and Sunderland and winning two England caps before a knee injury forced him to retire at 28.
Left-winger: Vocal supporter of the Labour Party – Malcolm Allison called him 'a Rolls-Royce communist'. Hates the tabloids, though he has written for the *Sun*. Philanthropist who insists his players get involved in charity work, but that hasn't stopped him building up a large personal fortune.
Other baubles: Awarded an OBE in 1991 and festooned with honorary degrees, but denied the prize he most wanted, the England manager's job, because he was too outspoken. 'The Football Association thought that I would want to take over and run the show. They were dead right.'
As if relegation wasn't enough: Clough is facing an FA investigation over an alleged V-sign to jeering fans. In 1989 he was fined £5,000 and banned from the touchline after manhandling fans who misbehaved at a cup tie.
Any other crises? Yes, he has been told that his TV advertising contract with Shredded Wheat will not be renewed.
No relation to: Arthur Hugh Clough; Algy Cluff.
Clough on management: 'In this business, you've got to be a dictator or you haven't got a chance.'
Clough on hooliganism: 'There are more hooligans in the House of Commons than at a football match.'
Clough on international politics: 'I hope you were as delighted as I was when Nelson Mandela was freed. But I hadn't bargained for the fact that his release was going to cut across the start of our Littlewoods Cup semi-final.'
Saying of A. H. Clough that Brian might quote: 'It is better to have fought and lost / Than never to have fought at all.'
Least likely to say: 'Well, that's a matter for the board, young man.'

24 March 1993. Forest were duly relegated and Clough resigned. The club won promotion back to the Premier League in the following season.

Phil Collins Inc.

Age: 20.

Appearance: Healthy.

Registered office: Hill House, 1 Little New Street, London EC4 3TR.

Job: According to its Report and Financial Statements for the year ending 31 December 1991 – the most recent lodged at Companies House – 'The principal activity of the company continued to be the provision of the services of Philip Collins in the entertainment field.'

Does Philip Collins provide a lot of services in the entertainment field? Yes. Turnover in 1991 was £17,835,628.

Profitable, eh? Actually, no. The company made a loss after taxation of £326,378.

How come? Well, there are costs and administrative expenses to take into account, but basically because Philip Collins Ltd paid its director a salary of £12,680,000.

Let me guess . . . Yes, Phil Collins is the director of Philip Collins Ltd.

Is £12,680,000 more than Andrew Lloyd Webber pays himself? Yes, about 10 times as much. It makes Phil Collins the highest-paid company director in Britain.

The tabloids say: 'He's the Mr Ordinary of pop.'

They should say: 'He's the George Soros of pop.'

Does he bother with a pension? Yes. In 1991 he paid £2,008,300 in pension contributions.

Anything else? Philip Collins Ltd has an investment in Fisher Lane Farm Ltd, representing 33 per cent of its equity share capital.

What does Fisher Lane Farm Ltd do? It provides recording facilities.

Does . . . Yes, Philip Collins Ltd paid the company £174,873 in 1991 to use its facilities.

Is . . . Yes, Phil Collins is a director of Fisher Lane Farm Ltd.

And . . . As of 9 November 1990, he is also director of Ashtray Music Ltd, Effectsound Ltd, Gelring Ltd, Genesis Music Ltd, Isle of Mull Salmon Farm Ltd, Pennyghael Estates Ltd, TGP 155 Ltd and TGP 156 Ltd.

What will Phil Collins's next album be called? *No Mortgage Required.*

And his next single? 'You Can't Hurry Capital Gains Tax'.

Jilly Cooper

Age: You're as old as you feel, aren't you?

How old does she feel? A young 14, still drooling over anything with four legs.

Appearance: Exploding fringe over apple cheeks and Wife of Bath gnashers.

Career: A brigadier's daughter and paragon of sixties madcappery who made her name in the *Sunday Times* as an expert on Jilly Cooper.

Specialities: Schoolgirl puns, scatty domesticity and the blissfulness of marriage to Leo, a portly publisher. The latter inspired her first book, *How to Stay Married*: 'If you keep your partner happy in bed, he's unlikely to stray . . . '

Jilly's fiction: Modest sizzlers called after posh girls – Bella, Octavia, Harriet – gave way to the longer, more thrusting *Riders*, *Rivals* and *Polo*, wherein stereotypical nobs rut their way round the shires.

Who buys them? Everybody. Jilly's laboriously padded sagas, coarse tributes to the class system, have a natural allure for dimwitted toffs and perverse appeal for the masses, who have, between them, bought 800,000 copies of *Polo*. This was the most successful British paperback of 1992, grossing almost £5 million for Corgi.

Jilly's hobbies: 'Merry-making, wild flowers, music, mongrels' (*Who's Who*). And being photographed in and around her dreamy Cotswold house, telling interviewers all about talented Leo. 'Leo is brilliant at sex,' she informed the *Daily Express* in 1985. Leo, too, has been generous with matrimonial advice. 'If anything looks like it's becoming an affair, by Christ, in come the fire engines,' he told the *Daily Mail* in 1989.

Dial 999: In 1990, Jilly told *Today* that Leo had been having an affair, or what she termed a brief 'dalliance'. Umbraged, one Sarah Johnson announced in the *Guardian* that she'd been dallying with Leo for six years. She was, she wrote, tired of reading Jilly's wittering about her 'idyllic marriage'.

Excuse me, isn't this appallingly prurient? From a literary angle, no. Soon after the Revelations, Jilly told *Tatler* that adultery would be the theme of her next book: 'I'm writing it because I know so many women in Gloucestershire who are miserable because their husbands are up in London having affairs.' Publicity for *The Man Who Made Husbands Jealous* has inevitably refocused on the home life of the Coopers.

Is it revenge? The suggestion makes her cry.

The moral of this story: Only saints should base their careers on personal revelation.

How to interview Jilly: Flatter the dogs, shout 'giddy up' and switch on the tape recorder.

Most likely to say: 'Send for the fish knives, Fergie.'

Least likely to say: 'No comment.'

Tom Cruise

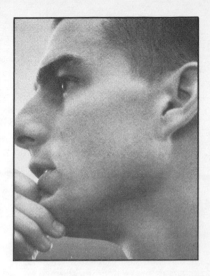

Age: For ever young (30).
Real name: Thomas Cruise Mapother IV.
Other names: The Happy Hunk; Top Gun; the thinking person's Michael J. Fox.
Marital status: Married – to the actress Nicole Kidman – with kid (adopted).
Previous marital status: Married – to the actress Mimi Rogers – without kid (not adopted).
Best performance to date: A tough one, but probably a toss-up between the trouser-dropping dance sequence to celebrate his parents leaving him alone for the weekend in *Risky Business* and virtually anything with Nicole Kidman in *Hello!*.
There have been more than a few turkeys haven't there? There certainly have: *Cocktail, Taps, Days of Thunder, Far and Away, Legend* (whatever that was).
There must be more to him than that? Well, *Born on the Fourth of July, The Color of Money* and *Rain Man* all did pretty well.
Appearance to date: Dumb but cute; Richard Gere's younger brother; vertically challenged Levi's Man.
New appearance: Bright but cute; Paul Newman's younger brother; vertically challenged Brooks Brothers whiz kid.
Why the change? He's playing a brilliant young lawyer who gets involved with the Mafia in Sydney Pollack's $150 million box-office smash *The Firm*, which is based on John Grisham's bestselling novel.
How does he do it? Method acting? Make-up? Glasses.
Glasses? But women don't make passes at men who wear . . . You don't understand, do you. Glasses equal clever. And clever is sexy this year in Hollywood. That's why Sly Stallone always slips a pair of specs on when he's doing his Renaissance man pose for *Hello!*.
But can Tom act? Are we working to the Nicole Kidman scale?
If you like: He's brilliant.
Really? Let's just say Nicole's major achievement to date is *The Bangkok Hilton*, an Australian mini-series.
I hear what you're saying, but can he act? Well, Dustin Hoffman said he was 'very compulsive and monk-like' about his work on *Rain Man*. But then Cruise has just signed to make *Top Gun 2* for $7 million.
Not many monks in the air force, are there? Few indeed.
Not to be confused with: Julia Roberts playing a brainy, whiz-kid lawyer in the film version of the John Grisham novel *The Pelican Brief*.
Will she be wearing glasses? Probably.
Least likely to say: 'Nicole and I are really looking forward to making the sequel to *Far and Away*.'
Most likely to say: 'Nicole and I think the script to *Top Gun 6* is very strong in a genuinely dramatic sense.'

The Dalai Lama

Appearance: Bronzed, podgy, slightly wrinkled but totally benign Mekon.

Age: 58.

In the news because: He's the hottest ticket in town; his public appearances on his UK visit are sold out.

How would you recognise him, apart from his yellow robes? You probably wouldn't: he's such a saint.

Previous incarnations: He is the 14th earthly incarnation of the Tibetan God of Mercy, known for his infinite tolerance.

Mannerisms: Given to giggling, chuckling and exclaiming 'Heavens!'

Profession: God-king and Buddhist monk.

Role in life: Professional exile; gentle thorn in the flesh of Western governments, reminding them of their failure to help Tibet, which has been occupied by China since 1950, and has led to the victimisation and death of countless thousands of Tibetans.

Image: The ultimate icon of non-violence. Awarded Nobel Peace Prize in 1989 for his unremitting devotion to a peaceful solution of the Tibetan problem.

How does he spend most of his time? In prayer and meditation for six hours a day. Sometimes he goes in for a four-day ceremony, the Kalachakra Tantra, which is supposed to speed the path towards the Buddhist state of Enlightenment.

Sounds the sort of quiet guy Hollywood has never heard of: Don't you believe it. At the Oscars, Richard Gere made an impromptu plea for an end to the Chinese occupation of Tibet. Harrison Ford has visited him and is rumoured to be planning a movie. What's more His Holiness has performed the Kalachakra in Madison Square Garden, New York.

Is Europe paying him due regard? Well, His Holiness has rapped with Wogan and fellow saint Bob Geldof. He's the subject of a Spanish pop song; and he was invited to edit the Christmas edition of French *Vogue*.

Is he into fashion then? Has a weakness for little off-the-right-shoulder numbers.

Address: Heavenly Abode, Dharamsala, Himachel Pradesh, India.

Not to be confused with: Lana Turner; the Lambada; the Lambretta; Salvador Dali; the Pope.

What does he have in common with the Pope? Both are addressed as Your Holiness.

Aphorisms of the Dalai Lama: 'Violence is like a strong pill. It may work in one way, but the side-effects may be equally strong.'

Least likely to say: 'Send in the troops.'

Leonardo da Vinci

Age: 541.
Appearance: Cross between God and Ivan the Terrible.
Status: Renaissance man.
Background: Born in Florence in 1452, the illegitimate son of a Florentine notary. Philosopher, painter, sculptor, scientist, engineer, astronomer, mathematician, anatomist and all-round smart alec. Was the first artist to be appreciated as a creative thinker rather than a skilled artisan working purely under commission.
Infuriatingly quick learner: He was taught by Verrocchio and first worked on the latter's *Baptism of Christ*. Leonardo painted the angel on the left so beautifully that Verrocchio turned to sculpture and never painted again.
Most famous for: The *Mona Lisa*, the world's most pastiched painting, and *The Last Supper*, model for endless Last Suppers since.
Have easel, will travel: Worked for Lorenzo dei Medici in Florence, then in the court of Ludovico il Moro in Milan. Moved to Venice, back to Florence, then to Rome, and eventually to France, where he died in 1519.
Little-known facts about Leonardo: He was dyslexic and left-handed.
Why is he in the news? A musical supposedly based on his life has just opened at the Strand Theatre in the West End.
Supposedly? The play bears no relation to the real Leonardo. It suggests he was passionately in love with Mona Lisa and that she had his child. Hence, presumably, the sly smile.
What's so implausible about that? Leonardo was gay. He was twice tried on charges of sodomy and had a retinue of pretty young men.
OK, forget the facts, is it art? Not if the critics are to be believed: 'Less exciting than watching Leonardo's paint dry' (*FT*); 'Leonardo's life in the West End is likely to prove nasty, brutish and short' (*Daily Telegraph*); 'No one who loves music, let alone theatre, would want to inflict this string of glucose jingles upon innocent audiences' (*Evening Standard*).
Did anyone enjoy it? Sub-editors, because they could all use the headline 'Painting by Numbers'.
Anybody else? The natives of the Pacific island of Nauru (pop. 8,000), who financed the show to mark the 25th anniversary of their independence. Happily, the £2 million is thought to be a drop in the ocean for the island, which gets its income from phosphate-rich bird droppings.
You mean shit? Ornithologists call it guano.
And the production: That's shit.
Has anyone else had a go at lionising Leonardo? Steven Spielberg, who in 1971 made a TV movie of his life starring Dennis Weaver.
Not to be confused with: Leonard Bernstein; Lennie Kravitz; Lenny Henry; Michelangelo.
Least likely to say: 'What shall I do for an encore?'

8 June 1993. The critics were proved right: the show had a short and inglorious run.

Sir Robin Day

Age: 69.
Appearance: Bow-tied bullfrog.
Status: Grand Inquisitor of British TV (semi-retired).
Catchphrase: 'But with respect . . . '
Latest spat: Verbal punch-up with Richard Madeley on *This Morning* over the latter's 'disgracefully intrusive' interviewing of Elaine Paige. Day called him a 'bastard' and mentioned a shoplifting charge on which Madeley had been acquitted: hundreds of viewers rang to complain.
Did Day apologise? Not likely. 'Viewers must have lost their sense of humour.'
Was it out of character? No. He once slapped Ben Elton during the Michael Aspel show to shut him up.
Background: Born in Hampstead Garden Suburb. President of the

Oxford Union. Became a barrister but was broke and disillusioned when he saw an ad for a job as a newscaster with ITN: 'The work', it said providentially, 'might appeal to a barrister who is thinking of giving up the profession.' Got it, joined the BBC in 1959, and did first set-piece interviews with party leaders in 1964, based on questions sent in by viewers.
Famous interviews: John Nott in 1982: the then Defence Secretary stormed off, throwing his microphone at Day, who had described him as a 'here today, gone tomorrow minister'. Margaret Thatcher in 1987: he was crushed – a steamroller flattening a blancmange, according to one critic.
Bon viveur: Member of the Garrick, Athenaeum, Royal Automobile and MCC.
What does he think of Jeremy Paxman? It is not known, though Day has said: 'There is a generation of interviewers who think that snide and insulting questioning is a substitute for incisive and well-informed questioning.'
Day on the Dimblebys: They are quite harmless and bland.
Day on Walden: 'I think you should ask questions that ordinary people can understand.'
Walden on Day: Like Dr W. G. Grace, he can justly claim to have raised to the level of an art something which, before his appearance on the scene, was a mere occupation.
Biggest mistake: Quitting *Question Time* in 1989. The programme suffered and so did his profile on TV, despite work for BSB, Channel 4, the BBC during the 1992 election, and a stint on *Central Lobby*, an ITV show similar in format to *Question Time*.
Second biggest mistake: Being a parliamentary candidate for the Liberals in 1959. 'I would have liked to sit on those green benches, having a ringside seat at history . . . but I chose the wrong party.'
Least likely to say: 'Pardon me for asking.'

Jean-Luc Dehaene

Age: 54.
Status: Belgian Prime Minister;
would-be President of the European
Commission.
Appearance: Chief taster in a
Bratwurst factory.
So he's a trifle rotund?
Exceedingly corpulent. He's also
fond of vulgar French anecdotes and
given to picking his nose in front of
TV cameras.
***Zut alors!* He can't be terribly
popular:** That's just where you're
wrong. His pragmatic political skills
endeared him to both the French and
German governments, who saw him
as the man to succeed Jacques Delors
and lead the EU into the next
millennium.
What was his appeal? Skilled
negotiator; representative of a small
country; keen federalist; not Leon
Brittan.

So will he get the job? Not now. Our man in Corfu, J. Major, has blocked
the appointment, claiming Dehaene represented a 'tradition of big
government'.
Dehaene must be devastated? Doubtless, though he cheered himself up
with a spot of commentary during Belgium's World Cup triumph over arch-
rivals Holland.
Did John stand alone? Totally – and proud of it. If 11–1 defeats could
always be proclaimed as victories, we'd be in the World Cup too.
Who's doing the proclaiming? Our Euro-sceptic press is in a flag-waving,
tub-thumping, Belgian-bashing rapture. The defeat of the 'Flemish Fatso'
was a 'barnstorming performance' (*Mail on Sunday*) by a 'leader who has
finally redeemed himself' (*Sunday Times*). The Belgian Plumber/Carthorse/
Big Ugly Slob (take your pick) was a threat to British sovereignty and Bill
Cash's blood pressure.
What happens now? A special summit will be held in mid-July at which
new candidates will come forward.
Like who? Many names mooted. Peter Sutherland, head of GATT; troubled
Spanish PM Félipe Gonzalez; veteran Italian diplomat Bernardo Buggins.
What about the poor old Belgians? By no means forgotten. Finance
Minister Philippe Maystadt has his supporters; and there is a growing lobby
for Tintin.
Key qualifications for the job? Large appetite; no problems with travel
sickness; some vague notion of what subsidiarity is.
Not to be confused with: Jean-Luc Godard; Jean-Paul Sartre; Hercule
Poirot.
Most likely to say: 'Just a few more dumplings for Helmut and me.'
Least likely to say: 'Corfu what a scorcher.'

27 June 1994. The more congenial Jacques Santer, prime minister of Luxemburg, was
eventually chosen to succeed Delors.

Gérard Depardieu

Age: 43.

Appearance: Gascon village idiot.

Background: Son of illiterate sheet-metal worker in small town south of Paris. Made a promising start as an oversize (11½ stone by age 12) small-time gangster, stealing cars and selling black-market goods before running off with two prostitutes. Found straight and narrow of sorts after joining Paris-based TNP (Théâtre National Populaire) at 16. Since then has appeared in more than 80 movies.

Career: Widely suspected to have appeared (not always with distinction) in every French film since the early seventies. Recently discovered by the non-Renoir crowd after an *annus mirabilis* in which he played Cyrano and established himself as the definitive thinking woman's bit of rough in *Green Card*. Now seeking to become every historian's bit of rough as Columbus in *1492*.

Some French films he has not appeared in: *Les Enfants du Paradis, La Grande Illusion, Le Jour se Lève, Jules et Jim.*

What the critics say: Raw presence, rough diamond, impetuous, stormy, primal energy.

What the audiences say: Isn't he that one from *Roxanne*? I liked his summer collection. Was that nose real?

Why men like him: He proves fat men can get the girl.

Why women like him: He is an intoxicating mixture of raw animal sensuality and touching sensitivity and he's French.

Profession listed in passport: *Acteur/vigneron* (actor/winemaker). Regrettably has taken to naming his wines after favourite roles. Hence Cuvée Cyrano, Cuvée Christophe Colombe.

Greatest line: 'Look and see what exuberance / I have with this protuberance' (Anthony Burgess's subtitles from *Cyrano*).

Gérard thinks: 'In my 80 movies there is a lot of *grosse merde*.' 'If I hadn't become an actor I would have become a killer.'

Gérard likes: Branagh, Mitchum, Brando, Gitanes, Food.

Don't mention: Rape – an apparently certain Oscar for Cyrano eluded him after (and probably because of) an interview in *Time* magazine in which he described taking part in a rape, aged 9, and several more later. It has since emerged that he was probably mistranslated. Dogs – he was mauled by an alsatian and had to undergo therapy to get over the resultant phobia.

Least likely to say: 'No, thank you, I'm on a diet.'

The Derby

Age: 214.

Appearance: Trailing horses, flailing jockeys, wailing punters.

Origin: First run in 1780. Dreamed up by the 12th Earl of Derby and Sir Charles Bunbury, who tossed a coin over dinner to decide its name. Much fun had since imagining whether the Bunbury would have survived for two centuries.

Status: A horse race with prize money of £800,000.

Don't you mean the greatest flat race in the world? Sadly, not any more. Like everything else, it isn't what it was.

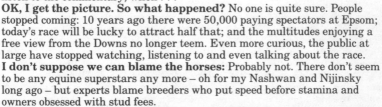

Well, what was it? It used to be a great national event, an institution, the day when thousands would descend on Epsom Downs to celebrate horse racing, when Gypsies and jugglers would hold an impromptu fair upon the sward, when offices and factories would stop to listen to the commentary, when . . .

OK, I get the picture. So what happened? No one is quite sure. People stopped coming: 10 years ago there were 50,000 paying spectators at Epsom; today's race will be lucky to attract half that; and the multitudes enjoying a free view from the Downs no longer teem. Even more curious, the public at large have stopped watching, listening to and even talking about the race.

I don't suppose we can blame the horses: Probably not. There don't seem to be any equine superstars any more – oh for my Nashwan and Nijinsky long ago – but experts blame breeders who put speed before stamina and owners obsessed with stud fees.

So what can be done to restore its reputation? Many theories: move the race to Sunday; run it in mid-July so that late-developing horses can enter; open it up to horses of any age, not just three-year-olds as at present; move it from Epsom to a decent course like Newmarket.

Look, this is all fascinating, but just tell me one thing? Who's going to win? Hard to predict: big field, no outstanding candidate, Saturn's influence is baleful, and we're using teabags. But Erhaab has a favourite's chance, Waiting looks good each-way value, and Party Season is a snip at 200–1.

I think I'll just put my quid on old Lester as usual: The inimitable Piggott, winner of a record nine Derbys, is now 58 and has won only one race this season. But your notion is not as mad as it sounds and Khamaseen should run well.

Not to be confused with: The French Derby, the Irish Derby, the Italian Derby, the Pitmen's Derby, the Greyhound Derby or any of the 300 other races around the world called the Derby.

Don't mention: The 34 false starts in 1863; the death of suffragette Emily Davidson, who threw herself under the hooves of the King's horse, in 1913; Shergar.

Do mention: The Queen; the Members' Lawn; Never Say Die.

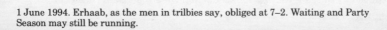

1 June 1994. Erhaab, as the men in trilbies say, obliged at 7–2. Waiting and Party Season may still be running.

Roddy Doyle

Age: 36.

Appearance: Jesuit train spotter.

Occupation: Novelist/screen-writer; manager of fantasy football side Dublin Moenchengladbach.

Achievements: Booker Prize winner 1993 for *Paddy Clarke Ha Ha Ha*; holds world records for frequency of variants of 'fock' and 'shite' per page and paragraph.

Has he written another mucky book? No, but his first TV series, *Family*, has just begun a four-week run on BBC1 and RTE. Its portrait of a dysfunctional family on a run-down Dublin housing estate has provoked angry reaction and a national debate in Ireland.

But those Rabbittes are rather jolly, aren't they? Like the Grundys, only saltier? These are their neighbours, the Spencers. The daughter goes on the game, the son is in trouble at school, the mother is a lush and the father is a wife-beating, philandering petty criminal with incestuous tendencies.

Golly. Has Roddy undergone some personal crisis that would explain this suddenly darker *Weltanschauung*? On the contrary. £70,000 from *The Commitments* and £20,000 from the Booker have enabled him to give up his teaching job; *The Van* will soon become the third book from the Barrytown Trilogy to be filmed; and Ireland are in the World Cup finals.

Ah, yes, the celebrated footie fetish. A PR ploy, surely? It's pretty convincing, anyway. He calls a Chelsea goal in a seventies FA Cup Final replay 'the highlight of my life', and snubbed a book industry awards ceremony to appear with Basil Brush on BBC2's *Fantasy Football League*.

A bit of a rebel then? His approach to screen versions of his novels is certainly uncompromising; and in Ireland his novels are often sniffily received by a spiky 'Dublin 4' cultural elite which dislikes his blue-collar subject matter and his formula for fiction.

Which is? 'An awful lot of dialogue, and an awful lot of gaps. And when in doubt, say F***.'

But doesn't the resulting narrative absence, the characteristic minimalist Doyleian metadiscourse, reflect a timid 'non-judgemental' post-Catholic zero degree ethic which culpably refuses to position proletarian degeneracy for the bourgeois audience? I hear what you say. But Doyle prefers 'to leave the reader to make decisions'. And he reckons the wordy narrators in Dickens and Tolstoy are boring gobshites.

Not to be confused with: Arthur Conan Doyle; T. Corraghessan Boyle; Dail Eireann; Roddy Frame; Roddy Llewellyn.

Most likely to say: 'Macaulay Culkin wants to play Paddy? Tell the little bollix he can kiss my green Irish arse.'

Least likely to say: 'And when I've completed the E. F. Benson adaptation, Paramount want a vehicle for Julia Roberts set in 19th-century Connemara, and then if there's a window in '96/7 we're looking at an international blockbuster exploring the existential dilemma of a top fashion designer . . .'

The Bishop of Durham

In the beginning: He was born in AD 1925. Or not. It depends.
Real name: David Jenkins.
But what do we mean by real? Very true. Let's just call him Dave.
Profession: Bishop and Doubter.
A somewhat unlikely combination? Indeed, which is why many Britons who have never set foot inside one of those weird rectangular buildings with pointy tops can immediately recognise Dave, the Man of God. Regular professions of disbelief have made him more celebrated than his line-manager, George Carey; better known, in some quarters, than his maker, God.

Tidings of Comfort and Joy: Dave appeared on *Breakfast with Frost* on the last shopping-Sunday in Advent with a special un-Christmas message. First, he said, the Three Wise Men are a myth. There was no Star of Bethlehem, no virgin birth, and as for all that rot about Jesus being instantly acknowledged – when he was born, nobody knew him from Adam.
So the animals didn't kneel around the manger in awe? No.
And there was room at the inn after all? 'Who knows?' says Dave.
And the shepherds didn't watch their flocks by night all seated on the ground? Well, probably they did. But you can be quite certain the Angel of the Lord didn't come down while Glory shone Around.
The voice of one crying in the wilderness: Dave's career has been one long mission to promulgate the truth as he sees it, whatever the cost to his Church or assorted Conservative governments. He's attacked Thatcherism, market theory, capitalism, yuppies and the Gulf victory parade. He's doubted the Resurrection, the Ascension and the uniqueness of Christ.
Bish-bosh, loads of tosh! Is it? Many liberal members of the Church of England probably agree with him that these are symbols, not facts.
Well, why is he a bishop? Good question. You might say that they too are important symbolic figures, and have a duty to nurture, not shake, popular faith, however crudely it is expressed. Consensus would be helpful.
Oh come, all ye faithful: George Carey has rebuked Jenkins for reopening 'these divisive issues'. Geoffrey Dickens, the Believer for Littleborough and Saddleworth, said: 'He is destroying the faith of millions of believers.' Also critical was John Gummer, who is noted for his own unusual interpretations of the Gospel, in particular of Jesus's injunction to 'sell whatever thou hast, and give to the poor'.
Christians say: Dear Lord and Father of Mankind, forgive our foolish ways.
Satan says: 'Yo, mass respekt!'
Unlikely to sing: 'How sweet the name of Jesus sounds in a believer's ear.'
Dave's fave-raves: 'We Three Kings of Orient Aren't'; 'Not in Royal David's City'; 'Away from the Manger'.

22 December 1993. To the consternation of tabloid editors, David Jenkins retired in July 1994.

Bob Dylan

Age: Could be anything between 40 and 83, but believed to be 51.

Appearance: Bag-person with mystical pretensions. Weird waxwork complexion, inexpertly applied dollops of eye make-up and taciturn manner suggest that Bob has been released into the community before completing course of treatment.

Early life: Born Robert Allan Zimmerman in Duluth, Minnesota, but busied himself systematically erasing his past. Visited dying Woody Guthrie in New York in 1960, a gesture which established his connection to American folk mythology. By 1965, had had enough of folk music, civil rights and being followed everywhere by Joan Baez, and was credited with inventing folk-rock on the *Bringing It All Back Home* album.

Original purpose of: To turn sixties pop from brainless, gormless din into adult medium exploding with social, political and psychological content. Even the all-conquering Beatles felt it necessary to follow Dylan's lead into psyche-probing imagery.

Purpose of Dylan in the nineties: To demonstrate that a living legend can 'sing' like a sealion with emphysema and still draw full houses. To demonstrate that even a living legend could use a holiday. To provide living proof of all the horrible things Norman Tebbit says about the sixties. To keep biographers, book publishers and concert promoters in work.

Great things about Dylan: Unimpeachable coolness, *circa* 1965–6. Hilarious press conferences with woefully 'square' reporters yet to be obliterated by the 'New Journalism'. Hired the Band (then called the Hawks) as backing musicians. Made several of the finest albums in rock history – *Highway 61 Revisited, Blonde on Blonde, John Wesley Harding, Blood on the Tracks*. Even managed classic 'religious' album, *Slow Train Coming*.

Things we can blame Dylan for: Donovan. John Cooper Clarke. Dylanologists. *Renaldo and Clara*, the original unwatchable movie. Ruining careers of several artists hailed as 'the new Dylan'. The Traveling Wilburys. Farm Aid, invented after Bob's classic un-performance at Live Aid.

Famous catchphrases: 'To live outside the law you must be honest.' 'Even the President of the United States must sometimes have to stand naked.' 'The Times They Are A-Changin'.' 'The ghost of electricity howls in the bones of her face.'

Worst line: 'Wiggle wiggle wiggle like a bowl of soup.'

Bitchiest remark: (To Keith Richards) 'I could have written "Satisfaction" but you couldn't have written "Desolation Row".'

Least likely to do: Marry a nice Jewish girl and open a bagel factory.

Least likely to say: Anything, especially, 'I love you London, you're a beautiful audience.'

Clint Eastwood

Age: 62.

Appearance: Lump of granite.

First reel: Born in San Francisco. His father, Clinton, 'pumped gas' all over California. Little Clint followed him, changing school every term and excelling only in athletics.

Second reel: Did army service and worked as a lumberjack before moving to Hollywood in 1955. Series of bit parts in B-movies, before landing the role of Rowdy Yates in *Rawhide*, which ran on TV for eight years. Moved into the big league in 1960s with Sergio Leone's 'Man with No Name' trilogy.

Third reel: Set up Malpaso Productions, began directing. Unusual habit of bringing films in under budget.

Oscar fever: Tonight the Western he directed and starred in, *Unforgiven*, could clean up. It has nine nominations, including best film, best director and best actor.

But is it any good? The critics raved, the public flocked. Credited with single-handedly reviving the genre.

So what's it about? Ageing bounty hunter with existential nausea and back trouble who renounces violence for kids and pigs.

How does it end? Mass shoot-out; lots of blood.

What knowing critics said about the ending: 'His genius is in realising that a Western always has to revert to type.'

What unknowing critics said: 'Bloody cop-out.'

Essential props for a Clint Eastwood film: Guns, tomato sauce, cheroots, ponchos, more tomato sauce, nooses, coffins, whores, horses, hearses, Mexicans who speak broken English, women who speak broken Mexican.

A role model for psychopaths? Yes, unwillingly. 'I wouldn't like it if some kid shot someone because of me . . . I'd have to live with it inside of me.'

Does he worry about being typecast? Nope. 'Type me any way you like as long as you cast me. I'll worry about untyping later.'

Man with No Brain? Not at all. 'If I say that I'm interested in history, architecture and jazz, people look surprised.'

Is he rich? He sure is. His personal fortune is estimated at $130 million.

What does he spend it on? Divorce suits (the split with his wife in 1984 cost him $25 million); a helicopter called the Squirrel; and a restaurant, the Hog's Breath Inn, which serves Dirty Harry burgers and Magnum Force omelettes.

What does he have in common with Mrs Thatcher? Little is known about his mother; enjoyed special relationship with President Reagan (financing a thoroughly barking paramilitary incursion into Laos to search for PoWs); wielded political power (as Mayor of Carmel in California, where he blocked a campaign to ban ice-cream vendors).

How frustrated profile writers sum him up: 'He remains an enigma.'

Most likely to say: 'I want to be a Leone.'

Least likely to say: 'Go on Academy, make my day.'

29 March 1993. The Academy did make Eastwood's day, naming him best director and *Unforgiven* best film.

The Duke of Edinburgh

Age: 72. Born on 10 June 1921 in Corfu, in a house called Mon Repos.
Occupation: Prince. Also Earl (of Merioneth). Consort to HM Queen, though, unlike Prince Albert, he has never been named Prince Consort. Environmentalist (before it became the fashion). Champion of science and technology. Gaffer.
Advantages over Albert: Albert for some time was wildly unpopular, partly because he was German. Philip was taken for a Greek, which caused less trouble (though he is more of a Dane). Also Albert, who died young, consorted for only 21 years. Philip has done nearly twice that stint.
Disadvantages, compared with Albert: No hall. No memorial.
Attempt a pithy assessment of his character: Peppery old salt. Speaks his mind. But a former aide says of him: 'No man has a kinder heart or takes more trouble to conceal it.'
Role on this day 40 years ago: Best supporting performance. One step behind the monarch.
Did he want the job?: Not really, but it went with the princess's hand. He once admitted he'd have been happier staying in the navy.
Did the romance which blossomed all those years ago between the demure princess and her dashing admirer flower in time into one of the great love stories of this or any age? Not outside the imagination of Barbara Cartland it didn't. Greville wrote of V & A (the couple, not the museum): 'The prince is become so identified with the Queen that they are one person.' E & P look a bit, well, semi-detached.
Are you hinting at Camillas? Certainly not. Though several have been alleged (actress Pat Kirkwood, cabaret star Helene Cordet). But Philip says it's impossible: wherever he went, there were always policemen present.
Likes: Horses; polo till arthritis prevented it, then carriage driving. Whales and most other wildlife. Painting (has exhibited at the Royal Academy).
Dislikes: Have you got 45 minutes? Trendies, Marxist revolutionaries, mortgage interest relief, the CAP, photographers, the *Daily Express* ('a bloody awful newspaper'). Philoprogenitiveness (in others: he's got four children himself). The words 'avant-garde', 'conurbation', 'macho' and 'camp'.
Why do you call him a gaffer? Because he's always making gaffes.
Give examples. Have you got two hours? Talked of the Chinese as 'slitty-eyed', the Hungarians as 'pot-bellied', and has compared the duties of wives with those of prostitutes. Visiting Adelaide, he even insulted a koala, declining to pat it in case it gave him some ghastly disease.
Has this been held against him? Naturally. Why do you think Australia is turning republican?
Is he revered? Undoubtedly. A signed photograph of His Royal Highness is an object of veneration among the Iounhanan tribe in the Solomon Islands.
Least likely to say: 'Now, Lilibet, how about an evening of Stockhausen?'

2 June 1993. Appeared on the 40th anniversary of his marriage to the Queen.

Prince Edward

Name: Edward Antony Richard Louis Windsor.
Nickname: Mavis.
Royal rank: Fifth in line to the throne.
Age: 29.
Appearance: Marred by candyfloss hair and teeth like lollipop sticks, but not as ugly as people think.
Job: The Really Useless Prince.
That's a bit unfair, isn't it? You're right. Last week his onerous royal duties included: attending a gala performance of *Phantom of the Opera* in Manchester in aid of Marie Curie Cancer Care; attending a reception at St James's Palace to mark the UK Commonwealth Games Appeal launch; attending a dinner at Trinity House, Tower Hill; attending a reception and dinner at Trinity College, Cambridge; attending a

presentation at Mobil North Sea Ltd as patron of the Haddo House Hall Arts Trust; and receiving, on behalf of the Queen, the British High Commissioners of the republics of Gambia and Uganda and Her Majesty's Ambassador at Quito.
And for that he gets how much from the Civil List? £96,000.
It's a rip-off. That's what everyone says, but compared to the royal laundry bill (£63,700) he's a bargain.
Why's he in the news? According to the *Sunday Mirror*, he's told friends he's 'fed up' to still be living in his parents' house.
That's Buckingham Palace, right? Right.
Is it too small or something? No, but it seems there is a cutlery shortage. The Queen is reported to be worried about 'the use of royal silver' during 'bashes with his showbiz pals'.
Which showbiz pals? The *Mirror*'s not letting on, but since his days with Lloyd Webber's Really Useful Theatre Company, Eligible Eddie has been linked with every minor celeb ever to don a *Cats* suit or a *Phantom* mask.
Name names: Ruthie Henshall, for a start. Ex-TV-am weather girl Ulrika Jonsson. And Michael Ball, of course.
The Queen's third son is gay? In tabloid-speak, theirs was 'a touching friendship'.
What does that mean? Anything you want it to. Clever, eh?
So is Eddie gay? Not according to former model Romy Adlington. 'It was quite obvious from the start that he was a normal heterosexual guy.'
Most likely to say: 'Busy? No, I don't think so. Let me check . . . No, Monday's OK. And Tuesday, if you'd like. Wednesday, too.'
Least likely to say: 'Hello? Is that Heaven? Hi, it's Mavis here. Can you put me and Ulrika on the guest list? Thanks. Ciao.'

Vivien Eliot

Age: Died in 1947, but immortality awaits.

In the news because: April is the cruellest month, breeding movies out of the dead ground.

That's an allusion, isn't it? To *The Waste Land*, of course, Mr T. S. Eliot's epochally significant poem and conundrum for Eng. Lit. students.

You said Mr Eliot's poem: Oops, I meant Mr and Mrs Eliot's poem, Tom and Viv as they are in the soon-to-be-released film, based on Michael Hastings's play. Vivien knocked off a few stanzas, it seems.

But Tom was profuse in his thanks? No. She was nuts, you see. Poured chocolate through the letter box at his Faber & Faber offices.

So he had Vivien locked up? Yes. She was committed for 'moral insanity'.

How women see it: 'Tom went mad and promptly certified his wife,' said Dame Edith Sitwell. Harley Street doctors (male) were implicated in her awful treatment.

How Faber & Faber sees it: T. S. Eliot wrote T. S. Eliot.

Gender and genius territory? Absolutely. And husband blaming. The ghost of Sylvia Plath stalks the land. Rewrite your thesis now.

But the rest of the poem is all Tom? Yes, if you don't count Ezra Pound (who knocked it into shape), Shakespeare, the Greeks, the Jacobeans, Dante, Baudelaire, Mallarmé, Laforgue, Henry James . . . I won't go on.

Poet, or the world's greatest plagiarist? 'The ordinary man's experience is chaotic, irregular, fragmentary. [He] falls in love, or reads Spinoza, and these two experiences have nothing to do with each other . . . in the mind of the poet these experiences are always forming new wholes,' Tom wrote.

And ordinary women? Ordinary men read Spinoza: ordinary women knit, have babies, nag, menstruate and go mad (in any order).

And write their husband's poems? Yes, damn it. Please don't drag up the business of Dorothy Wordsworth helping William.

Verse in divers hands: 'Their handwriting is so similar it is difficult to be sure who is writing' – Eliot's biographer, Peter Ackroyd.

Who play Tom and Viv in the movie? Willem Dafoe (Eliot was born in the USA) and Miranda Richardson.

Her works not to be confused with: T. S. Eliot; *Middlemarch*; Sir Thomas Elyot (ancestor from whom T.S. also borrowed: 'Immature poets imitate, mature poets steal').

Most likely to say: 'April is the cruellest month, etc.'

Least likely to say: 'Tom, darling. Have you read "Pass Notes" this morning?'

Pablo Escobar

Age: 43.

Appearance: Aspiring Las Vegas crooner, *circa* 1975.

Childhood: Stole tombstones, filed off inscriptions, sold them as new.

Job: The hunt for Somali warlord Mohammed Farah Aideed is off, so Pablo is once again the World's Most Wanted Man.

Why? He's the only Colombian drug baron everybody's heard of.

But . . . Cali has replaced Medellin as Colombia's cocaine capital. The town now controls four-fifths of the country's drug exports.

Why isn't its boss famous then? Well, there's four of them, and they've got polysyllabic names that are pretty difficult to pronounce for people who don't speak Spanish.

Such as? Miguel Rodriguez Orejuela.

I see what you mean. Also, Pablo never denied being involved in the narcotics trade. Despite what the US Drug Enforcement Agency (DEA) says, the Cali bosses all pose as legitimate businessmen.

So what's Escobar worth? To you and me, £4.25 million. That's the reward for information leading to his arrest.

I mean how much cash has he got? *Forbes* magazine has him on its list of the world's richest men, with a fortune of around £1.8 billion.

That's more than Andrew Lloyd Webber: And then some. The DEA says that he once supplied 80 per cent of America's cocaine and two-thirds of the world's supply. That would give him a yearly income of £8 billion.

So, does money buy happiness? It's doubtful. Pablo is on the run, and his wife and two children tried to flee to Germany in a Boeing 747.

What does it buy then? Rolls-Royces. And dynamite.

He car-bombs his own cars? No, he uses other people's. But a group called Los Pepes recently took up the challenge. They've burned six of his Rolls-Royces, shot five of his lawyers and blown up his mum's farmhouse.

Why? Los Pepes is an acronym for People Persecuted by Pablo Escobar.

The long-suffering Colombians are finally fighting back? It'd be nice to think so. Sadly, Los Pepes is clearly financed by the Cali cartels.

Has he ever been to prison? Yes. He surrendered to the police in 1991.

What an idiot: Actually, it was safer for him on the inside. His architect designed the prison. He walked out of the front door after 13 months.

But the conditions must have been intolerable: Really terrible. One sauna, 2 jacuzzis, 12 exercise machines, 4 chefs, plus phones, fax and his own football pitch. Truly a cruel and unusual punishment.

He likes football? Put it this way, when the pitch was dug up last week, a lot of Persons Missing, Presumed Dead were found.

29 November 1993. **Escobar was murdered three days later.**

Eton College

Age: 554.
Fees: £12,000 a year.
Appearance: Bastion of privilege and ludicrous ritual.
Is it? Not according to headmaster Dr Eric Anderson: 'A fifth of the boys are on bursaries or scholarships and their parents could not possibly be described as toffs.'

Just how egalitarian is it? During the holidays it invites 40 Harlesden 16-year-olds to sample the good life.
What about all that fagging and flogging? Thing of the past, dear chap.
Eton revisionism? According to a new history by vice-provost Tim Card, supposedly reforming sixties headmaster Anthony Chenevix-Trench was 'pushed out' because of a fondness for alcohol and beating young boys.
Surely a necessary qualification for the job? Certainly not.
Card on Chenevix-Trench: 'He was obviously affected by his time on the Burma railway.'
Nicholas Soames, food minister and Old Etonian, on Mr Card's claims: 'I was beaten by almost everyone at Eton but never by him.'
Those ludicrous rituals: Pupils still wear a uniform of Victorian mourning dress. Poppers (elected prefects) get to wear multicoloured waistbands and are allowed to roll up their umbrellas. On 4 June (George III's birthday) they sail down the Thames standing in wooden boats and tossing flowers into the river from their boaters.
Eton wall game? Two teams of pupils – Oppidans and Collegers – duff each other up in a polite sort of way in front of a large wall. No team has scored a goal since 1907.
The things Old Etonians say: 'You cannot walk around two towns in tailcoats for five years without coming to some decision as to your importance in relation to the untailcoated pedestrians' (Craig Brown). 'I first met the Secretary of State for Foreign and Commonwealth Affairs looking backwards at him through my legs while spreadeagled, frightened, over a chair' (Philip Howard). 'It's not like people imagine' (all of them).
Those old public-school clichés? 'Every now and then somebody would be sacked for buggery' (Lord Charteris, former private secretary to the Queen).
Does that have anything to do with the practice of beaks (teachers) holding on to each other's tails? No, that signifies that the beak wishes to talk to the master whose tails he is holding.
Eton and girls: 'There is, to my mind, no philosophical or other justification for having girls' (Dr Anderson).
Not to be confused with: Harrow; Winchester; Slough.
Do say: Centre of academic excellence, meritocracy, creative traditionalism.
Don't say: Chenevix-Trench, bloody good chap.

Eurovision Song Contest

Age: 37.

Appearance: The entire cast of *Eldorado* modelling Freemans catalogue special-occasion wear.

Background: A grotesque mutation of the San Remo Song Festival. The first one was held in 1956 in Lugano, Switzerland. Britain's first-ever entry was a song called 'All', sung by Patricia Bredin. Subsequent British representatives included Matt Munro, Kathy Kirby, Kenneth McKellar and Lulu. The latest £2 million *schmalzfest* is in Ireland. It will go on for more than three hours and around 300 million will watch it. For the first time eastern European countries will take part.

Typical themes: Love; unrequited love; spurned love; anything with La la la in it. Spain's song in 1968 had 138 La la la's; Ireland's in 1982 had 111.

Stupid winning titles: 'Ding Ding a Dong' (Netherlands 1975), 'A-Bi-Ni-Bi' (Israel 1978), 'Diggi Loo Diggi Ley' (Sweden 1984), 'Didai Didai Dai' (Turkey 1985).

Bonus points for: Frenetic dance routines (Brotherhood of Man), fragile waifishness (Dana, Mary Hopkin), gorgeous Swedes (the blonde one from Abba), whipping dresses off to reveal miniskirts underneath (Buck's Fizz), no shoes (Sandie Shaw).

Nul points for: Earnest accordion solos, national costume, smutty lyrics, political and protest songs. Finland's anti-nuclear song scored nothing in 1982. Norway's Laplanders bemoaning their fate gained them 15 points and 16th place in 1980, and the Portuguese singer who wanted to perform in military uniform complete with pistol was refused permission to do so.

Controversies the organisers don't wish to be reminded of: When the 1984 UK entry Belle and the Devotions were greeted by boos because of European hostility to British football hooliganism in Luxembourg that year. When the Italians (in '81, '82 and '86) and French (in '82) withdrew from the contest because they were unhappy about the standard of music.

Italy's attempt at improving things: A song called 'All Together', in 1990. 'More and more free we are / It isn't a dream any more, you aren't alone any more / Higher and higher we are / Give me your hand and you'll see you fly.'

Britain's lowest ebb: In 1987, when Rikki Peebles came 13th with his own composition 'Only the Light'. Was last seen driving a taxi in Glasgow.

What the Eurovision Song Contest needs: Angst, black rollnecks.

Likeliest contender: Morrissey.

Record releases that will never happen: *Sonia: The Concept Album*; *Eurovision!*, the eight-album commemorative boxed set.

13 May 1993. Ireland won in 1993 and again in 1994 to complete a hat-trick of wins. Forty-six countries wanted to compete in 1994, including many from eastern Europe, and if all had done so it is estimated the event would have lasted more than six hours.

Chris Evans

Age: 26.
Appearance: Slightly nerdish hyperactive child with ginger hair.
Position: Presenter of Channel 4's hit programme *The Big Breakfast*. Currently pulling in an audience of about 1.2 million as against 200,000 for its predecessor, *Channel 4 Daily*.
Background: Born Warrington. Mother a nurse, father a hospital administrator. Left school at 16 and had 21 jobs in less than four years, including his own Kissogram company. Became obsessed with inane Manchester radio presenter Timmy Mallett, who gave him first break in radio. Nearly fired for telling sick joke about a cat. Moved to London to present own radio programme on GLR. He has also had abortive stints as a presenter on BSB and TV-am.

What does the programme lack: Sofas and soft chat. Presenters with the 'F-factor' or moustaches. A mission to explain. Gravitas. News.
What explains its success? Lack of the above. Restlessness, brazen, iconoclastic in age of channel grazing. Relentlessly silly and happy.
Most commonly used adjectives to describe Chris: Madcap; wacky; mad; geeky; cheeky; daft as a bottle of crisps.
Contribution to fashion: T-shirts under multicoloured shirts; NHS specs.
Fans: Jeremy Paxman, who has suggested that the rival station, GMTV, should poach him a.s.a.p.; Michael Parkinson, who predicted that he could be GMTV's nemesis; Michael Grade.
Critics say: A ghastly mix of pretentious nonsense and ludicrous imagery. Glorified children's TV. It's great if you're 6 years old, deaf and colour-blind.
Chris on *The Big Breakfast*: 'It's a show which screams "Yes, yes, yes, life, life, life." '
Chris on Chris: 'I have never made a career move mistake, only mistakes while on the actual stepping stone.'
Favourite word: Fan-tas-tic.
Typical Chris joke: Did you hear about the Russian guy who went up to the Kremlin and asked 'Is Len in?'
Least likely to say: 'Have we done quite enough on GATT?'

Mount Everest

Age: Approx. 25 million years.
Formed when the Indian
subcontinent converged with the
Tibetan Plateau.
Status: Highest point on earth, at
29,028 feet. Named after Sir George
Everest, surveyor-general of India in
the 1840s.
Why is it in the news? Because it's
there. Oh, and because Rebecca
Stephens has just become the first
British woman to climb it.
So what? Ms Stephens's ascent has
caused national rejoicing,
particularly among middle-market
newspapers who have the sniff of
serialisation in their nostrils. Ms
Stephens is the archetype of *Daily
Mail* woman – 31, journalist, fond of
hang-gliding, ballooning and gliding,
Home Counties background, lives in
Fulham.

But what about Hillary? He was a man, stupid.
So, how tough is it? It depends: most go up the easier south route (the 'yak
track'); the north face and south-west face are trickier.
Main dangers to climbers: Bumping into other climbers: on one day last
week 38 mountaineers reached the summit, and there are 19 expeditions
vying to reach the top for the 40th anniversary of the Coronation. Falling
over flags. Being attacked by a yeti. Being attacked by Brian Blessed.
But we mustn't belittle her outstanding achievement. Of course not,
though curiously last year it was conquered by a Frenchman, Thierry
Defrance, on his first and only climb.
The air must be incredibly thin: The oxygen of publicity helps.
At least it produced some great quotes: 'I'm on top of the world'
(Stephens); 'I'm so delighted' (Ms Stephens's mother); 'It's a phenomenal
achievement – history in the making' (John Major); 'How quickly can we get
the book out?' (publishers everywhere).
Politically correct behaviour on Mount Everest: Don't drop litter; avoid
defecation and fornication; don't chisel 'I wuz here' on the nearest ridge; take
corpses away with you.
Song inspired by Everest: 'Yakkety-Yak, Don't Talk Back'.
Famous people who haven't yet climbed Everest: Bob Geldof; Martyn
Lewis; Raine Spencer; Sting; Jocelyn Stevens (no relation).
Not to be confused with: Ben Nevis; K2; Kenny Everett; Everest Double
Glazing.
What will Ms Stephens's next challenge be? Staying awake during a
Michael Aspel interview; ditto at reception in Downing Street; deciding
between offers from the *Mail* and *Express*; calculating her bank balance.
And what's the future for Everest? Thomas Cook are exploring the
possibilities. Book now. Chair-lifts will be provided.

Nicholas Fairbairn

Age: 60.

Appearance: Eccentric country GP.

How he describes himself in *Who's Who*: Author, forester, painter, poet, television and radio broadcaster, journalist, dress designer, landscape gardener, bon viveur, raconteur and wit.

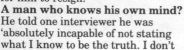

That all? He has been MP (Con.) for Perth and Kinross since 1983, for Kinross and Perthshire since 1974. Owns a 13th-century castle.

With all those jobs he must have little time for political infighting: He found time to describe John Major as '*vin ordinaire* when he should be chateau bottled' and call for him to resign.

A man who knows his own mind? He told one interviewer he was 'absolutely incapable of not stating what I know to be the truth. I don't want to be at the top lying and crapping with all those bus driver spooks in the cabinet.'

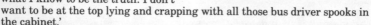

What kind of views has he expressed? He is opposed to what he calls 'economic immigration' to Britain, fought sanctions against South Africa and said women who made rape allegations were 'tauntresses'.

Sir Nicholas on allegations that he was racist: 'Several Pakistanis wrote to support me.'

Early signs of extremism? At 11 he smashed the windows of the local Co-op with a catapult on hearing of the 1945 Labour election victory.

Dazzling career? Became youngest-ever Scottish QC at 38. Appointed Scottish Solicitor-General in 1979 but resigned in 1982 over handling of a Glasgow rape case and the attempted suicide of an alleged lover.

Bit of a one for the ladies then? 'One day winter will come, but in my sexual energy I am still in the autumn of my life.'

Family values and all that? 'Monogamous marriage is a facile rule.'

Any evidence of his allegedly prodigious sex appeal? He claims his school matron fell in love with him at the age of 7.

Sir Nicholas on women's clothes: What is a skirt but an open gateway?

Sir Nicholas on women MPs: Cagmags, scrub-heaps, old tattles.

Sir Nicholas likes: Women (except MPs), vodka, being shocking.

Sir Nicholas dislikes: Lord Whitelaw ('Sanctimony, guile . . . slime and intrigue under a cloak of decency'); Edwina Currie ('the hag'); Labour.

That 'dress designing'? Makes his own outfits, mostly loud and tartan.

Recreations listed in *Who's Who*: Drawing ships, making quips, confounding whips, scuttling drips.

Yuk! He used to list 'growling, prowling, scowling, owling'.

Yuk squared: He used to list 'making love' too.

What they say: 'The finest cad of our times' (*Independent*); 'Bizarre prophet from one of the less reliable books in the Old Testament' (*Times*).

Not to be confused with: A box of shortbread biscuits; Old Nick; Alan Clark.

6 April 1994. Shortly afterwards he announced his decision to leave the Commons at the next election, attacking Parliament as 'a sea of classless lookalikes'.

Guy Fawkes

Age: 422.

Appearance: Fanatical munchkin sporting pointed witch's hat with matching chin.

Background: Born a Protestant. Became zealous Catholic under influence of stepfather. Became a mercenary in the Spanish army before going to live in Maastricht.

Claim to fame: Planting 20 barrels of gunpowder, camouflaged with coals and faggots, underneath the Houses of Parliament.

Why? To blow up James I and his cronies for oppressing Catholics.

Was it his idea? No.

How did he get involved? Religious zeal and foolhardiness won him a reputation for being something of a psychopath. Robert Catesby and fellow plotters needed an unknown Terminator to do the dirty work in London so they dispatched an agent to recruit Fawkes.

Did Fawkes know what the plot was when recruited? No.

What happened next? Tresham (one of the plotters) sent a letter to his brother-in-law Lord Monteagle, a Member of Parliament, warning him of the plot so that he could save Monteagle's skin. Monteagle spilled the beans, the cellars were searched and Fawkes was busted before the explosion, taken to the Tower and tortured on the rack.

Most heroic moment: Fawkes was tortured on the rack 'per gradus ad ima' for four days before revealing anything about the plot and did not disclose any of the names of his co-conspirators until 9 November, by which time they had already been captured anyway.

Sticky end: He was dragged through London on a hurdle and executed, weak from torture and illness.

Biggest mistakes: Getting involved. Living in Maastricht for over 10 years without blowing it up.

His legacy: Annual festival for pyromaniacs, bonfires, fireworks, guys, burned fingers, boom business around 5 November for toy shops.

Paradox: That we have an annual festival celebrating a failed plot, named after a man who wasn't even the chief, involving blowing things up, which he failed to do.

What he'd never say: 'Penny for the guy?'

Ranulph Fiennes

Full name: Sir Ranulph Twistleton-Wykeham-Fiennes (3rd Bt).
Age: 48.
Appearance: Bigglesian. Stiff upper lip due to character. Stiff upper limbs due to frostbite. Bit of toe missing due to same.
Job: Explorer. He and polar partner Dr Michael Stroud were the first people to walk across the Antarctic land mass without dogs or vehicles. They travelled 1,275 miles in 88 days, pulling 400lb sleds without the aid of dogs or air supplies.
What he would rather have done: Commanded his father's regiment, the Royal Scots Greys.
Background: Born into a family which traces its lineage back to Charlemagne. Father (same name) died of war wounds before Ran was born. Spent childhood shinning up

trees and church towers. Went to Eton, but failure to pass A-levels prevented him getting into Sandhurst. Short-service commissions in Scots Greys (including SAS) but disgraced, aged 21, for letting off bomb in Castle Combe as protest against the filming of *Dr Dolittle*.
Medical risks involved in job: Crippling piles, muscular strains, ulcerating blisters, bacterial sores, crotch rot (no change of underpants for 100 days), sensory deprivation, severe loss of body weight, dehydration, snow blindness, frostbite.
Why does he do it? 'I am not going to walk for three months across the Antarctic because I want to. I do it because that's what the people who read books about travel adventures or read newspaper accounts of expeditions or watch us on television dictate.'
In the end Ran's heroic expedition displaced from front pages by: News of Major Ron Ferguson's alleged amatory adventures.
Family: Married to Virginia for 21 years. He calls her Ginny the Germ.
Ran on Germ: 'She gives the impression of being happy about what I do. I don't know what's going on, behind. With females, one doesn't, really.'
Mike Stroud on women: 'That's because they've got half a brain, and most of that is fat, isn't it?'
Friends say: 'I am not saying that Ran is thick, but he is not overly philosophical.'
Ran says: 'Some people are born brainy, and others aren't.'
Products Ran could endorse: Damart, Deep Heat, Lip Salve, Dr Scholl's corn plasters, Odoreaters, Anusol.
Likes: Chocolate – capable of eating four Mars bars at a sitting. Britain – he won't drive foreign cars or buy foreign goods if avoidable.
Homes: London and Exmoor.
Least likely to say: 'Let's send out for a pizza and watch *The Late Show*.'

The Football Association

Birthdate: 26 October 1863.
Birthplace: A pub called the Freemasons' Tavern.
Motto: If at first you don't succeed, form a subcommittee.
In the news: Rarely out of it. About to appoint Terry Venables as the new England manager, on the recommendation of a subcommittee, despite a Premier League inquiry into alleged irregularities at White Hart Lane during his time there.
Chairman: Sir Bert Millichip.
Nickname: Bert the Inert.
Birthdate: Roughly the same as the above.
Isn't that a bit ageist? Perhaps. But the 12-strong International Committee have an average age of 67½. The youngest is Noel White, 58. The oldest Charles Thomas, 82.
No thrusting young men? Well, there's Graham Kelly.
Dynamic, bubbling with ideas, right? Err. Nice bloke, interests of football at heart, but hamstrung by the internal inertia of the FA. Won brownie points for turning up at a *When Saturday Comes* award ceremony to receive the prize for the man who has done most to harm English football. Acceptance speech included thanks to the International Committee 'who have done so much to help me win this award'.
His predecessor? Ted Croker.
Famous for: (1) Inventing a snow-clearing device called the Croker Sno-Blow. (2) Telling Margaret Thatcher at a post-Heysel meeting that 'we don't want your hooligans in our stadiums'.
What does the FA actually do? Everything and nothing. Formerly guardian of the amateur spirit of football. Now guardian of the amateurish spirit of English football administration. Controller of the game from muddied park to hallowed turf.
Great FA decisions (part 1): England didn't compete in the World Cup until 1950. They allowed themselves to be expelled from FIFA in 1928 with all the home countries and didn't rejoin until 1946. Thus England never got the chance to rack up a few World Cup wins while the rest of the globe were still kicking a tin can around.
Great FA decisions (part 762): Withdrew English clubs from Europe after Heysel, but kept the England team in (while asking supporters not to travel with them). So every two-bit hooligan attached themselves to the team, attracting yards of publicity and delaying English football's rehabilitation.
Least likely to say: 'What do you think of the new Lemonheads album, Bert?'
Most likely to say: 'And now gentlemen, the report from the Biscuits Subcommittee. It's jammy dodgers again, I'm afraid.'
Not to be confused with: Sweet FA.
On the other hand: . . .

19 January 1994. Venables was exonerated of all allegations of financial irregularities.

E. M. Forster

Dates: 1879–1970.
Famous for: A posthumous movie career more glittering than his literary achievements during his life; his filmed works have had more Oscar nominations than he had published novels. *Howards End* was nominated for seven Oscars.
Life: Born middle-class, middle-aged. Home counties, private income. Only child. Never able to flee influence of his widowed ma and a gaggle of maiden aunts till death dispatched them. Two great escapes: to Egypt and India (where he was secretary to a minor prince). Lodger at and fellow of King's College, Cambridge, for so long that he became part of the architecture.
Appearance: Bit of an old biddy with granny glasses and a stoop.

Why do (a) Penguin Classics (b) school examiners and (c) film-makers Merchant–Ivory like him? Because: (a) his books expose the hypocrisy of the Brits while redeeming them with a bit of liberalism; (b) they contain no explicit sex to titillate teenagers; (c) his brand of Edwardian England effortlessly translates into Laura Ashley lookalike movies.
Was Forster in a position to throw stones? Not entirely. He kept quiet about his homosexuality, stipulating that *Maurice* should be published only after his death.
Biggest mystery in Forster's life: Why he wrote no more novels after *A Passage to India* in 1924.
Possible answer: Because he wanted to write about gay relationships but dared not publish *Maurice* (finished in 1914) because he feared it would ruin his reputation.
Best decision Forster ever made: To write no more novels; some critics say his literary reputation increased with every novel he didn't write.
Likes: Travel, writing, friendship, especially with young policemen.
Was his own life anything like that portrayed in Merchant–Ivory's adaptations? In no way. He once said: 'I warmed both hands in front of the fire of life. And put it out.'
Essentially English movies that would be very different if there had been a Forster novel to base them on: *Damage.* Any of the Carry Ons.
Forster script for British Telecom commercial: Only connect.
Philby motto from Forster: If I had to choose between betraying my country and betraying my friend, I hope I should have the guts to betray my country.
Least likely to say: 'Would Clint Eastwood be interested in doing *The Longest Journey*?'

Lynne Franks

Age: 45.
Appearance: Alters daily. If it's
Friday, it must be flares and a
mauve throw. Jennifer Saunders's
portrayal of her in *Absolutely
Fabulous* was flattering.
Background: Jewish daughter of a
north London butcher. Worked for
Eve Pollard at *Petticoat* magazine
before setting up her own PR
business. In 1988, she sold the firm
for £2.6 million, retaining control. It
was later acquired by a French
company, BDDP, for £6 million.
Reputation: The PR from hell.
But is she good at her job? Is
Vivienne Westwood bonkers? Franks
is a consummate schmoozer, a
hustler of some repute. Besides
handling, over the years, such design
luminaries as Katherine Hamnett
and Jean-Paul Gaultier, she has
managed to make street-credible must-haves out of such unpromising
products as Brylcreem and Asda.
Rare disaster: Took on the Labour Party in 1986 but the relationship was
short-lived. You can lead Neil Kinnock to an acrylic poncho but not even
Lynne Franks could make him wear it.
Things she always carries with her: Cordless phone, phial of ginseng,
Lenny and Dawn's phone number.
Eighties obsessions: Shouting, negative stress management, money,
bumbags, Nicheren Shosu Buddhism, chanting for parking meters.
Nineties obsessions: Crystals, consciousness-raising, having her offices
doused by a Chinese lady 'to release trapped energy', transformational
psychology, the Earth Goddess principle.
Typical stunt: Bussing 150 fashion editors to a dank warehouse on an edge-
of-town industrial estate to attend a thrash sponsored by Red Stripe.
Entertainment provided by little-known but very happening acid-ragga band
from Ladbroke Grove. Guests include Lenny, Dawny, Ruby . . .
What's in it for the fashion editor? A plastic tumblerful of warm booze, a
free I Am a Really Caring Person T-shirt and a heartfelt air-kiss from
Franks.
That's all history now though, right? Right. Franks announced that she
was ditching her role as head of the agency named after her to concentrate on
her interests in broadcasting, despite a failed bid earlier this year for an all-
women commercial radio station in London.
Most likely to say: 'Nam myo ho renge ko' (repeat 50 times before
breakfast).
Least likely to say: 'Buddhism schmuddism.'

French and Saunders

Ages: Jennifer is 34 and Dawn is 35.
Appearances: Crush-worthy games mistress in Angela Brazil novel (Jen); almost-beautiful Sumo (Dawn).
Backgrounds: Very similar – each is the daughter of an RAF officer and both grew up in comfortable, middle-class rural England. Met at London drama school Central. Hated each other on sight, but later became friends and shared a flat. Eventually teamed up and formed, among other acts, the Menopause Sisters.
Example of early Comedy Store form: Dressed as *Thunderbirds* characters, one said 'What's the time, Brains?' and the other replied 'Six o'clock, Mr Tracey.' End of sketch.
Have they improved? Yes. Apart from the double act, Jennifer scored a success with *Absolutely Fabulous*, and Dawn is making a new series of the less-celebrated *Murder Most Horrid*.
Does the BBC like them? Very much. It has announced a £2 million golden handcuffs deal tying them to the Corporation for five years.
Status: Leading lights of the comedy establishment once known as 'alternative'.
Is that world in any way incestuous? Think of a Cornish fishing village. Jen is married to Ade Edmondson, the punk from the *Young Ones* (three daughters); Dawn's husband is Lenny Henry (one adopted daughter). Their friends are Ben Elton (who directed Dawn on stage), Ruby Wax (with whom they appeared in a sitcom), Rik Mayall (Ade's partner), etc., etc.
Strength as double act: Acutely observed parody of films and TV shows.
Weakness as double act: Observation sometimes too accurate, so that it becomes over-clever imitation rather than parody; some sketches too long.
Which of them is the Ernie Wise? Difficult to say for sure. It used to be Jennifer, but on current form the short hairy legs are moving Dawn's way.
What do all double acts say about their partnership? That it is a kind of marriage.
How do showbiz writers describe F and S? They are 'a kind of marriage'.
But don't Lenny and Ade resent all this marriage cobblers? No. What they may come to resent, new men though they famously are, is being completely eclipsed by their wives.
How long before the girls, their husbands, Ben, Rik, Ruby and the gang inaugurate the Comic Relief Pro-Am Golf Tournament? Not long now.
Other British female comic double acts: Gert and Daisy; any doubles team in the Federation Cup; Samantha Fox.
Would French and Saunders approve of that last gag? No. It's obvious, ancient, not funny and sexist.
Least likely to say: 'To be honest, I've been carrying the bitch for years.'

David Frost

Age: 53.

Status: Workaholic breakfast televiser. Ex-cabaret performer (school of Peter Cook). Ex-satirist, ex-iconoclast, ex-classless citizen. Since 1962, interviewer on 25 TV series or programmes with his name in the title.

Most provenly enduring gifts: Glad-handing. Getting his name in the title.

Current role model: The Greek mythological character Sisyphus, whose stone-rolling task in hell was akin to his in trying to get the British public to watch John Major at 8.15 on a Sunday morning.

Favourite phrases: 'Hello, good morning/afternoon/evening . . . and welcome.' 'Super.' 'That's fantastic.' 'Bon voyage.' 'I was born into a Methodist minister's home where we didn't have any money.'

Taxable status: Multimillionaire.

Early life: Reared in Methodist minister's home in Beccles, Suffolk. Said he refused public-school place out of dislike for 'posh' people, into whom he subsequently married. Went to Gillingham and Wellingborough grammar schools, then Cambridge.

School nickname: Little pudding-face.

Modesty quotient: 'I arrived in Cambridge at five in the afternoon and by six I was in the swing of things.'

Glittering prizes: Undergraduate cabarets when P. Cook not available. Junior role in fabled Cook–Eleanor Bron–John Bird *Footlights* revue which helped launch satire craze. Spotted when Ned Sherrin was setting up *That Was the Week That Was*. Compère's job put him on crest of craze.

Broadcasting assets: 'A nasal voice, a muddy complexion and buck teeth' (Bernard Levin, *TWTWTW* collaborator and friend).

Early praise: 'The most remarkable man to emerge since television began' (Donald Baverstock).

Early goals: 'I want to raise the level of public debate. We are really trying to get down to the roots of things. I care passionately about TV as an instrument of a participating democracy.'

Early warning signs: 'Princess Margaret wrote him a lovely letter in her own handwriting' (Frost's mother, 1966).

Mid-career misgivings: ' . . . the steady debasement of life into question and answer, the process by which a power-worker is made to justify his behaviour to a multimillionaire' (Clive James).

Married to: Lynne Frederick, 1981; Lady Carina Fitzalan-Howard, second daughter of Duke of Norfolk, 1983, three sons.

Own assessment: 'I was born with this innate curiosity about people and how they operate and I think that explains why my interviews work.'

Least likely to say: 'Whereof one cannot speak, whereon one must remain silent.'

Stephen Fry

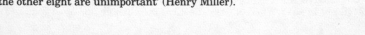

Age: 36.
Appearance: Trainee Billy Bunter.
Occupation: Comedian
(*Blackadder*, *Fry and Laurie*, *Jeeves and Wooster*) and writer. *The Hippopotamus*, his second novel, has just been published.
About hippos? No. About a young boy and his seminal fluid.
Odd topic for one so tweedy and vicarish? The donnish appearance is deceptive: he spent three months in prison during his teens for using stolen credit cards, and he used to take cocaine. Now he just chain-smokes.
So he's not as straight as he seems? Gay, actually – somewhere between 90 and 100 per cent depending on which supplement you read.
Doesn't he like girls? He insists it's nothing personal: 'To be attracted to girls is the norm, it is nature: it has the blessing of God, mummy, daddy, Hollywood, Westminster, Rupert Murdoch and MTV.'
Is he, you know, promiscuous? Far from it. He is notoriously celibate.
Why? He says he likes his friends but 'I just don't want to rub the wet slimy bits of my body all over them.'
Perhaps he should try a different technique? Very possibly.
So what does he do for fun? Fun? The very thought is anathema to him: 'The idea of spending six months a year in Barbados is horrible.' He works so much that friend Douglas Adams thinks there must be two of him.
Maybe the other one has sex? Indeed.
But he does have friends? Hundreds, including Hugh Laurie and Emma Thompson, whom he met at Cambridge. He calls them things like 'poppet'.
I thought he was supposed to be clever? He is. One of the things that depresses him is the *Daily Mail*, and his triumphs include the anagram 'I'm an evil Tory bigot' for Virginia Bottomley. Comedian Jimmy Mulville says that Fry knows so much 'he'd be the perfect luxury item to take away to a desert island'.
His witty repartee wouldn't do him much good there: He wouldn't stay – he'd fly back to warm beer and cricket in his Tiger Moth.
He's got one? Cars too; a Saab, an Aston Martin and a taxi.
How come he's so rich? He rewrote the script for *Me and My Girl* and is still receiving 3 per cent of the colossal profits.
Not to be confused with: C. B. Fry; Roger Fry; Hugh Laurie.
Most likely to quote: 'A cigarette is the perfect type of a perfect pleasure. It is exquisite, and it leaves one unsatisfied. What more can one want?' (Oscar Wilde).
Least likely to quote: 'Sex is one of the nine reasons for reincarnation . . . the other eight are unimportant' (Henry Miller).

Galileo Galilei

Age: 428.

Appearance: 17th-century heretical astronomer mathematician.

Occupation: Mathematician, astronomer, heretic.

Background: Son of musician born within spitting distance of leaning tower of Pisa. Began studying medicine but developed sudden interest in mathematics after observing a lamp swinging in Pisa cathedral (the lamp always took the same amount of time to complete an oscillation, however far it swung). In 1592 appointed professor of mathematics at University of Padua.

Discoveries: Falling bodies accelerate at the same speed, the Milky Way is not a chocolate bar, Jupiter has satellites, Saturn has rings, the sun has spots.

Things he did not discover: Gravity, America, the Sony Walkman.

On the earth and sun: From observing sun spots concluded Copernicus was right and Ptolemy wrong: the earth orbits the sun and not vice versa.

How the Vatican took it: Bad. Ordered by Pope Urban VIII before the Inquisition and forced to announce that he 'abjured, cursed and detested' his Copernican beliefs. Sentenced to imprisonment but commuted to house arrest for the rest of his days.

Supposedly muttered: 'Eppur si muove' (It does move all the same).

Galileo and the Vatican now: Firm friends. Pope John Paul II has apologised for the rash behaviour of his predecessors, pleading 'tragic mutual incomprehension'.

The bestsellers: *Siderus nuncius* (The Starry Messenger: in which he reveals that the moon is not made of cheese and other unsettling astronomical observations); *Dialogo sopra i due massimi sistemi del mondo, tolemeico e copernicano* (Dialogue Concerning the Two Chief World Systems, Ptolemeic and Copernican: in which he delivers veiled but compelling endorsement of new idea that the earth rotates around the sun and cooks his goose).

Biggest mistake: Didn't accept Kepler's 'discovery' that planets followed elliptical (rather than circular) orbits.

Some things named after him: A spacecraft *en route* to Jupiter, a moderately successful racehorse, a ticket reservation system operated by British Airways and United Airlines.

Don't say: 'Did you see the one he scored against Juventus?' 'Does the earth rotate around the sun then?' 'A fiver to win at Newmarket please.'

Do say: 'Of course his biggest mistake was not accepting Kepler's . . .'

George Galloway

Age: 39.
Profession: Labour MP for Glasgow Hillhead.
Appearance: Fading northern comedian.
So he's interested in mother-in-law jokes? No, Marxism's more his line.
Bit of a firebrand then? As he put it to Saddam Hussein: 'Hatta al-nasr, hatta al-nasr, hatta al-Quds.'
Was he in pain? The rough translation from Arabic runs: 'Until victory, until victory, until Jerusalem.' He was delivering an address to the publicity-conscious tyrant for the benefit of Iraqi television.
So he's a fan of Saddam? He denies it. Claims he only expressed support for the long-suffering Iraqis. His critics are adamant that he paid homage to his host by declaring: 'Sir, I salute your courage, your strength, your indefatigability.'
What does George say? 'What else do you call a president, other than "sir" or "Mr President"?'
What else indeed? Well, there's 'butcher' for starters.
Has George always been willing to court unpopularity? You bet. An outspoken supporter of most Islamic nations, in 1980 he twinned Dundee with Nablus, a West Bank town reputed for resistance to the Israeli occupation.
So he's not exactly popular in Israel? While visiting Nablus he was threatened with death by an Israeli soldier and detained for two hours.
His fellow Labour members must have been concerned: Sort of. They were hoping for a rather longer period of incarceration.
He's not popular with his parliamentary colleagues then? The whips were furious with his 'grovelling' to Saddam and meted out a 'severe reprimand'. They were especially aggrieved that while sojourning in Baghdad he missed at least two important votes in the Commons.
What about the Conservative side? More equivocal but once, after a heady night of debate in the Commons on the future of Scottish bus services, the Tory MP Barry Porter unsportingly took a swing at him.
The government must condemn his behaviour too? Strangely, John Major's his biggest fan at the moment, since it gives him a respite from his own renegades.
Any other supporters? Pakistan awarded him the country's highest civil award, the Hillal-i-Ovaid-i-Azzam (a.k.a. Order of the Founder of the Nation).
He's a dedicated reader of the Koran then? Hardly. The tabloids christened him Gorgeous George after he confessed to having 'carnal knowledge' of two delegates at a conference in Greece in 1985 run by the *World Marxist Review*.
He likes to mix politics with pleasure? Certainly appears to enjoy his time in the company of world figures. Compared Benazir Bhutto to a swan, and described with glee his breakfast with Fidel Castro on a recent fact-finding mission to Cuba.
Better than sausage and eggs with George Foulkes? What isn't?
Not to be confused with: Ron Brown.
Most likely to say: 'Can we do another take, boys?'
Least likely to say: 'Hatta, schmatta. Pass me a bagel.'

Paul Gascoigne

Real Name: Gazza. (It means Magpie in Italy.)

Age: 25.

Appearance: 'Priapic monolith in the Mediterranean sun' (Karl Miller, *London Review of Books*).

Only man in world who has not heard of Gazza: Mr Justice Harman. In a court case in 1990 he professed ignorance of the great footballer, and asked: 'Is there an operetta called *La Gazza Ladra*?' (There is.)

Plays for: Lazio in Italy, who bought him from Tottenham for £5.5 million.

Best friend: Jimmy 'five bellies' Gardiner, wearer of round-the-clock shellsuit and gargantuan beer gut. Met on Newcastle United terraces.

Favourite evening entertainment was to adjourn to the Godfather restaurant in Newcastle, where Gardiner would hide under a table and watch Gazza walking up and down trying to find him.

Income: Financially secure for life. £3 million five-year contract with Lazio. 'My father's got his pint-money for the rest of his life.'

Favourite food: Mars bars.

Famous for: Getting into trouble; crying during the 1990 World Cup; sticking his tongue out; kamikaze attack on own knee during the 1991 FA Cup Final; being as daft as a brush. Also the most talented British footballer of his generation.

Daft as a brushisms: On first evening in Rome, he gave his minder the slip and hid in a cupboard, leaving his shoes by an open window. During training he panicked his manager and doctor by crumpling to the ground clutching his knee – only to jump up and jog off as if nothing had happened.

Is that as daft as he gets? No. In September 1991 he was conditionally discharged for punching a man he claimed knocked over sister Lindsey. Subsequently punched while in a nightclub, falling and redamaging his knee, necessitating another operation. When asked if had a message for the people of Norway, he replied: 'Yes, f*** off.' Later apologised.

Testimonials: John Sheridan, the Tottenham physio and his constant companion during his rehabilitation, was in tears when he left for Lazio. The then England manager Graham Taylor likened him to a hand grenade, capable of damaging friend or foe. Romans call him Il Matto, the madman. 'He is not pretty but he has steel in his soul and passion in his heart' – Lazio fan Bettina Salvini, 21.

Has moving to Italy changed his attitude on the pitch? 'No more patting referees on the backside for me.'

Least likely to say: 'Let's nip off and have a look at the *Pietà* after the game.'

Bill Gates

Age: 37.

Real name: William Henry Gates III. Known to his parents as 'Trey', after the III. Referred to as 'Chairman Bill' and 'Billionaire Bill'.

Appearance: 19-year-old 'nerd' or 'propeller head' (derogatory terms for computer freaks). Has done well out of being underestimated, becoming America's youngest billionaire and one of its richest men.

Character: Described as 'one part Albert Einstein, one part John McEnroe and one part General Patton'.

Occupation: The Henry Ford of personal computer software. Gates co-founded and runs Microsoft, a personal computer software company based at One Microsoft Way, Redmond, Washington. His shares are worth roughly $8 billion.

Does that make him one of the world's most eligible bachelors? Not for long: he's recently become engaged to Melinda French, 28, a Microsoft product manager.

Career: Started as a schoolboy programmer whose mother sometimes helped with sales presentations. When the MITS Altair, the first personal computer, was launched in kit form in 1975, Gates dropped out of Harvard to finish and market a version of the Basic language for it. Gates and his friend Paul Allen then founded Microsoft.

So he's gone from being a poor little rich kid to being an impossibly rich big kid? Yes.

Lucky breaks: Sold IBM the Microsoft Disk Operating System (MS-DOS) for the IBM Personal Computer, launched in 1981. Microsoft didn't have such a thing at the time, but Bill knew someone who had already done the basics . . .

What's good about DOS? Microsoft sells a copy every three seconds. It also sells a copy of Windows – a friendly front end for DOS – every four seconds. Then it makes even more money selling DOS and Windows applications like word processors, spreadsheets, data bases and games.

Lifestyle: Workaholic who still eats pizzas at his desk. However, his taste in celebratory drinks has progressed from the Shirley Temple (grenadine and 7-Up) to Dom Perignon. Donates money to charity.

Hasn't he anything to spend his money on? Fast cars. He's also building a futuristic $10 million mansion on 415 feet of Lake Washington waterfront, but it won't spoil the view: 80 per cent of it is below ground. It has a 60ft swimming pool, a 20-seat movie theatre and parking for up to 28 cars.

Like Xanadu? Quite. The local press call it San Simeon North, with reference to the William Randolph Hearst original.

So everything's perfect, right? Not quite. Microsoft is still at war with parts of IBM over OS/2, a jointly developed operating system that flopped. The company's allegedly unfair trade practices are also being investigated by America's watchdog, the Federal Trades Commission.

Least likely to say: 'You know, if I'd stayed on at Harvard and got a degree I might have made something of my life.'

18 May 1993. Married Melinda on 1 January 1994 in Hawaii.

James Gilbey

Age: 36.
Appearance: Knitting pattern model.
Job: Car salesman.
Best known for: Long mobile telephone chats with Princess Diana.
Isn't he yesterday's man? He was, until snatches of conversation, previously considered too raunchy by the British press, turned up in Australia.
Such as? It may be best to ask an Australian.
Family motto: Honour and Virtue.
Isn't Gilbey's the name of a popular brand of gin? It is.
Are they by any chance related? Distantly.
Background: Son of a wine merchant. Brought up near Bishop's Stortford, Herts. Educated at Ampleforth (nickname 'Fatty'). Did not go to university. Started car dealership, which went bust. Joined Lotus Cars in February 1993.
How long has he known Diana? Since she was 17.
Has he made any other significant contribution to the public's understanding of royal life? He was the main source of Andrew Morton's book revealing Diana's suicide attempts, her empty home life and her concerns about Camilla.
James's nickname for Di: Squidgy, Old Bossy Boots.
James's nickname for himself: Chinless.
Favourite words: 'Darling' (he calls Diana this 53 times in the 20-minute conversation), 'shit-hot', 'bummer', 'jellybags'.
What is the meaning of 'jellybags'? When one has had a bummer of day one might go all jellybags.
James's friends say: 'He's a very good bloke. He's extremely nice to girls' (Tom Dodd-Noble, former business associate); 'He's a gentle Sloane' (Frances de Salis, known to her friends as 'Tuft').
Enemies say: 'I think he was simply a mouthpiece of a disgruntled wife and that he willingly passed on highly dubious stories' (rival biographer Lady Colin Campbell); 'His behaviour is extremely common and vulgar. He should be thrown out of his club' (Barbara Cartland).
Friends: Andrew Morton, Lisa Butcher, wife of Marco Pierre White.
Enemies: Prince Charles, Marco Pierre White.
Not to be confused with: Monsignor James Gilbey, celibate 91-year-old Catholic priest resident at Travellers' Club; Camilla Parker-Bowles.
Does he have any other lady friends? There was a liaison with Alethea Savile, daughter of the Earl of Mexborough.
Is he the nicest person in the world? Diana thinks so, and she has met Mother Teresa.
Least likely to say? 'Your great achievement is to love me.'

Gary Glitter

Real name: Paul Gadd.
Also answers to: The Leader.
Age: Old enough to know better.
Appearance: Mutton dressed up as Glam.
Lookalike: Andrew Neil after transvestite night at Tramp.
Background: With a sartorial style that made Liberace look like a bank clerk, Glitter made his name by adopting the hairstyle and facial expressions of a permanently startled rodent. Thudding round a stage with all the grace of a well-stacked quarterback, his stagewalk became known as the Glitter Stomp.
Typical Glitter sound: Multi-track handclaps; plenty of bass, drums and reverberation; primordial football terrace chanting.
Typical lyric: 'Hey, hey, hey, hey, oi, oi, oi!'
Glitter on Glitter: 'I'm a terrible singer. Or let's say, as a singer, I'm a great shouter, and I can pull marvellous faces.'
High: Between 1972 and 1975, he sold 18 million records and had 11 top 10 hits. 'I'm the Leader of the Gang (I Am)' and 'I Love, You Love, Me Love' reached number one and sold a million copies each.
Low: In 1978 his finances, like his trousers, started to show the strain. He declared himself bankrupt, owing £170,000 to the Inland Revenue and £60 to the Fulham Road Tandoori. Spent much of the eighties submerged in a boozy, druggy hell before taking an overdose and threatening to slash his wrists with a meat cleaver.
Comebacks to date: Four.
Do You Wanna Touch Him? Not personally, no, but while Glitter is not possessed of conventionally good looks ('I've got eyes like a garage mechanic and a body like a truck driver') he still makes women of all generations swoon.
What he should be doing at his age: Tending an allotment; playing bowls; making speeches at Rotary lunches; wearing beige leisurewear from BHS; subscribing to the *People's Friend*; going on Saga holidays.
What he is actually doing: Backcombing his hair; wearing platforms, skin-tight jumpsuits and opening a chain of sandwich bars selling Do You Wanna Munch Me pizza and Gary's Platforms doorstep sandwiches.
Gary Glitter dress-alikes: Duchess of York, Joan Collins, Flash Gordon, Christmas turkeys countrywide.
Surprising fact: He once challenged Prince Charles to a hairy chest competition.
Surprising fact no. 2: Glitter lost.
Likes: Hairspray, Bacofoil, dressing up – 'I still wear sequins at home.'
Most likely to say: 'Hello Hello, I'm Back Again' (and again, and again).
Least likely to say: 'Me? I just Wash 'n' Go.'

King Goodwill Zwelithini

Age: 46.

Appearance: Sixties soul singer with optional sunglasses and leopard-skin head-dress.

Full title: King Goodwill Zwelithini kaBhekuzulu Ingonyama Yamazulu.

What does that mean? King Goodwill Zwelithini, son of Bhekuzulu the Lion of the Zulus.

Occupation: Zulu monarch.

And where does he reign? Moot point. He is a king without a country, ruling only over the region of KwaZulu/Natal, which he says was a sovereign state before 1834 under King Shaka.

So why is he in the news? Before last Friday, Nelson Mandela thought he represented the solution to the problems in KwaZulu/Natal, currently under a state of emergency.

What does Mandela think now? That he represents a major problem.

Friday must have been a bad day. What happened? Nothing. That's the point. Mandela, King Goodwill, Chief Mangosuthu Gatsha Buthelezi and F. W. De Klerk all met in Kruger National Park to hammer out an agreement but failed to agree on anything. Mandela says he offered Goodwill the same rights, status and privileges as Queen Elizabeth II.

And what did King Goodwill say: 'I have examined your proposals and find them unacceptable.'

He's not interested in being like Elizabeth II? Probably keener to be like Elizabeth I.

But didn't Mandela offer him more powers than he enjoys under the present constitution? Yes.

So who in their right mind would turn an offer like that down? Ask Gatsha Buthelezi.

What's he got to do with it? He is not only Goodwill's uncle and leader of the Inkatha Freedom Party, but also Chief Minister of KwaZulu/Natal.

Are you suggesting King Goodwill's goodwill can only be won with his uncle's support? Well, since you ask, yes.

Have King Goodwill and Gatsha always been in cahoots? Hardly. In 1975 Goodwill tried to set up a separate party with other tribal chiefs. Smelling a rat, Buthelezi forced him to sign an oath that would prohibit him from participating in party politics.

What does the King do in his spare time: attend charity galas, go on lots of foreign trips, that sort of thing? His rather complicated domestic arrangements don't leave him with much time for socialising.

What are the complications? He has five wives, the youngest of whom is 21. Each lives in a private royal residence.

He'd better be careful or he'll have scurrilous royal biographers on his tail: He says that having five wives is better than having one and lots of 'private girlfriends'.

Not to be confused with: Goodwill to All Men.

Least likely to say: 'Shlalakahle, Madiba' (Stay well, Nelson).

12 April 1994. At that point Inkatha looked likely to boycott the election and provoke a violent stand-off. A few days later, however, they suddenly announced their participation – such is the power of Pass Notes to make international leaders see the error of their ways.

Henryk Gorecki

Age: 58.
Who is he? A reclusive Polish
composer who has achieved
something close to cult status as a
result of his Third Symphony.
Pronounced? Henrick Guretski.
Background: Grew up in Katowice,
Poland, near to Oswiecim
(Auschwitz). Studied composition at
the Katowice Conservatory and in
Paris (though not, as has been
popularly supposed, with Olivier
Messiaen.) Much of his music is
infused with sorrowful resonances of
the Second World War. He now lives
and works in Katowice. He is a
reluctant icon, and had to be forcibly
persuaded to visit America for the
first time this year to receive homage
from a mass audience. In recent years
his work has been slowed by illness.

**Is there a useful pigeonhole to
hand?** Holy minimalism.
Who else writes holy minimalist music? John Tavener, the Greek Orthodox
British composer; Arvo Part, the Estonian composer; and Giya Kancheli, the
Georgian symphonist.
How can you spot it? Pious subject matter, harmonic stasis and snail-like
progress (a.k.a. 'time suspended').
Influences: Webern influenced early music. Scriabin, Stockhausen, Terry
Riley, Szymanowski, Ives and Messiaen for later music. The big change
happened about 1963, when he was challenged to prove he could write a tune.
He did (Three Pieces in Old Style) and has since increasingly concentrated on
simplicity and modal music derived from folksong.
That Third Symphony: Composed in 1976, and took 10 years to find a
publisher. Introduced to Britain in 1987 and the USA two years later. It has
been recorded four times. The latest version, by the London Sinfonietta, has
sold 115,000 copies worldwide. Much of this has been achieved by word of mouth
and through plugs on Classic FM. It has, for instance, never been reviewed in
Gramophone. It is titled *The Symphony of Sorrowful Songs*. All three
movements are slow. The music, which lasts for 55 minutes, is scored for
soprano, strings and piano and uses 15th-century Polish prayers, Aeolian
modes, folksong and a poem written by a woman imprisoned by the Nazis.
Why do people like it? Popularity attributed to a thirst for spirituality and the
material West's need for a moral message. Plus, it's tuneful.
Useful phrases when talking about Gorecki: At last mystic minimalism has
acquired a heart and soul. Voluptuously ascetic. Revisionist. Symbolic art
which expresses the deepest and most permanent of human metaphysical
longings.
Has the Third Symphony been used as a soundtrack yet? Yes. It was used
by Maurice Pialat for his 1985 *Police*, starring Gérard Depardieu.
Other Gorecki recordings: Harpsichord Concerto, op. 40. *Lerchenmusik*, op.
53. *Already It's Dusk* (String Quartet No. 1).

Teresa Gorman

Age: State secret. Not given in *Who's Who*. But reckoned to be 60-ish.

Appearance: Getting younger by the day (thanks to hormone replacement therapy).

Status: Conservative MP for Billericay, Harvey Proctor's old seat, since 1987. Doyenne of the New Right, virulent critic of the PM and touted as a possible stalking-horse candidate to run against Major.

Why is she in the news? Has written *The Bastards*, an everyday story of Westminster folk.

Sex, drugs, power-mania, that sort of thing? Er, no – the stirring tale of Tory rebels' attempts to wreck the Maastricht Treaty, actually.

Available from all good bookshops? Of course, but strangely absent from the Conservative Central Office bookstall at the Blackpool conference. They wanted to see the book before stocking it; the publishers refused.

What her leader thinks of her: Barmy.

Is she? Not in the slightest, unless you think that political views which make Michael Portillo look dangerously left wing are a sign of mental instability.

Such as? Hang 'em, flog 'em, but most of all privatise 'em.

Where did she develop her fundamentalist worldview? America, of course. She saw the light in the mid-sixties while teaching there. 'America changed my life; it was the first time I'd lived in a capitalist society; it was like coming out from behind the Iron Curtain.'

So she threw herself into anti-socialist politics? Not exactly. Her first election was in 1974, when she stood in Streatham as an anti-Heath  Independent against the official Conservative and lost heavily.

Did she learn the lesson? Sort of. She joined the Tories in 1975 but remained a rebel, fulminating against constituency selection committees that failed to pick her.

An example of this fulmination please: 'The average selection committee doesn't want a woman; it wants a man of 35 in a neat business suit with an obedient, attractive wife and two nice children.'

Any other *aperçus*? 'I hate this nagging society we've got. We've all got to go to hell our own way.'

Likes: Wimbledon ticket touts; she defended them as 'risk-takers'.

Dislikes: (1) Conservationists for ever banging on about the greenhouse effect: 'We legislate on the environment because we are all put under pressure by eco-terrorists.' (2) Old-fashioned Conservatives: 'The enemy is the old wet Tories who think they were born to rule.'

Most likely to praise: Adam Smith.

Least likely to praise: John Smith.

David Gower

Age: 35.
Appearance: Surfer turned stockbroker.
Background: Born on April Fool's Day 1957, in Tunbridge Wells. Early years spent in Tanganyika (father was in the Colonial Service). Public school in Kent. Studied law at University College, London, but left after two terms to concentrate on cricket. Joined Leicestershire and played first Test in 1978. Hit his first ball for four, in what John Arlott called a 'princely entry'. Went on to captain England, winning the Ashes in 1985 but then losing eight Tests on the trot.
Gap in the diary: Left out of team to tour India despite being England's highest-ever run scorer and averaging 50 in Pakistan Test series.
Why was he left out? Selectors wanted to blood younger players. Youthful South Africa rebels Mike Gatting (also 35) and John Emburey (40) were included, and skipper Graham Gooch is 39.
Real reason: Gooch resents his lackadaisical style, thinks he's bad for morale.
Evidence against him: Hired a Tiger Moth and buzzed the ground during a match between England and Queensland – was fined £1,000. Visited a casino with Allan Lamb and Kerry Packer the night before a Test against Australia. Loves champagne. Hates net practice. Criticised Gooch's fitness regime. Prone to get out to airy swishes outside the off-stump at vital moments. Attacked by the *Times* for having his hands in his pockets between overs.
Saving grace: He's a world-class player and, at his best, bats like an angel. 'If Shakespeare had been there, he would have written a sonnet,' Henry Blofeld said of a typical Gower century.
Supporters: Surrey businessman Dennis Oliver, who has won a special meeting of MCC members to vote on a motion of no confidence in the selectors; the *Observer*, which is running a Restore Gower campaign; Harold Pinter; wine merchants everywhere.
Consolation: Two weeks after his omission he married Thorunn Nash. Asked if Gooch had been invited, he replied: 'No, he wasn't selected. He's too old.'
Interests: Wildlife photography, wine, winter sports, flying, lawn mowing.
How does he relax? 'With a bottle of Bollinger and something or someone to nibble in the sunshine.'
Least likely to say: 'OK, chaps, time we were in bed, we've got a big game tomorrow.'
Friendly obituary: 'He can now play in heaven, where his talents will be most at home.'
Critical obituary: 'A player of great innings but not a great player.'

7 December 1992. The Restore Gower campaign failed, he was not picked for England in the disastrous series against Australia in 1993 and at the end of that season announced his retirement.

Hugh Grant

Age: Depends who you believe – the *Daily Express* says 33, *Today* says 30, the consensus is 31.

Appearance: Stiff upper lip with a floppy fringe on top; public schoolboy who never grew up.

Eton, country estate, that sort of thing? No. Latymer Upper in Hammersmith, then a scholarship to New College, Oxford. Joined the Piers Gaveston Society.

Sorry? One of those socially advantageous Oxford clubs.

Sounds like a good move: He was able to practise his Merchant–Ivory vowel sounds.

Why is he in the news? The tabloids have been full of pictures of him at a gala West End screening with a scantily clad young woman.

What was she doing there? She's Elizabeth Hurley, Hugh's partner.

And Hugh? I'm glad you asked. It was the première of *Four Weddings and a Funeral*.

Er . . . Oh come on, the most successful, funniest, most sophisticated, etc., etc., British film since, well, since the last one.

Does it have a complicated plot? There are, unsurprisingly, four weddings and a funeral, but not necessarily in that order.

Sounds pretty dull. Why has it been so successful? According to the director, scriptwriter, other actors and anyone who knows him, the film's success is down to its star, Hughie.

What else has he done? From a debut on the BBC school quiz *Top of the Form*, he went on to *The Remains of the Day* and Polanski's *Bitter Moon*.

Unimpressive: Well, he did star in *Maurice*, the life of a Cambridge homosexual based on E. M. Forster's posthumously published novel.

And? Oh all right, it earned him a spot as cover star for *Gay News*.

So he's gay? He did say 'No one kisses like [co-star] James Wilby – the things he could do with his tongue.' And he did turn down Madonna . . .

Ah-ha . . . because he didn't want anything to come between him and girlfriend Elizabeth.

Prospects? Currently Hollywood's, nay, the world's, hottest property.

Passions? Liz, Fulham FC, not necessarily in that order.

Who was the last British film star to cause such a stir? Rupert Everett.

Who? Exactly.

Not to be confused with: Cary Grant; Bernie Grant; Eddie Grant; Russell Grant; Ulysses S. Grant; Grant of *EastEnders*; Barry Grant of *Brookside*; anyone called Grant.

Most likely to say: 'We are Fulham, we are Fulham . . .' (repeat for 20 minutes to the tune of 'Sailing').

Least likely to say: 'Please, no photographs.'

John Gummer

Name: John Gummer (Selwyn
sometimes inserted to give it a ring).
Age: 52; looks 15; talks as if 70.
Appearance: Precocious head
prefect. Bearded till someone told him
Thatcher hated facial hair.
What's he done now? Resigned from
the General Synod over women's
ordination: 'The Synod has finally
turned the Church of England into a
sect.'
**Are the liberal bishops dancing
with delight?** Probably. But the
Bishop of St Edmundsbury and
Ipswich has promised to pray for him.
So will we be hearing less of him?
No such luck. There'll be more
righteous declamations if he leaves
the C of E altogether, and he's still
Secretary of State for Agriculture.
Background: Son of a canon, but
never fired (in government for 11

years and the cabinet for three). At school was bad at sport but good at essay
prizes. Went (coincidentally) to Selwyn College, Cambridge, and was Union
president in 1963. Tossed up between priesthood and politics: politics lost.
Political career: Won inner London seat in '70, lost it '74, re-emerged in rural
Suffolk from '79 on. At the 1975 referendum ran Christians for Europe, since
when has recklessly mixed religion and politics (Bible in office anteroom,
prayer card in sun visor of official limo). Succeeded Cecil Parkinson as Tory
Party chairman in '83 (Mr Clean to follow Mr Dirty) but was dumped in favour
of street-fighter Tebbit. Pushed through the poll tax (calling it 'morally
superior') before surprising the world in '89 cabinet promotions and making a
pig's ear of the scare over mad cow disease.
Political principles: Also catholic; so devoted to Heath he married his
secretary; so devoted to Thatcher he blubbed when she fell; so devoted to Major
. . . well, we'll see.
Specialities: Pomposity; ineffable sanctimoniousness; going over the top.
Talents: Hard-working, nimble-minded, approachable, quotable, as concerned
for animal welfare as a zealous carnivore can be.
Things they say about him: 'Little squit' (Dennis Skinner); 'an
inconsequential little creep who's never grown out of student politics' (Sir
Edward du Cann); 'a mediocre school swot' (a senior Tory Party official).
Things he says about them: Bishops purvey 'condom culture', modern liturgy
is 'Tesco-speak', Dave Nellist is a 'red fascist', and vegetarians are 'unnatural
faddists' at odds with biblical teaching.
Daftest stunt: Forcing daughter Cordelia to eat a beefburger for the cameras
during the mad cow scare.
Daftest remark: 'When I'm in Brussels sitting down, I'm standing up for
British interests.'
Remark he's least likely to make: 'For Christ's sake, child, eat your
vegeburger.'

3 December 1992. Gummer became Environment Secretary in May 1993. In February
1994, he left the Anglican Church and converted to Rome.

Darius Guppy

Age: 28.

Appearance: Model for Brylcreem advert *circa* 1983.

In the news because: He is part of the distressing wave of youth crime sweeping the country.

Ramraiding and drugs? A bit more sophisticated, actually. Fraud to the tune of £1.8 million and a VAT fiddle which netted him and his accomplice £200,000.

Is that enough to justify all the headlines? No. They are on account of the fact that he was best man at Earl Spencer's wedding. This gives him a walk-on part in Di-mania.

Background: Son of Nicholas and Shusha. He is a writer and explorer who lost heavily on Lloyd's. She is an Iranian folksinger and writer.

Educated: Eton and Magdalen, Oxford (first-class honours in French and history).

The glittering prize: Alleged to have spent his time at Oxford drinking and seducing women. Describing himself as 'poet and socialite', he swanned around in spats and a monocle. Women were reported to have been enslaved to him – particularly an aristocrat in her late 40s. Fell out with his landlord and retaliated by detonating giant fireworks through his letterbox.

Career: First job as bond dealer at Credit Suisse ended when he refused to do routine office tasks. Started a company selling monocles. Turned to crime.

The things they say about him: Byronic good looks . . . born in the wrong century . . . a demigod . . . a romantic brought down by arrogance . . . like an evil genius from a Bond movie . . . golden youth led astray . . . Rasputin glamour . . . lives by a Homeric code of honour . . . clearly bonkers.

Darius's role models: Sir Philip Sidney, Napoleon, Alexander the Great, Darius the Great (he built Persepolis), Raffles.

Family: Married Patricia, a girl he met in the Groucho Club in 1989.

Hobbies: Kickboxing, scuba diving, flying, sculpting.

Strange fact: Darius's great-grandfather, the Rev. Lechmere Guppy, discovered a diminutive, flamboyant, aggressive, sex-mad fish and named it the guppy.

Earl Spencer on Darius: 'I knew he could be a millionaire or would have visited the cells by the time he was 30.'

Darius on the press coverage: 'People are just jealous of my friendship with the royal family. It's pathetic.'

Judge Andrew Brooks says: 'You are going to prison for a very long time.'

Darius on prison: 'I expect it will be a bit like Eton.'

5 March 1993. Guppy appealed unsuccessfully against his five-year gaol sentence but did have his fine cut from £539,000 to £227,000. *Hello!* magazine was censured for paying for a gushing 'at home with Guppy' article in his cell.

Sir Peter Hall

Age: 62.

Appearance: Falstaffian restaurateur. 'Genghis Khan' – Michael Blakemore; 'Fu Manchu' – Jonathan Miller.

Reputation: Seen alternatively as the elder luvvie of British theatre, whose achievements are so great as to put him beyond criticism; or as the grey man of the South Bank whose replacement by Richard Eyre in 1980 as the National Theatre's artistic director gave the lumbering institution a breath of creative life.

So who's right? Both. He's a pushy radical who joined the establishment.

Act one: In the fifties and sixties he was a leather-jacketed tyro, who gave *Waiting for Godot* its first British production, and at 29 set up the RSC, the first British subsidised theatre.

Act two: In 1972 he pushed aside Peter Blakemore, Olivier's protégé, for the National job. His eight years there were fraught with conflicts with unions, with his associate directors and with building contractors. Glenda Jackson said of him then: 'I do wish he'd stop pretending to be so bloody nice, when really he's a dictator.'

Act three: Now he is responsible for filling the West End with respectable if dull productions (Wilde's *An Ideal Husband*, Rattigan's *Separate Tables*).

The final curtain? He also seems to be developing a line in high-class smut: he directed, one hopes with regret, *The Camomile Lawn* for television. His bawdy production of Aristophanes's *Lysistrata* provoked walk-outs at the Liverpool Playhouse. Objection taken to its graphic depiction of men wielding excruciating erections under their baggy trousers, driven mad by a female sex strike in ancient Greece.

Luvvie's love labours: He's a serial monogamist, married four times – every time to someone whom he worked with. He has swapped the gamine wife (actress Leslie Caron, opera singer Maria Ewing) for the willowy blonde (Nicki Frei, former NT publicist) – maybe striking a menopausal blow for freedom. His failed marriages (such as to PA Jacqueline Taylor) weren't up to the stress of his high-powered lifestyle.

Hall's well: Harold Pinter once urged him to lead a more 'sensible life – having time off, time to read, or time to do nothing, or time to see friends'. He has scrupulously ignored the advice.

Rich? For an honest luvvie, very. He astutely transferred many money-spinning plays from the subsidised sector to the West End.

Least likely to say: 'I'm thinking of a profit-share production at the ICA.'

Hamlet

Created: Not by Shakespeare. The story of Amleth featured in a 12th-century history of Denmark, later in Belleforest's *Histoires Tragiques*. Thomas Kyd also thought to have pre-empted Shakespeare with the lost *Ur-Hamlet*.

Age: 30, in Shakespeare.

Home address: Elsinore Castle, Denmark.

Occupation: Unemployed Danish prince. Formerly student at the University of Wittenberg.

Appearance: 'Fat, and scant of breath', dressed in 'customary suits of solemn black', lachrymose.

Why? Hamlet's father, Old Hamlet, has been dead two months and succeeded by his brother Claudius, who has already married Gertrude, Old Hamlet's wife. The ghost of the old king tells Hamlet that Claudius murdered him.

So what's Hamlet's problem? Good question if you agree with T. S. Eliot, who thought the play lacked an 'objective correlative' – a set of events sufficient to explain Hamlet's behaviour: 'So far from being Shakespeare's masterpiece, the play is most certainly an artistic failure.'

What does it all mean? That Shakespeare was a cuckold, betrayed by Anne Hathaway and his brother (James Joyce); an expression of sexual disgust, caused by the arrival of syphilis from the New World (D. H. Lawrence); premature male menopause – 'he is at a crossroads in his life and Shakespeare dramatises that very human situation' (Kenneth Branagh).

Hamlet on the House of Windsor: 'I say we will have no more marriages.'

Hamlet on Madonna: 'To a nunnery, go.'

Hamlet on David Mellor: 'Our indiscretion sometimes serves us well when our deep plots do fail.'

Hamlet's letter to 'Notes and Queries': 'How long will a man lie i' the earth 'ere he rot?'

What it's like playing Hamlet: 'A warm-hearted and life-enhancing experience' – Kenneth Branagh (pictured), who is having his third go at the part.

Suitable jobs for Hamlet: Researcher on *The Late Show*; Samaritans counsellor.

Some titles nicked from *Hamlet*: *The Mousetrap, Single Spies, Very Like a Whale, Rosencrantz and Guildenstern Are Dead, Murder Most Foul*.

Other things called Hamlet: Small villages, mild cigars, disappointing portion of ham.

How not to greet Hamlet: 'Cheer up, it may never happen.'

Lord Hanson

Age: 70.

Appearance: Young for his age. Lean, tall (6ft 5in) and dressy. He exudes wealth. If it were possible he would wear his black Rolls-Royce.

Background: Yorkshire merchant class. His family was too sophisticated to say 'where there's muck there's brass' but nonetheless worked on that principle. His father built up a successful haulage firm which young James Hanson believed he would end up running with his brother. Hanson's background taught him the value of money but did not instil in him much ambition. He got that from wild young Gordie White (now Lord White), a friend of his swashbuckling brother Bill he came to know after Bill's early death from cancer.

Main strengths: Very good administrator and with a good financial mind. Has a frightening clarity of purpose. Is generous to Lord White, whom he credits with the inspiration of the operation.

Biggest faults: A terrible temper and hypersensitivity. There are few people who exude quite the air of terrible menace that Hanson does when irritated by an opponent or journalist. During interviews he is likely to break off to say: 'We sue for libel when we see it, so please take trouble over the facts in this story.' Can be horrible to managers who do not meet his growth targets. Has a regrettable taste in light music, which he has piped into his office from his own Melody Radio (he was a presenter with Forces radio).

Best friends: Lord White, Frank Sinatra, Lord King, son Robert, Jim Slater.

Enemies: The entire board of ICI, which Hanson failed to take over in 1991.

Passions: Hunting, show jumping, Lady Thatcher, things that money can buy and his home in Palm Springs, crooners, the deal.

Single most surprising fact about him: He was engaged to Audrey Hepburn for a year in the fifties when White and he cut quite a swathe through Hollywood. He broke it off and married Geraldine Kaelin in 1959. He had also escorted Jean Simmons.

First joint venture with White: Importing humorous birthday cards from America.

Achievements: His part in creating a company which is worth $10 billion and employs 80,000 people worldwide. Keeping Gordon White as part of Hanson when his friend left for America and set up on his own to make the corporate-raiding operations of the eighties. But for Hanson's guile, Gordon would have kept all that money to himself.

Least likely to say: 'Coal not dole.'

Sir Peter Harding

Age: 60.
Appearance: Prosperous butcher.
Occupation: Chief of the Defence
Staff until yesterday; aide-de-camp
to HM the Queen.
**Why has he resigned – was one of
our planes missing?** No, no, it's
more serious than that. He allegedly
had an affair with Lady Buck, née
Bienvenida Pérez-Blanco, 32, while
she was still married to ex-Tory MP
Sir Antony Buck, 65. The *News of
the World* said the besotted Harding
ignored security and blackmail
perils in arranging trysts and
penning love letters to the blonde
Spanish 'fashion designer'. And he
said John Major was 'nice . . . but
just not strong enough'.
**Ouch. But it all sounds a bit
flimsy?** Alas, no. Both Bucks spoke

to the press. The *NoW* printed pics of
the star-crossed duo snogging after a platonic tête-à-tête last week at the
Dorchester, and cited examples of Sir Peter's purple prose.
Let's have a sample: 'Your skin so very fair and satin to touch, your nipples
so delicately pink, like a girl, your breasts so petite, your legs so gazelle-like,
your smell so overpoweringly intoxicating . . .'
Phew. But tell me about Bienvenida. Are her legs really gazelle-like? The
black lingerie she posed in for the *NoW* makes it hard to tell. She married
Buck in 1990, seeing him as 'a cultured English gentleman who could recite
Shakespeare'. Now they are sorting out custody of their pet spaniels, Pebbles
and Cocoa. Her background is obscure: her father is supposedly a retired
lawyer called Francisco Pérez, but Spain's law society lists no such figure.
**Anything else that made her a perfect partner for Britain's war
supremo?** Her former friendship with Valerio Viccei, who pulled off the £60
million Knightsbridge safe deposit robbery.
So how did she meet Pete? Initially, at a dinner held by the Indian High
Commissioner; later at well-known hotels such as the Meridian and the
Halcyon. Harding eschewed more discreet rendezvous at his club, the Army
and Navy.
Is he the classic upper-class air force type? Not at all. His background
resembles Norman Tebbit's: a Chingford lad who trained as a pilot after
leaving school.
Doesn't the RAF turn a blind eye to Brylcreem Romeos? No longer.
Three months ago the MoD issued its own Back to Basics code, fingering
adultery as 'the most serious form of social misconduct'.
Is Sir Antony mortified about the resignation? Well, yes and no: 'It's
absolutely tragic, he's a brilliant officer. But in the circumstances you cannot
expect me to be overwhelmed with grief.'
Not to be confused with: Tonya Harding; Septimus Harding; Biggles.
Most likely motto: Per ardua ad Jobcentrum.

Tonya Harding

Age: 23.

Appearance: Sickly-sweet cheerleader. Ideal for a fizzy drink commercial.

Occupation: Ice skater.

Why is she in the news? She has just been crowned America's ice queen in the National Figure Skating Championships and will be travelling to Lillehammer in Norway to fly the star-spangled banner in the Winter Olympics.

Good old Tonya, she must be delighted: Indeed, but there was a tiny cloud over her triumph.

What was that, one judge thought her triple salko was a bit sloppy, that sort of thing? Not exactly. Her bodyguard, Shawn Eckardt, has been arrested for knocking her arch-rival Nancy Kerrigan out of the competition by hiring a hitman to bash her on the knee.

Wow, that's a pretty damning charge: There's more. Harding's ex-husband, Jeff Gillooly, is also implicated.

What's the evidence? The FBI were set on Gillooly's trail after a church minister in Portland was played a tape of the plan to injure Kerrigan by a concerned parishioner. The tape is believed to be a recording of a three-way conversation between hitman Shane Stant, Eckardt and Gillooly.

Did any of them confess? Eckardt spilt the beans to the police when the hitman, who'd been denied his whack, got nasty.

Is Tonya involved? Not directly, but investigators suspect that the $6,500 used for the hit came from her US Figure Skating Fund, donated by supporters and supposed to be used for training and competition.

So this doesn't count as competition? No, not even in America.

Anything else in her closet? Numerous sequined strips of material which pass for ice-dancing costumes . . .

No, skeleton-wise: I see what you mean. She has a colourful past: her father was a drifter and her mother has been married seven times. Harding divorced last year after four years of tempestuous marriage.

Like mother, like daughter? Maybe not, she was recently reconciled with Gillooly.

Has she faced any other problems? She froze at the last Winter Olympics, falling several times and failing to win a medal.

And Kerrigan won bronze . . . ? I hope you're not putting two and two together.

Not to be confused with: Sonja Henie, ice skater and actress (remember *Sun Valley Serenade* and the Norwegian classic *Svy Dager for Elisabeth*?).

Most likely to say: 'I love Nancy and hope she makes a speedy recovery.'

Least likely to say: 'He was only trying to break the ice.'

---

18 January 1994. Harding was allowed to skate for the USA in the Winter Olympics but failed to win a medal. Kerrigan won silver. In March 1994 Harding pleaded guilty to obstructing police investigations and was fined $100,000 and ordered to do community service. She was later stripped of her US title.

Stephen Hawking

Age: 51.

Position: Lucasian Professor of Mathematics at Cambridge.

Good job? It was good enough for Isaac Newton.

Boldly going where no astrophysicist has gone before: Hawking has been offered a cameo role in *Star Trek: The Next Generation*, programming the USS *Enterprise*'s computer to create a poker game between himself, Einstein and Newton.

And move over Beattie: He is appearing in Saatchi & Saatchi's 90-second commercial for British Telecom.

The popularising prof: His *A Brief History of Time* has sold 22 million copies worldwide and stayed on the UK bestseller lists longer than any other book except *The Country Diary of an Edwardian Lady*.

So it's a good read? Few people have actually got to the end. Even though the book has only one equation ($e = mc^2$), it is extremely heavy going, partly because of the complexity of the subject, but mainly because of his convoluted style. His next book, *Black Holes and Baby Universes*, will be simpler – it includes a transcript of his interview on *Desert Island Discs*.

A brief history of Hawking: Born in St Albans, he cruised to a first at Oxford in physics, appalling fellow students with his habit of binning his brilliant essays. Beamed up to Cambridge, where he did postgraduate research in cosmology. In his first term there his speech began to slur and his movements became clumsy. Tests revealed he had motor neurone disease, a wasting condition that slowly paralyses the body. Now he can only communicate through a voice synthesiser.

Profile writers' cliché: 'From his wheelchair he roams the universe.'

A (very) brief history of modern cosmology: Most astrophysicists think the universe is expanding, so that if you imagine the creation running backwards you return to the beginning – the Big Bang. Hawking says there was no moment of creation: this is an illusion fostered by the framework of space and time through which we view the cosmos.

A star is born? His work amounts to an audacious union of opposites – quantum theory (the study of small particles and their movement through space-time) and general relativity (Einstein's theory of gravity, dealing with planets, stars and galaxies).

But will his theories be exploded? Hawking's colleague Professor Roger Penrose says: 'My feeling is that you should wait 25 years to see if the book stands the test of time.'

Hawking the democrat: 'If we do discover a complete theory, it should be understandable in broad principle by everyone. Then we shall all be able to take part in the discussion of why it is that we and the universe exist.'

Hawking the dictator: When he left his wife Jane Wilde after 25 years in 1990, she said at least she wouldn't have to keep 'telling him he's not God'.

Least likely to say: 'So does the sun go round the earth, or what?'

19 April 1993

Sir Edward Heath

Age: 77.
Appearance: Retired brigadier who likes a snifter.
Status: Sailor; pianist; conductor; former Prime Minister; MP for Old Bexley and Sidcup; Father of the House; Knight of the Garter; unofficial envoy to Baghdad.
But we don't have diplomatic relations with Iraq, do we? Exactly. The Foreign Office prefers to leave it to Ted, who is happy to share a sofa with Saddam.
Saddam, the well-known butcher? The very same.
So how can he justify doing business with such a dictator? 'Saddam Hussein is not Hitler. We'll have to see what he says. I don't think it would be very polite to get up and walk out.'
How does that line play down in Old Bexley and Sidcup? They seem to lap it up. His majority at the 1992 election rose to 15,699.
What about his colleagues? Not quite so enthusiastic. At the time of the Gulf War, one Conservative MP referred to Ted and Saddam as 'a couple of rogues together'.
And the tabloids? They christened him Ted the Traitor.
Are there any dictators Ted won't do business with? Just one.
Who? Gadafy? Deng Xiaoping? Kim Il Sung? No, Margaret Thatcher.
There was a falling out? That's one way of putting it.
The little matter of Mrs T. toppling him as Tory leader in 1975? These things happen.
And not offering him a cabinet post in 1979? Well, yes.
And rubbishing everything his government stood for? Yip.
And attacking his grand vision of Europe at every opportunity? Oui.
And . . . ? Please, we're running out of space.
What does she say about him? 'I don't feel it is a man looking at a woman; more like another woman looking at a woman' (source: Sir John Junor).
What does he say about her? 'A footnote in history.'
He doesn't sound the ideal diplomat: Ted is endearingly brusque. He called Norman Tebbit a 'ghastly man', branded Daniel Barenboim a 'monkey with a stick' and told Placido Domingo he could sing quite well.
So what qualifies him for his difficult and dangerous missions to Iraq? According to the Queen, he's expendable.
Not to be confused with: Ted Heath (bandleader), Blasted Heath, Hampstead Heath, Heath Robinson, Mr Blobby.
Most likely to say: Something in Franglais.
Least likely to say: 'You're so right, Margaret.'

9 December 1993. Two days later, thanks in part to Heath's intervention, Iraq released three Britons it had been holding.

Heathcliff

Age: 147.

Appearance: Dark, brooding, menacing, pretty good for his age.

Status: Gypsy of doubtful parentage turned wealthy northern landowner.

Key characteristics: Insane pride; vengefulness; brutality.

You're pulling my leg, aren't you? Isn't he a character in a book? Thank goodness the national curriculum has achieved something. Of course he's a character in a book! He's the primitive antihero who makes everyone's life hell in *Wuthering Heights*.

Wasn't that a Kate Bush song? Yes, but I wouldn't mention that in your GCSE paper. Emily Brontë had the idea first.

So why is he in the news? Has the song been re-released? Thankfully no. But there is to be a new rock show based on the book, with music by John Farrar and lyrics by Tim Rice

***Heathcliff the Musical*?** No, just *Heathcliff*.

With a dashingly dangerous leading man? Well, with a leading man anyway.

Let me guess: Daniel Day-Lewis, Sean Bean, Kevin Costner, Oliver Reed? Close. Cliff Richard, actually.

But why Cliff? Well, the name has a certain resonance.

Yes? And he's always wanted to do it.

Umm? And he's been planning the show for 15 years.

Uh-huh? And he was prepared to put up £5 million to finance a tour starting in the autumn.

But isn't Cliff sort of, well a bit, you know, just a touch, ah, nice for the part? He doesn't think so. 'I can be vicious. I can be nasty. I can be cruel.'

Any evidence of Cliff's cruelty? His Christmas records.

How are the critics likely to respond to Killer Cliff? With derision unfortunately. 'When I mooted the project I was almost laughed out of court,' he says. 'People said: Oh, that nice little Cliff Richard, he can't possibly play Heathcliff. Now that angered me.'

What's Cliff like when he's angry? God knows.

Who else has played Heathcliff? Laurence Olivier magnificently (pictured); Timothy Dalton passably; Ralph Fiennes dismally.

Who should play Heathcliff? Ted Hughes: dark, passionate, poetic and a northern accent.

Heathcliff/Cliff not to be confused with: Each other.

Cliff most likely to say: 'What about Sue Barker for Cathy?'

Heathcliff most likely to say: 'Turn that bloody music down.'

Michael Heseltine

Age: 60.
Appearance: Youthful model for Saga Holidays.
Occupation: President of the Board of Trade and potential future Tory Party leader.
Eh? He wants to be Prime Minister. Always has done, always will do.
But hasn't he just had a heart attack? That was four months ago. He claims to be well on the road to recovery.
Ideology: The caring capitalism candidate. Obsessively pro-EC. Wet, but not a drip. Highly interventionist.
Interventionist, you say? Yes. He promised the Tory Party conference that in order to help British companies 'I'll intervene before breakfast, before lunch, before tea and before dinner.'

What happened next? A week later he announced that 31 coal pits would have to shut, with the loss of 30,000 jobs.
Did he intervene before or after breakfast? Neither. Nor before lunch, nor tea, nor dinner, nor before retiring to Bedfordshire with a cup of cocoa.
Is that not a mite hypocritical? Do bears excrete in the woods?
Did the subsequent flak contribute to his heart attack? Almost certainly. He was being written out of the script by political journalists and often appeared broken and lost for words in trying to defend his blunder.
So all this talk about being Prime Minister is whistling in the dark? Yes. He is seen as a satanic figure by the right, who will never forgive him for standing against Mrs T.
Any Steve Norris tendencies? Apparently not. A long and faithful marriage to Ann, a gregarious socialite who dabbles in art.
Does he have any interests outside politics? Before his heart attack he had devoted himself to creating a magnificent and historic garden at his 400-acre country seat, Thenford, with more than 300 varieties of willow tree and a giant lake.
Would money be a worry? He is loaded. He started off in property, renting boarding houses in London, and then moved into magazine publishing.
Least likely to say: 'Why don't you and Norma come over for the weekend and we'll go and bag a few grouse?'

12 October 1993. Thought to have refused post of Conservative Party chairman in July 1994 reshuffle. Likes being President of the Board of Trade; would like to be prime minister even more but John Smith's fatal heart attack made that far less likely.

Major James Hewitt

Age: 35.

Appearance: Edward Fox meets the Barbour mail-order catalogue.

Background: Prep school, Millfield public school. Parents divorced 12 years ago. Hasn't spoken to his father since and lives with his mother.

Occupations: Officer in the Guards since leaving school, mentioned in dispatches during the Gulf War. Retires this month with the rank of major and a £40,000 lump sum.

Any other assets? Friendship with the Princess of Wales, which blossomed after he gave her riding lessons.

Is that really an asset? I thought she'd retired as well? Gone but by no means forgotten. The *Express* is paying Hewitt a reported £100,000 for his revelations.

What revelations? Well, that the Princess is jolly attractive for one thing. 'I'd defy a lot of men not to find her attractive but you have to learn to control your emotions and feelings,' he told the *Express*.

And? That she's 'astute, intelligent, loyal, affectionate and caring'.

That's a lot of adjectives: The *Express* has a lot of space to fill.

Any other famous pupils he has had round the enclosure for a gallop? Sally Faber, the TV weathergirl and wife of Conservative MP David Faber.

TV weathergirl, Tory MP, Di's riding instructor, didn't they . . . ? That's right. James and Sally are supposed to have had an affair.

Did the earth move? It didn't for her husband. He named James as a co-respondent in the divorce.

So, Major Hewitt is a bit of a ladies' man? Perish the thought. 'Everyone thinks I'm a seducer but I don't ever brag about my conquests.'

Isn't that nice. This macho 'lady-killer' nonsense is so passé these days: Not so fast. He reportedly said to one girlfriend: 'I ought to tell you that I have known at least 50 women in the past six years.'

OK. He's confused, but what do his friends think? 'The trouble with him,' said one, 'is that in finding his way through life he keeps his compass in his trousers.'

Thank goodness Princess Diana wasn't attracted by such a shallow approach to forging meaningful relationships: Thank goodness indeed, though she did take him for a reciprocal gallop round the shops of South Kensington. 'Hewitt,' she told her friend James Gilbey on the Squidgy tapes. 'Entirely dressed him from head to foot, that man. Cost me quite a bit.'

Not to be confused with: Major News Story.

Most likely to say: 'It was time to put the record straight and I thought it best to talk to the *Express* . . . Diana, *Diana*, are you there? . . . Can you believe it, she's hung up on me.'

Least likely to say: 'Will you marry me?'

Shere Hite

Age: 51.
Real name: Shirley Diana Gregory.
What's wrong with that? Try writing a snappy headline with Gregory in it. Whereas Shere Hite has given us: 'Hite list'; 'The Hite of sex'; 'Sheer Hype'. And worse.
Appearance: Hooded eyes, powerful nose, blanched face – Margaret Thatcher in *Les Liaisons Dangereuses*.
Job: Self-appointed sex expert.
What does that mean? The expert amasses thousands of anonymous sexual experiences, calls the result a Report, sells it for newspaper serialisation, then travels the world talking about sex to gaping hacks.
Dear Jim, can you fix it for me to be a sex expert? Are you an ex-*Playboy* model? With Pre-Raphaelite blonde mane, red lips and mouth-

adjacent beauty spot? If so, marvellous career opportunities await. If not, forget it.
What's she discovered? Almost all women are unhappy in marriage. Most people have affairs. Women prefer clitorally to vaginally induced orgasms.
Do they? Dunno. Why don't you write to 4,000 discontented women and ask?
The Hite methodology: Put 100,000 questionnaires in the post. Wait for the replies. Open the envelopes. Let the senders write your book for you.
Scientific status of this research: Nil.
Results of her research: Millions of dollars for the US postal system. Even more millions for the miraculously preserved Shere.
Her achievement: Making smutty gossip look respectable. Making the faithful feel like freaks. Making women even crosser. Passing off anecdotes as statistics.
Rivals: Nancy Friday, who asked women for their fantasies. Anaïs Nin and Nicholson Baker (who supply their own). *Marie Claire* magazine.
There's one born every minute: Her new opus, *The Hite Report on the Family*, is being serialised in the *Daily Telegraph*, that respected family newspaper. Methods as before: 'Men and women, teenage boys and girls answer the intensive Hite questionnaire . . . '
Complete S Hite: Summarising their confessions, Hite informs us that 45 per cent of girls have masturbated to orgasm by the age of 7 – 'yet nobody talks about this'.
Why's that? Answers on a postcard please, c/o the *Daily Telegraph*.
Surprise surprise! 'The traditional family does seem set for trouble,' says S Hite. She was abandoned by her mother and raised by grandparents.
Is she a feminist? No, she's an American.
Not to be confused with: Shere Khan, Golan Heights, eight denier tights.
Most likely to say: 'Hi! Are you clitoral or vaginal?'
Least likely to say: 'A woman is only a woman, but a good cigar is a smoke.'

Bob Hope

Age: 91.
Appearance: Serial pro-am golfer.
Occupation: Comedian.
Stand-up? Just about these days.
What sort of subjects – life, death, racial bigotry, embarrassing bodily functions? I think you may be confusing him with Lenny Bruce. His preoccupations are golf and/or US Presidents.
Let's hear a joke then: 'The last time I played golf with President Ford he hit a birdie . . . and an eagle, a moose, an elk, an aardvark . . . '
That's not bad. Any Clinton jokes? Sadly not. Clinton is much less keen on golf than his predecessors. And he's a Democrat.
So what? Hope is a staunch Republican.
How staunch? He makes Barry Goldwater look like a liberal.
Who's Barry Goldwater? I knew you wouldn't understand that allusion.
Why are you blathering on about Hope anyway? The legendary comic is coming to Britain to take part in the D-Day celebrations.
Was he a GI? Honorary. He spent a large part of the Second World War entertaining the troops in Europe and the South Pacific.
And his role now? To relive those glorious days, but this time in the comfort of the Normandy-bound *QEII*, in front of an audience of vets and celebs.
Vera Lynn will be there too, of course: Of course.
Any other old stagers? Sir John Mills, Richard Todd and, er, Jeremy Irons.
Jeremy Irons??? Yes, bizarrely; he'll be performing 'A Nightingale Sang in Berkeley Square'.
The troops love old Bob presumably: The D-Day generation adore him; his carefully scripted 40-minute routine is guaranteed an ovation. But he is unlikely to be attending any Saigon singalongs.
What do you mean? Whenever the USA has gone to war, Hope has been in tow in a gags-and-grenades offensive. The strategy backfired in Vietnam, where he couldn't cope with America's disillusioned draftees.
But he went down a storm in the Gulf War, didn't he? Not exactly. He planned to appear as a sheikh in a Christmas show, but his scantily clad female co-stars were banned by the Saudi authorities.
Wasn't there a biography recently? You mean Arthur Marx's *The Secret Life of Bob Hope.*
That's the one. A bit of a hatchet job, if I remember correctly: More a machete, actually. Hope was portrayed as a stingy sex-mad egoist who relied entirely on a battalion of script-writers.
And is he? I'm sorry, I can't quite see the autocue from here.
What do his critics say? Abandon hope all who enter here.
Most likely to say: 'Thank's for the memory – and the cheque.'
Least likely to say: Something spontaneously witty.

Michael Howard

Age: 52.
Appearance: Sleek.
Job description: Home Secretary. HM Chief Erector of Prisons.
Objectives: To be Prime Minister. Also to go down in history as the man whose 27-point plan, unveiled at the Tory conference, swept the menace of crime from our streets and made Britain a rose-strewn land of discipline, order and tranquillity.
Any hope of that happening? Nope. It's a well-established delusion which goes with being a Tory Home Secretary (compare Clarke, Baker, Waddington, etc., etc., right back to Sir William Joynson-Hicks).
Where did Howard spring from? Llanelli, where he went to grammar school; Cambridge, where he was part of the Fowler–Gummer–Clarke–Lamont–Lilley–Cobbley Mafia which has done so much to put the Great back into Great Expectations.
Presumably, being a Welshman, he was commonly known as Taffy? It wasn't as simple as that. He's really a Romanian Jewish Welshman: his father came from Romania, changed his name and set up a ladies' fashion house in Llanelli with the help of Michael's mum.
Was she Welsh? No, eastern European – hailing, Howard once said in an interview, 'from what used to be Russia'.
Does that explain his unusual accent? Presumably. He talks about pee-pul, not people. And constable, a word which ex officio he uses quite often, comes out as constab-ule (compare Bluebottle in *The Goon Show*).
Would this hinder him in a bid for the leadership? The Jewishness might: never underestimate the anti-Semitism of the Tory Party (compare Brittan, Lawson). There's no known objection to Romanians, though. Curiously, another hope of the Right, Michael Portillo, is a foreigner too – he's Iberian. Advantage, ace foreigner-basher Peter Lilley?
Where did he start on the ladder of opportunity? As PPS to Patrick Mayhew. Don't laugh: John Major started that way too. After spells at the DTI and Environment he landed a cabinet job (Employment) after less than five years in the Commons. Then Environment Secretary, now the Home Office. It's the sort of career which put the grease into 'greasy pole'.
Name a few of his triumphs along the way: The poll tax: he helped invent it, and later helped to get rid of it. He also handled water privatisation.
And now he's getting tough with squatters? Right. Under new legislation he'll give them 24 hours to get out. Exactly what the Police Federation, the Howard League (no relation), Lord Woolf and others would like to give him.
Least likely to say: 'Society needs to understand a little more and condemn a little less.'

Lord Howe

Age: 67.
Appearance: Cuddly, owlish, jowlish.
Vocation: Assassin.
Assassin? Surely you mean revered world statesman, accomplished diplomat, architect of the Thatcher economic miracle? No.
List his actual and potential victims: Much of British manufacturing industry in the early eighties. Mrs M. Thatcher: his resignation speech in November 1990, by opening the way for Michael Heseltine's leadership challenge, effectively did for her. The Scott inquiry on arms to Iraq.
What has he got against Scott? A lot. He doesn't like the way the inquiry is being conducted. Lord Justice Scott, he complains, is acting as detective, inquisitor, advocate and judge. Because of these imperfections, he warns, ministers and civil servants may simply ignore the inquiry's conclusions.
Who instigated this unjust inquiry and wrote its disgraceful ground rules? Ministers and civil servants.
Are there any precedents for a senior lawyer acting as detective, inquisitor, etc., etc.? Yes, the banning of union activity at GCHQ.
Who was the senior lawyer in question? Geoffrey Howe.
What did he say about Thatcher? Before they fell out? 'A skilled and resolute battler for British interests at home and abroad.'
And after? The sort of captain who sawed through her openers' bats before they went out to the middle. Others too, he said as he plunged in the dagger on 13 November 1992, should consider their own response to the tragic conflict of loyalties with which he himself had wrestled for perhaps too long.
Meaning? It's time we got rid of this frightful old termagant.
What did she say about him? 'In the cabinet he was a force for obstruction, in the party a focus of resentment, in the country a source of division. And we found each other's company almost intolerable' (her memoirs).
Why did she hate him so? She thought he'd gone soft on foreigners and especially on Europe. After he and Chancellor Nige ganged up on her over the ERM at the Madrid summit, she demoted him to Leader of the House and Deputy Prime Minister.
Does he have a hang-up about masterful women? Can't have: he's happily married to Elspeth, who is Thatcher-class formidable. Some alleged she had written much of Geoffrey's resignation/assassination speech.
Does he have trouble keeping his trousers on? Not in the Yeo/Norris sense. But he once managed to lose a pair on a London-to-Scotland sleeper.
Not to be confused with: Earl Howe, junior minister in the Lords; Don Howe; Dr Who.
Least likely to say: 'Great Scott!'

Saddam Hussein

Age: 55.

First name: Derived from Arabic verb meaning 'to clash violently'. Official White House pronunciation is 'Sod 'em'.

Appearance: Uglier than Mussolini, better looking than Noriega.

Address: c/o Revolutionary Command Council, Baghdad.

Occupation: Ruler of Iraq, or rather those parts that lie north of the 32nd parallel and south of the 36th parallel.

Background: Playground bully who graduated at the age of 10 from iron bars to guns. Turned into gangster and hit man and then regraduated with an Ll.B. at Baghdad University, finally discovering an outlet for his talents in the Ba'ath Party.

Less well-known activity: Author of bestseller entitled *One Trench or Two* (buy a copy or else).

Contributions to the arts: Sponsors monumental sculptors in Baghdad; provides employment for portrait painters; plans to restore the Hanging Gardens of Babylon (possibly with working gallows).

Likes: Cigars, children, nuclear physics, halal butchery.

Dislikes: Kurds, Shi'ites, Iranians, Kuwaitis, Saudis, Americans, Israelis, Syrian Ba'athists, *Observer* journalists, etc.

Dress sense: Proto-grunge; berets, pistol holsters and belly-hugging khaki shirts.

Survived: Death sentence for attempted assassination of General Qassim (1959), arrest for plotting coup (1964), Iran–Iraq War (1980–8), more bombs than the USA dropped on Vietnam (Jan.–Feb. 1991).

Catchphrase: 'The Mother of Battles has begun.'

His view of the United Nations: An advertising agency used by the United States.

Ambition: To repeat his pilgrimage to Mecca, this time accompanied by tanks.

His gravest miscalculation: Invasion of Kuwait (and subsequent war) came too late to give Margaret Thatcher a fourth term and too soon to give George Bush a second term.

America's gravest miscalculation: It thought it had beaten him.

Deserves: Queen's Award for services to British exports.

Other services to the West: Keeping Iranian ayatollahs in check, providing test facilities for new weapon systems (Patriot, etc.), reducing unemployment in the engineering industry.

Most likely to say: 'Crisis, what crisis?'

Actually did say: 'God is on our side.'

Least likely to say: 'I resign.'

Marmaduke Hussey

Age: 69.

Appearance: Crusty squire straight from Fielding. Immensely tall (6ft 5in). False leg dates from war wound in 1944. When fitted with new artificial leg in Germany said: 'First they shoot it off, now they put it back on. Doesn't make any sense, does it?'

Married: William Waldegrave's big sister, Lady Susan, fifth daughter of the Earl Waldegrave.

Job: Chairman of the BBC.

Wife's job: The Queen's Woman of the Bedchamber.

Wife calls him: Dukey.

Background: Rugby and Oxford. Went into newspaper management after war. Blamed as hatchet man who closed down *Times* Newspapers for a year over union dispute. Plucked from Times to bring BBC to heel after Mrs Thatcher became convinced Beeb was being run by pinko English literature graduates under feeble management of Alasdair Milne. First thing he did was to sack Milne. Board stopped Hussey replacing him with David Dimbleby: had to make do with an accountant called Checkland.

Strengths: Barking voice; good at cocktail parties; courageous; knows everyone; gives BBC veneer of Establishment respectability; affable manner conceals fact that he is tough as old boots.

Weaknesses: Age; friend of Rupert Murdoch; interfering management style; autocratic; out of touch; no good on TV; thinks FM stands for fuzzy monsters.

Favourite saying: 'The innovator has for enemies all those who have done well under the old conditions and lukewarm defenders in those who may do well under the new' (Machiavelli).

Favourite programmes: *Songs of Praise, Trainer*, racing.

Michael Grade on Hussey's management style: Brutalist, pseudo-Leninist, politically appeasing.

Hussey on Grade: A Bourbon with red braces.

Other Marmadukes: Marmaduke the cat; alias of Lord Snooty in the *Beano*.

Don't mention: His age.

Risky metaphor for Hussey to use of BBC: 'It is in danger of becoming a fossilised relic.'

Least likely to say: 'Come round for a bevvy and we'll take a squint at *Eldorado*.'

Ray Illingworth

Age: 61.

Appearance: Hard-bitten manager of a club in the Northern Premier League.

Occupation: Annoying members of the Establishment; selecting the England cricket team. His first side take the field today against the might of New Zealand.

Are New Zealand mighty? No, I was being ironic. At present, they would struggle to give the Shetland Islands a game.

I see, so Ray should enjoy some sunshine? Inded, though the capacity for English cricket to shoot itself in the foot is legendary.

Illy's a Yorkshireman, isn't he? You certainly know your cricket.

And famed for blunt speaking? As you said, he is a Yorkshireman.

What did he make of the team he inherited? Too young, not hungry or hard-working enough, preoccupied with money, too many batsmen, too few bowlers, no decent all-rounders, totally useless really.

Any new blood in the side now he's in charge? Graham Gooch.

I thought he was ancient: He is pushing 41 – but Illy likes old-timers. He's hoping to get Fred Trueman fit for the Tests.

You're joking? Always on the ball.

No need to be rude. Doesn't Illy think he should be more diplomatic? 'Diplomatic' is not a word much used by the Uncle Morts back home in Pudsey. In any case, Illy thinks he's blameless: 'I've only ever offered constructive criticism. I've never slagged anyone off.'

Is that true? Ask Hick, Tufnell, Lewis, Ramprakash, Russell, Smith, Fraser. Oh, and Fletcher.

Who he? Keith 'the Gnome' Fletcher, the England manager, who has already had a ticking off from his new boss over his handling of Gooch.

Fletcher feels threatened presumably? Only in the sense that Troy felt threatened by the Greeks.

So Illy plans to be hands on? Indeed. Probably on the throats of underperforming players.

When did Illy play? In the balmy days of the sixties and seventies when a pint of Theakston's was fourpence and English cricket the best in the world.

And Illy himself? Good player, great captain: regained the Ashes in 1970–1.

How to describe him: Gruff, bluff, rough, tough, in a huff.

Not to be confused with: Geoffrey Boycott.

Definitely not to be confused with: M. J. K. Smith; A. C. Smith; M. C. C. Smith; I. Zingari-Smith.

Most likely to say: 'Get that booger out of the team. He couldn't hit a barn door with a bluddy football.'

Least likely to say: 'Jolly bad luck, Hicky. Curtly's yorker is always difficult to spot.'

Bernard Ingham

Age: 61.

Disposition: Like a late autumn day on a Yorkshire moor. One minute the sun is shining and all is genial. The next, black cloud and thunder.

Name some targets of his wrath: John Biffen (described as 'semi-detached' after hinting that Margaret Thatcher might be less than totally perfect). Francis Pym (called 'Mona Lott' for exhibiting gloom in public during Thatcher's premiership). Michael Heseltine (should have been sacked over Westland). Mark Coyle.

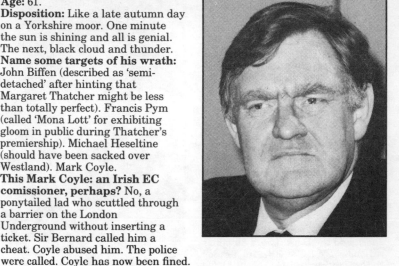

This Mark Coyle: an Irish EC comissioner, perhaps? No, a ponytailed lad who scuttled through a barrier on the London Underground without inserting a ticket. Sir Bernard called him a cheat. Coyle abused him. The police were called. Coyle has now been fined.

So Sir Bernard is opposed to abuse? To abuse directed at respectable citizens by ponytailed lads on stations, certainly. But he does make exceptions in other cases (see above).

Describe the origins of the knight: Hails from Hebden Bridge. Joined the local paper. Later a labour reporter on the *Guardian*; then in government press relations.

Assess his politics: Once wrote a column, signed Albion, on the left-wing *Leeds Weekly Citizen*. Sample: 'As a party [the Tories] do not give a tinker's cuss for the consequences of capitalism – the crawling anthill of the South-east and the underemployed, underprivileged muckheap of the North.'

Does he still see the Tories as lower than vermin? Some of them (see targets of wrath, above). To others he is besottedly loyal, especially those who were Prime Minister from 1979 to 1990.

Give examples of this loyalty: Some lobby correspondents regard him as the best Downing Street press secretary ever, because when he spoke you could hear Maggie speaking. Others believe he misused this office by slagging off ministers, foreigners, etc., under the cloak of non-attributability.

But surely the duty of civil servants is impartiality? Not exactly: more an unswerving commitment to serve whoever happens to be in government. Some say he might have been just as unswervingly loyal to Neil Kinnock.

Do you really believe that? No.

And didn't he sanction the leak of a letter damaging to Heseltine during Westland? That's what was said at the time. He blames the DTI for the leak – though he says that with hindsight he ought to have stopped it.

But wouldn't you say that was cheating? Well, it certainly wasn't cricket as played in Hebden Bridge.

Not to be confused with: St Bernard of Clairvaux; a St Bernard.

Least likely to say: 'Is that the *Guardian*? I'd rather like to rejoin.'

Eddie Izzard

Age: 31.

Occupation: Stand-up comedian.

Appearance: Oikish, bleached blond Essex boy built like a scrum-half.

Sartorial idiosyncrasies that set him apart from Daryl from Romford: He wears frocks and pink nail varnish.

Just for the hell of it? No, because he's TV. Has been since the age of 4.

Any relation to GMTV, HTV, ITV? Not likely. He claims to loathe television and turned down Wogan twice, Paramount City twice and Jonathan Ross five times.

Shy or what? No, just hard to get. Known in the business as Eddie the Ego.

Not to be confused with: Eddie Shah; Edd the Duck; Izzard Shipping of London SW7; Ralph Izzard, former *Daily Mail* journalist.

But funnily enough: When Ralph Izzard was filing reports from Lord Hunt's Everest exhibition in 1953, a rival journalist was the *Times*'s James Morris, now Jan Morris, the transsexual.

Background: Former street entertainer whose patches included shopping centres in Woking and Peterborough, and the piazza in Covent Garden ('I've died on the street; I just wasn't funny enough in the early days'). First stand-up appearance was at Hysteria in 1988. Subsequently went down a storm at the Edinburgh Festival, the London comedy circuit and venues nationwide.

So he tells cracking jokes, right? Wrong. His act is a stream of unconnected one-liners such as 'What do batteries run on?' 'Why is the alphabet in that order?'

Izzard on Izzard: 'People think I talk bollocks. Initially I talked bollocks, but now there is an underlying truth to what I say, with bollocks on top.'

But is it funny? The punters seem to think so. His show at London's Ambassadors Theatre, originally a one-month run, was extended twice. 'The funniest comedian in the country today,' said the *Sunday Times*.

Useful terms for critics: Surreal, stream of consciousness, life-enhancing, unreproducible humour.

Mannerisms: Prowls the stage, stares at the floor, mutters in a monotone.

Dislikes: Trousers, scripts, smiling.

Likes: Skirts, improvising, scowling.

Least likely to say: 'Heard the one about the Englishman, the Irishman and the Scotsman?'

26 March 1993. In May 1994 Izzard made his 'straight' acting debut in David Mamet's *The Cryptogram*.

Michael Jackson

Age: 35 and getting younger all the time.

How come? He sleeps in an age-defying oxygen tent.

Appearance: Despite all his efforts, nothing like Diana Ross.

Lookalike: The world's worst shaving accident.

Background: As an angelic, Afro-haired 11-year-old, he sang memorably shrill, high-register vocals with the Jackson Five on such Motown classics as 'ABC' and 'I Want You Back'. Later developed the Moon Walk dance and falsetto yelp that were to become his trademarks. As his fame escalated, so did his barmy, reclusive behaviour and desire to be white. It earned him the nickname Wacko Jacko. Now he lives on a Californian ranch called Neverland.

Surgery so far: Nose certainly, and, it has been said, chin, eyes, cheekbones and jawline, but these he denies.

Is there anything left? His ears present an exciting new area for development.

What's between them? God alone knows, but behaviour that suggests Jackson is two sandwiches short of a picnic includes visiting Disneyland in a smog-mask and wheelchair; buying a $40,000 antique clock for his pet chimp, Bubbles; attending surgical operations for kicks; trying unsuccessfully to purchase the mummified remains of the Elephant Man, John Merrick.

Fashion pointers: Epaulettes, military braid, fascist-style armbands, single gloves, white towelling socks crammed into scuffed penny loafers.

Peak: His album *Thriller* sold 45 million copies – the most successful record of all time.

Trough: *Dangerous*, last year's album, sold a piffling 15 million. 'It was kind of sad, as if Bob Dylan had decided to imitate Bruce Springsteen' – David Wild, *Rolling Stone* magazine.

Close friends to date: Brooke Shields, Liz Taylor, Macaulay Culkin.

Platonic? Of course. When asked during an appallingly toadying Oprah Winfrey TV interview if he was a virgin, Jackson went as pink as it is possible to go under eight layers of Vim, giggled hysterically and said: 'How could you ask me that? I'm embarrassed. You can say I'm old-fashioned. I'm a gentleman.'

So he enjoys gentlemanly pursuits? Er, no. He likes chimps, fairground rides, grabbing his crotch, ex-child stars, the very very young and the extremely old.

Why is he in the news this time? He is being investigated for child sex abuse after a mother's claim that her son was molested at one of his homes.

Not to be confused with: Michael Jackson, beer correspondent for the *Independent*; Michael Jackson, controller of BBC2.

Least likely to say: 'I'm black and I'm proud.'

25 August 1993. In May 1994 Jackson shocked the world by marrying Lisa-Marie Presley in a secret ceremony in the Dominican Republic.

Jesus Christ

Full name: Jesus Christ. Middle name unknown, though widely believed to begin with the letter 'H'.
Age: 1,997 or 1,998. Probably. Scholars think he was actually born in 5 or 6 BC. They also point out that he could not have been born in December, but it's much too late to reorganise Christmas now.
Appearance: Ascetic New Age traveller prone to irritability.
Politics: Liberal Democrat, on the beard-and-sandal wing of the party.
Religion: Jewish.
Brief history: The subject of one of history's earlier paternity disputes. Candidates were Joseph, someone quite modest in the furniture trade, and God. Mother had him in a manger because all Bethlehem hotels were full – well, it was Christmas. Precocious as a child,

Jesus grew up to be baptised by John (the Baptist) in AD 28–9, but his flamboyance (see miracles below) brought problems with Jewish reactionaries and Rome. Imperial Procurator Pontius Pilate eventually got him for action against the Temple in either AD 30 or 33, and after a brief though impressive comeback (known by fans as his 'Resurrection'), he made the Ascension to heaven.
What are the sources? Mainly the Gospels – hagiographic accounts by the tabloid hacks of the day – and contemporary Roman historians.
Profession: Lord and Saviour of the world; sideline in catering.
His Big Things: The oppressed, the poor, redemption, democratising the Kingdom of Heaven, forgiveness of sins.
Would he be welcomed by the present Conservative establishment? Probably not. Expect apoplectic *Daily Mail* leader within days of his return railing against false prophets and dangerous subversives.
Was he a typical Capricorn? Yes – he was ambitious and got to the top.
But was he an exhibitionist? Yes, indeed. (See miracles below.)
Famous sayings: 'Forgive them for they know not what they do'; 'Let he who is without sin cast the first stone'; 'It is easier for a camel to go through the eye of a needle than for a rich man to enter the Kingdom of God.'
In common with Robert Maxwell: Both were Jewish boys who made it big from humble beginnings.
Not in common with Robert Maxwell: Jesus could walk on water.
Top five miracles: Lazarus, walking on water, feeding the 5,000, water into wine, restoring sight to the blind.
Likes: Showing off, parables, wine, redeeming prostitutes.
Dislikes: Pharisees, bankers, shaving, haircuts, fig trees.
Least likely to have said: 'String 'em all up, that's the only language they understand.'
Least likely to have sung: 'So Here It Is, Merry Christmas'; anything seasonal by Cliff Richard.

James Joyce

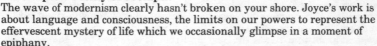

Age: Born 1882. Died 1941.
Appearance: Boozy general practitioner.
Reputation: Literary colossus of the 20th century. Today is Bloomsday, an anniversary tribute to his greatest novel, *Ulysses*.
A sober literary affair? Hardly. Enthusiasts meet in Dublin and stumble from bar to bar tracing the steps of Stephen Daedalus and Leopold Bloom.
Nothing to do with Bloomsbury? Thankfully, no.
So who's this Bloom? A fictional character, whose mental peregrinations on one day in 1904 form the bulk of *Ulysses*.
Must be a short read: You're joking of course – 1,000 pages, excluding notes.
Decent plot? Plenty of ooomph? The wave of modernism clearly hasn't broken on your shore. Joyce's work is about language and consciousness, the limits on our powers to represent the effervescent mystery of life which we occasionally glimpse in a moment of epiphany.
And people *read* it? Academics turn cartwheels of joy. So many papers to write, lectures to give – Joyce and language, Joyce and the phallus, intransitive verbs in Joyce, Bloom and potty-training: a feminist critique . . .
What do students think? Divided. Half are so enamoured that they cling to his books wherever they go. The other half panic and seek solace in a thumping tome by Stephen King.
They're the lightweights: Not at all. The poet Sylvia Plath in *The Bell Jar* describes how her *alter ego* plummets into suicidal depression after attempting to read the first page of *Finnegans Wake*.
A touch melodramatic? You open a book on which you plan to write a long thesis. It's summer, the birds are singing, the first words you see are "riverrun, past Eve and Adam". Then you stumble over the "commodious vicus of recirculation", and fall flat in front of "bababadalgharaghtakammin arrommnkonnbronntonnerronn . . ."
Enough, enough. What does it all mean? It imitates the sound of a fall, dumbo. Joyce used free association to get to the heart of meaning. His avowed task was 'to create the uncreated conscience of my race'.
A bit like Jack Charlton and the Irish football team? More or less.
All down to a tormented childhood, I suppose: Spot on. Like all great writers, his home was a cauldron for the imagination. Initially prosperous, they moved down the social scale after his father lost his job. Faced with poverty, Joyce Snr hit the bottle.
Joyce escaped? He left Ireland in 1904. *Ulysses* was written in Zürich.
Most likely to say: 'Burgundyguinnessbrandyscotchandsodawouldbelovely.'
Least likely to say: 'But that isn't a real word, is it?'

Radovan Karadzic

Age: A closely guarded secret.

Appearance: Greying, big-hipped man with a quiffed new romantic hairdo and a nose flared red with Montenegran wine.

Position: Head of the Bosnian Serbs.

Background: Son of a soldier from the mountains – made it on a Tito scholarship to Sarajevo but not into the inner circle of the city's elite. Has never forgiven them for it.

Occupation: One-time shrink, likes working with neurotics; former official doctor to the Sarajevo football team (half of them now dead); PR man for his Serbian butchers.

Record: Spent nine months in prison in 1975 for flogging false sick-notes.

Home: A hillside hotel in the mountain village of Pale outside Sarajevo, where he once told a journalist from *Le Figaro*: 'The Bosnian Serbs have no armed forces.'

Favourite TV programme: *Newsnight*. Except when Jeremy Paxman says: 'Come on Mr Karadzic – why do you keep lying to us?'

Greatest ambition: To run the Serbian Republic of Bosnia from the presidential palace in Sarajevo that his men keep trying to blow up.

Favourite saying in public: It wasn't us, Mr Owen.

Favourite saying in private: Up yours, David.

Modus operandi: Lie, deny and cry jihad.

Nickname: Call him K.

Offspring: Sonja, the singing pop star in black leather, who gave it all up to go into the family PR business. Now runs the press office in Pale with a man who answers the door in a black bathrobe.

Speaks with: The flowing cadences of the man who warns London commuters to mind the gap.

Favourite sayings: 'There are no civilians in Serb-run camps in Bosnia . . . ' 'The Serbs have no snipers.'

His defence of ethnic cleansing and genocide: 'The press have it in for us.'

Future plans: To avoid being tried as a war criminal (he has been on the telephone to Alan Dershowitz, who defended Claus Von Bulow and Mike Tyson and managed to get TV evangelist Jim Bakker a reduced sentence).

Hobbies: Playing the lyre, writing bad poetry about singing cannons, lying to Jeremy Paxman.

Retirement speech: 'We came, we saw, we wiped most of them out and nobody did a damn thing about it.'

Least likely to say: 'Economic sanctions really bother us.'

Likely to end up: Getting away with it.

28 April 1993

Paul Keating

Age: 49.
Appearance: Chevy Chase crossed with an albino raisin.
Career: Speedy. Joined the Labor Party at 15. Member of Parliament at 25. Minister for Northern Australia at 31. Treasurer at 39. Prime Minister at 47.
So he's never done anything except politics then? Wrong. At 22, he managed a rock band called the Ramrods.
Why's he in the news? He compared the British monarchy to a 'horse and cart' that should be affectionately and gracefully retired – and traded in for something better. Like a Nissan Micra or a Renault Clio, probably.
That's not news: You're right, he's been banging on about Australia becoming a republic since he became PM in 1991.

But didn't he touch the Queen's bum? Her back, actually. He says he is one of her greatest admirers but he did slag off our war record.
The tabloid newspapers must hate him. They do. The *Sun* calls him 'the Lizard of Oz'.
But isn't he a gifted insult-monger himself? That's correct.
For example? His parliamentary opponents are 'Harlots, scumbags, pigs, pansies, clowns, perfumed gigolos, stunned mullets, half-baked crims, bunyip aristocrats, pissants, gutless spivs, nongs, vermin who think they are born to rule, dummies and dimwits . . . who could not raffle a chook in a pub . . . or operate a tart shop.'
Bunyip aristocrats? Uh-huh. It's a derogatory conflation of 'bunny rabbit' and 'turnip'. From the 19th century, apparently.
And nongs? An all-purpose Aussie insult for anyone who looks Oriental, or who behaves in an Oriental – i.e. fiendishly cunning – fashion.
You're just making these up, aren't you? Yes.
What else? He's an expert on antique French clocks.
Pull the other one: He is. He has lectured on the subject at the Australian National Gallery in Canberra.
What lessons can Britain's Labour Party learn from his continued success? Submit to the logic of market-oriented economic policies, but insist that organised labour will always play a big role in decision-making, policy formulation, everything.
Least likely to sing: 'Rule, Britannia!'

2 August 1993. In June 1994 the loquacious Keating got into trouble when he was reputed to have called Australia 'the arse-end of the world'.

Harvey Keitel

Age: 54.

Occupation: Screen actor.

Appearance: Warthog (with clothes on); front end of a Minotaur (with clothes off).

Is this guy a luvvie? Don't even ask.

So he's macho, right? With knobs on. De Niro, Schwarzenegger, Stallone? Wimps by comparison. Never challenge him to a staring contest.

Check out the workload: *The Young Americans*, in which he plays a tortured American cop in London, has just opened; coming soon: *Rising Sun*, in which he plays a tortured, racist cop alongside Sean Connery and Wesley Snipes; and Jane Campion's Palme d'Or-winning *The Piano*, in which he plays a tortured Scot lusting after Holly Hunter in Victorian New Zealand.

Most likely to play: Tortured cop, tortured crook, tortured Catholic – or a mixture of the three, with a few nude scenes thrown in.

Least likely to play: Michael Tolliver in Armistead Maupin's *Tales of the City*; Felix Unger in *The Odd Couple*; any character in a Merchant–Ivory film.

Reel one – method in his macho: Born in Brooklyn to a Romanian mother and Polish father, Keitel was expelled from school for truancy so joined the Marines (natch). After seeing service in Beirut, he studied at the Actors' Studio – home of the Method. In 1968 he had his screen debut in Scorsese's thesis film, *Who's That Knocking at My Door?*. In 1973 he leapt to fame (with Robert De Niro) as a Noo Yawk mobster in Scorsese's *Mean Streets*.

Reel two – so De Niro, so far: As De Niro's career went from strength to strength in a series of successful macho movies (*Taxi Driver*, *The Deer Hunter*, *Raging Bull*), Keitel appeared in a series of well-regarded box-office disasters: Ridley Scott's *The Duellists*, James Toback's *Fingers*, Paul Schrader's *Blue Collar* – regularly choosing to work with talented first-time directors who went on to greater things.

Reel three – the Maverick Makes Good: Starring roles in two extraordinary movies have given him the status of elder statesman of movie macho. In Quentin Tarantino's *Reservoir Dogs* he was Mr White, a world-weary hood; in Abel Ferrara's *Bad Lieutenant* he bared all (physically and psychically) as a bent junkie cop seeking redemption.

What they say about him: 'Guys like him are on the edge, man, right out on the edge. And they are there without a net' (Abel Ferrara).

Least likely to say: 'More tea, vicar?'

Most likely to say (at least when in conference with De Niro): 'Whatsa madda whichoo?' 'Whatsa madda wi me? Whatsa madda whichoo?' 'Whatsa madda wi me? Whatsa madda whichoo?' 'Eeeey!!' 'Eeeey!!!' (contd p. 94).

Graham Kelly

Age: 46.

Appearance: Glum bear nearing his hibernation date.

Is he happy about it? 'If I've got what appears to be a miserable face, I can't do much about it. I suppose I could go to Harley Street.' He is fond of repeating the quote about himself: 'Not even his friends would say he has charisma.'

Background: Son of Blackpool tram driver, three A-levels, failed Accrington Stanley goalkeeper. Remembers as a fan sleeping in Euston Station several times on nights before FA Cup Finals.

Current job: Chief executive of the Football Association.

Became famous for: Leading the richer clubs in Premier League breakaway from the Football League.

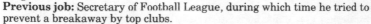

Previous job: Secretary of Football League, during which time he tried to prevent a breakaway by top clubs.

Experience for these jobs: Bank clerk and accountant.

Kelly on Kelly: 'I don't get by with flair or genius. I depend on hard work and careful analysis of situations.'

In the headlines for: Defending in court a Brentford player whose elbowed challenge shattered a Torquay player's cheekbone and eye socket and threatens his career. Said he would see 200 similar aerial clashes in a week by watching just four matches.

How did that go down? 'Kelly has given the impression that football is the equivalent of a bar-room brawl' – Mike Bateson, Torquay chairman. He has 'caused immeasurable harm to the game' – referees' and linesmen's association.

Good at: After-dinner speaking. Sample joke when Aston Villa were going through a bad spell: 'The fences at Villa are not working because the players are still getting on to the pitch.'

Low point: Endured accusations of murder after the 1989 Hillsborough disaster because of the FA's choice of end for the Liverpool supporters.

How did Hillsborough affect him? 'I'll never forget meeting the bereaved and what was etched on their faces, the grief, the anguish and the questioning look of confusion.'

Social life: Limited. Drinks very little, is not a great socialiser, very much a loner.

Rumours of female love interest: Recently slimmed down and swapped his specs for contact lenses.

Concession to anger: A tut and a sigh.

Testimonials: 'Graham, you'll always be a banker' – former player Emlyn Hughes.

Least likely to say: 'Let's give the fans what they want.'

Least likely to sing: 'Shiny, Happy People'.

Charles Kennedy

Age: Still only 34.
Occupation: Liberal Democrat MP for Ross and Cromarty; just completing his second term as president of the party (he became President Kennedy at 30, 13 years younger than JFK managed it).
Appearance: Stocky, with a shock of red hair. Seems that's how they recognised him in the betting shop.
Which betting shop was this? One just round the corner from the Lib Dems' Westminster HQ. In one of the most fateful high street drop-ins since Norman Lamont didn't go into Threshers', President K. wandered in during the Euro-election campaign and bet on his party collecting a paltry two seats. As it then did, netting him a cool £2,500.
Clearly a man of prudence: Maybe, but that wasn't the point some of his colleagues – particularly those who have always said he overdoes the fun-loving – were making yesterday. It's not kosher to bet on your party doing badly, especially when you're publicly boasting that stupendous gains will be yours. Charles himself is clearly embarrassed: he has been hiding from the media, rather than hurling himself, as is his normal practice, headlong into its mushy embrace.
What is his Captain saying? Nothing, so far. But a spokeswoman said that Kennedy 'had already intimated that any winnings would go to party funds'. You can always tell spokespeople are in trouble when they use words like 'intimated'.
Wait a sec, though: aren't the Lib Dems going to court to prove they should have had three Euro-seats rather than two? Indeed. They believe they only lost Devon and East Plymouth because some fellow called Huggett stood as a Literal Democrat, and made off with 10,000 votes.
So if they win the court case, Charles won't have won his bet after all, and party funds will suffer accordingly? In theory, yes. Still, it looks as though the party could keep the money. As far as the bookies are concerned, the bet is over and done with.
Will this dent his hopes of becoming party leader? A tinge perhaps: but he's not as safe a bet for that job as the world outside assumes. Some colleagues think he's a bit of a flibbertigibbet: they compare him unkindly with the super-diligent (and even younger) Matthew Taylor.
And how are they likely to take it back in Ross and Cromarty? Not too well. This is God-fearing territory, as Kennedy's voting pattern suggests he is well aware. He opposed the relaxation of Sunday opening laws, and last month voted against the legalisation of betting on race tracks on Sundays.
Not to be confused with: Nigel Kennedy; Teddy Kennedy; Sir Ludovic Kennedy; the Moderator of the Free Church of Scotland.
Most likely to say: 'Is that William Hill? I wondered what odds you would give me on losing my seat at the next election?'

Kim Il Sung

Age: 81.

Occupation: Communist dictator of the Democratic (not) People's Republic of North Korea.

Appearance: Octogenarian Mutant Ninja Turtle. Short, wears Chinese-style tunics, birthmark on neck. According to his Soviet-born ex-tutor in Marxist ideology he's like 'Stalin but 10 times smaller'.

Other titles: Suryong (Great Leader), Beloved Leader, Ever Victorious Captain of the Korean People, the Greatest Genius Mankind Has Ever Had, Outstanding Leader of the Revolution and, most recently, Generalissimo.

Claims to fame: He's the world's longest-serving dictator. Hoisted to power by the Soviets in 1948, he is teasing the world with the nuclear weapons his country is believed to have created in defiance of the Non-Proliferation Treaty.

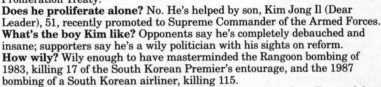

Does he proliferate alone? No. He's helped by son, Kim Jong Il (Dear Leader), 51, recently promoted to Supreme Commander of the Armed Forces.

What's the boy Kim like? Opponents say he's completely debauched and insane; supporters say he's a wily politician with his sights on reform.

How wily? Wily enough to have masterminded the Rangoon bombing of 1983, killing 17 of the South Korean Premier's entourage, and the 1987 bombing of a South Korean airliner, killing 115.

Are the duo popular at home? Economic disaster since the collapse of the Soviet Union means many of North Korea's 23 million people are starving, and discontent is growing.

What is the Pyongyang administration doing about its starving people? Ignoring them: the domestic media prefers to run stories of people whose stomachs explode through overeating.

Are the Kims popular abroad? No. President Clinton feels distinctly chilly towards them and has said that any attack on South Korea will mean 'the end of their country'. Also unpopular with Amnesty International, to which they tactlessly admitted holding public executions 'at the crowd's request'.

Why doesn't someone assassinate them both? It's been tried. There have been numerous coups and assassination attempts, but they always emerge unscathed.

Not to be confused with: South Korean President Kim Young-Sam; North Korean defector Kim Young-Sun; South Korean ex-spy Kim Hyung-Wook; North Korean jet bomber Kim Hyon-Hui; Kim Jae-Kyu, assassin of President of South Korea; North Korean football team – half of them called Kim – who reached quarter-finals of 1966 World Cup; Kim Philby; Kim Basinger.

Least likely to say: 'No nukes is good nukes.'

Most likely to say: 'Like father like son.'

9 November 1993. Kim Il Sung died in July 1994. Kim Jong Il succeeded him and relations with South Korea and the US gradually began to improve.

Hanif Kureishi

Age: Child of his times (39).

Appearance: Seventies rock star. Che Guevara of the west London word-processor set.

Occupation: *Épater* of bourgeoisie.

Street credentials: Born in Bromley, Kent. Philosophy degree. Publishing contract with Faber & Faber (T. S. Eliot, W. H. Auden and other major socialist workers). 'It's the lefties who hate me most because I can never satisfy them,' he says.

Key words: Racism. Revolution. Drugs. Sex. Thatcher. Royalties.

Directions to home: Right on.

Came to fame: By writing the screenplay to *My Beautiful Laundrette*, an Oscar-nominated film which told the story of young gay Asian's relationship with a peroxide blond bovver boy played by Daniel Day-Lewis. Lauded by the chattering classes, the film's triumph was to make the National Front look like the Von Trapp family in *The Sound of Music*.

Came to grief: By writing the screenplay to *Sammy and Rosie Get Laid*, a risible non-Oscar-nominated film that was tangentially about Thatcher's Britain (weren't they all in those days?).

Came seriously to grief: By writing and directing *London Kills Me*, a film about a young drugs dealer in search of some shoes in order to get a proper job. Said he was influenced by de Sica's *Bicycle Thieves*. He was wrong.

Why is he in the news? The BBC has adapted his bestselling and Whitbread Prize-winning novel *The Buddha of Suburbia* for television.

What's it about? Usual fare: sex, drugs, suburbia, rock music, angst, politics, sex, suburbia, sex. Anti-hero is called Karim Amir – a.k.a. 'creamy jeans'. David Bowie's done the soundtrack.

Critical response: Angela Carter was impressed, invoking the 'glorious, scabrous, picaresque, savage, sentimental tradition that stretches from Chaucer to dirty postcards on Brighton Pier'.

Author response: 'I can only reflect what English society is like. I write about riots and street life and so on because I feel that writing is a way of forming a discussion about the sort of society we live in.'

So what's he like? Rebel without a clue. Biggest disappointment must have been Lady Thatcher's dethronement – nobody left to *épat* any more.

And colleagues say? 'Provocative little sod' – film director Stephen Frears; 'Very cool, very watchful' – author, and friend, Nigel Williams.

Not to be confused with: Salman Rushdie.

Most-famous-for-five-minutes cameo: Telling the bourgeoisie on *Start the Week* that the poll tax riots were 'terrific'.

Least likely to say: 'Is that Merchant–Ivory? I've just finished the adaptation of *Portrait of a Lady*.'

Most likely to say: 'I may not write as well as Salman Rushdie but I'm much better looking.'

Norman Lamont

Age: 50.
Appearance: Twenties masher after a heavy night.
Impending dates with destiny: Tomorrow's budget, his third as Chancellor; the next reshuffle.
Early sightings: Born in the Shetlands. At Cambridge in era of Ken Clarke, Michael Howard, Gummer, Lilley, Leon Brittan. President of the Union. 'He was so frivolous, a fantastic dancer, with an eye for the girls' – unnamed female contemporary.
Where did this frivolity lead him? Towards journalism, of course. He applied for a job with the *Guardian*, which said no. To research at Central Office; to merchant banking with Rothschild's; to Kingston-upon-Thames, where he beat Rhodes Boyson for the Tory nomination.

Was that when he got the black eye? No, that wasn't till '85, when he'd been an MP for 13 years and was minister for defence procurement. He said he'd walked into a door.
What did the door say about it? It said it was an art dealer called Connolly, and they'd had a 2 a.m. clash over a beautiful widow.
Has he walked into any more doors? No doors, but several gates. When staff of a Paddington Thresher's said he'd stopped off for a bottle of cheap champagne and cigarettes (Threshergate). They later retracted. When he inadvertently let his Notting Hill house to a sex therapist (Notting Hill Gate). When he turned to a pricey solicitor to advise him on her eviction (Carter Ruckgate), and accepted part of the cost from public funds (Taxpayergate).
When he got the call to Number 11, what was he doing? He was Major's campaign manager.
Was he the obvious man for the job? He was Major's campaign manager.
Has he not had notable triumphs? He was hailed as the party's saviour for his 1991 budget, when he cut the poll tax by half (but put up VAT to pay for it). And again for his 1992 budget, when he wrong-footed Labour by bringing in a reduced tax band. Some Tory MPs believed that won them the election.
So why have they gone off him now? It could be something he said. Such as: 'There is reason to think the recession will be relatively shallow and short-lived' (December 1990). 'The green shoots of economic spring are appearing once again' (October 1991). 'There is going to be no devaluation and no leaving the ERM' (August 1992).
Does he have a life outside politics? He's a cinema buff, supports Grimsby Town and plays table tennis ('I've seldom met anyone who can beat me'). Reads poetry – especially Tennyson.
Most likely Tennyson quote: 'The man's the true Conservative who lops the moulder'd branch away.'
Most likely misquote: 'I would that my tongue would stop uttering the thoughts that arise in me.'

15 March 1993. Lamont was sacked two months later and in his resignation speech attacked John Major's government, which he said was 'in office, not in power'.

k d lang

Age: 31.

Background: Canadian-born singer/songwriter whose recording career began in 1987 with the release of the album *Angel with a Lariat*. Nashville was thrown into turmoil by Lang's punkish hairdo and less than reverent attitude to country music. Last year she made her acting debut with a five-second nude scene in the film *Salmonberries*.

Don't give up your day job: Once performed a tribute to Barney Clark, the world's first artificial heart patient, which involved re-enacting his time on the operating table. Like Clark's surgery, it lasted 12 hours.

Possible reasons for leaving small cattle-farming community of Consort, Alberta (pop. 650), where she was brought up: Declared herself gay, vegetarian, started wearing men's suits.

Current address: A cabin on a Hollywood hillside: 'I like to pretend I am a farmer. Always ready to feed the cows, drive the tractor, fix the trucks.'

Clothes: Has been known to wear cowgirl outfits with plastic barnyard animals attached and spectacles with no glass in them.

Country-music clichés she has avoided: Flouncy gingham blouses, big hair/breasts, rhinestone-studded cowboy boots, whiney little womanishness, names like Patsy, Tammy and Dolly.

What has she got in common with the poet e e cummings? A lower-case affectation.

Why initials? Probably to disguise the fact that her full name is Kathy Dawn.

Anything wrong with that? No, except that it's a name that calls to mind page-three girls and holiday reps, not lesbian cult heroines.

Love match: Was romantically linked with former Wimbledon champion Martina Navratilova, who payed out undisclosed 'palimony' to Dallas housewife Judy Nelson – last girlfriend but two – after they split.

Likes: Swiss cough drops, the Carpenters, plastic combat boots, animals; 'Nature is my teacher – it's also my God.'

Dislikes: Humans, 'one of my least favourite species on the planet'.

Right-on credentials: Makes TV commercials for Peta (People for the Ethical Treatment of Animals); made a video of 'So in Love' for the Red, Hot and Blue Aids project.

Madonna on Lang: 'Oh my God, she's the female version of Sean (Penn). I could fall in love with her.' 'Elvis is alive – and she's beautiful.'

No relation to: Jack Lang, David Lange, 'Auld Lang Syne', Jessica Lange, R. D. Laing.

Least likely to sing: 'Stand by Your Man'.

Tim Laurence

Age: 37.

Appearance: Paddy Ashdown's younger brother.

Background: First graduate to marry a royal. Tim is the son of a marine engine salesman who brought up his children in military fashion, insisting they 'fall in' for inspection every morning. At prep school he won prizes for efficiency and table tennis. Went on to Sevenoaks where contemporaries remember him as 'a straightforward plodder'. Read geography at Durham University and edited college magazine. Nicknamed 'Tiger' Tim for habit of chasing students for contributions. Joined the navy, moving in 1979 to post of household liaison officer on the royal yacht *Britannia*. Said to have caught Queen's eye, resulting in promotion in 1986 to royal staff as military equerry. Currently has desk job at MoD.

What is an equerry? It is pronounced ekwerry, with the accent on the second syllable, and is not derived from *equus*, the Latin for horse. An equerry accompanies the Queen on all engagements and introduces guests.

Home: Terraced house in Winchester. Drives a classic MG sports car.

Earnings: £40,861.

Family tree: Great-great-grandfather was Joseph Levy, son of Zaccaria Levy, a merchant of Venice, who changed name to Laurence in 1826. Great-grandfather was Rev. Percival Laurence. Grandfather was barrister.

Romance: Blossomed after Anne separated from Mark in the same year that love letters from Tim to Anne fell into the hands of a tabloid newspaper. Tim carpeted by Sir William Heseltine, Queen's private secretary. Queen herself is said to have stood by Tim.

Princess Anne is: Bubbling with joy.

John Major is: Delighted.

Supporters of Tim within royals: The young royals.

Opponents of Tim within royals: The courtiers. They are reported to be furious at having to call Tim 'sir' in future. One aide told the *Daily Mirror*: 'Former equerries just don't marry Princesses Royal.' Though Group Captain Peter Townsend jolly nearly married Princess Margaret.

How does he compare with Mark? Plusses: Brighter and more sociable. No unsuitable close friendships with women in New Zealand. Minuses: Not so handsome as Mark, and not so good on a horse.

How does he compare with other royal incomers? Never lived with racing driver. Does not suffer from bulimia. Does not have a 'financial adviser'. Father was not in the SS. Not related to Barbara Cartland.

Old flames? None found so far. Only girl anyone can remember Tim talking to is Gillian Malpass, now senior editor at Yale University Press. That was 20 years ago. She remembers him as a 'nice guy'.

Least likely to say: 'Is that the *Sun* newsdesk?'

Mike Leigh

Age: 50.

Appearance: Bloodhound in mourning.

Background: Born in Salford, went to Salford Grammar, then RADA. Has made lots of celebrated TV films (*Abigail's Party, Meantime, Nuts in May*, etc.) but only four cinema films in 23 years. Married to actress Alison Steadman.

Why is he in the news? His latest movie, *Naked* – about angry, antisocial man living angry antisocial life – has won him best director and David Thewlis best actor at Cannes.

Why so few films? He makes them in Britain. Also, when he approaches would-be backers he can't tell them what the film's going to be about.

What are his films about? Crippled communication/normal life depending how good you're feeling. The working class/lower-middle class. What Leigh calls 'the nose-picking, arse-scratching world'.

Why this obsession with the working class? 'Because they're the kind of people I know best.'

Really? No. His parents are affluent-ish middle class, dad a doctor.

Are titles like *High Hopes* and *Life Is Sweet* serious? No. They are ironic.

Typical conversation in Mike Leigh film: ' . . . ' 's'pose so.' ' . . . ' 'OK, then.'

Another typical conversation: 'Hahahahahhaaa, heehehehehehehe.' 'Ahhahahahahahah, hehehchchhe . . . '

Why are his films remarkable? They are made for threepence and improvised (see typical conversation). Actors build up characters with Leigh and then are placed in dramatic situations. Eventually story evolves. Leigh turns this into a script and then credits himself as the author.

Is he having his cake and eating it? Most certainly.

What critical critics say about his films: Working-class types are patronising and sentimental, toffs are caricatures. No one's really like that.

What friendly critics say: No one understands real life like Mike Leigh.

How does he take criticism? Badly; has been known to ring journalists first thing in the morning to tell them they're 'complete bastards'.

Has he as many hang-ups as his characters? Probably.

Such as: Not really being working-class, being Jewish, not making as many films as he thinks he should have.

What favoured actors say about him: 'Wonderful'; 'Amazing'; 'Discovered depths I never knew I had.'

What out-of-favour actors say: 'I disagreed with him, so he sent me home.'

Not to be confused with: Vivien Leigh; Francis Lee; Dairylea.

Least likely to say: 'I think Pass Notes got me off to a tee.'

Most likely to say: 'Complete bastards . . . '

Jean-Marie le Pen

Age: 64.
Appearance: Chubby scoutmaster.
Has he always looked like that?
No, in the 1950s he wore army
fatigues and a black eyepatch.
Background: Son of a Breton
fisherman; ex-paratroop officer.
Marital status: Remarried. After
leaving him in 1984, his first wife
humiliated him by posing semi-nude
in a maid's outfit for *Playboy*.
Why did Pierrette leave him? 'He
was always hard to live with, but he
changed the most in 1976 when he
was left an inheritance by a rich
supporter of the National Front. All
his faults became accentuated. He
became a dictator, an authoritarian.
I was a maid, no more.'
Current occupation: Leader of the
French National Front and the
European Right grouping of the
Euro-Parliament.

How European is the European Right? It has members in France and
Belgium.
Anywhere else? No. But it has conventions all over the Continent.
At whose expense? Ours. In 1991 the European Right spent £390,000 of
European taxpayers' money on conferences in Paris, Dublin, Rome, Vienna,
Venice, London, Madrid and Nice.
Least favourite newspaper: The *Guardian*, whose exposure of his latest
freebie in Corfu earned it the description of 'nauseating dishcloth' on Radio le
Pen, the Paris phone-in line of the National Front.
Most recent hobby: Being refused accommodation for future EC-sponsored
junkets in Edinburgh and Dublin.
Does he let this put him off? Not a bit. Yesterday he spent all of two hours
in Britain, signing books at Heathrow Airport.
Most infamous remark: 'The gas chambers are a mere detail of the Second
World War.'
Is it fair to call him 'the spiritual son of Adolf Hitler'? A French court
recently turned down his £12,000 claim for damages and ruled that the
description was quite legal.
Warning to visitors: Don't approach him from the left.
Why not? He has a glass eye.
Not to be confused with: Mont Blanc pens; John le Mesurier; Sean Penn.
Most likely to say: 'Pass the ouzo, Adolf.'
Least likely to say: 'Vive la différence.'

Bernard-Henri Lévy

Age: 44.

Appearance: Hero in a Jilly Cooper novel called *Thinkers*.

Status: Philosopher, playwright, novelist, *Elle* sex symbol, *un médiatique* (television star), editor of literary-political journal, former *enfant terrible*.

Otherwise known as: B.H.L. to his friends, BHV (French equivalent of BHS) to his enemies.

Why is he in the news? Has assumed the role of fashion guru in current Paris fashion week. Such a brain has never got so close to a catwalk.

Famous for: Chest hair, attacks on 'messianic' intellectuals (Marx, Sartre et al.), liberal pragmatism.

Most famous works: *Les Aventures de la Liberté* (as book or television documentary); *Les Hommes et les*

Femmes (with former minister Françoise Giroud; a bestselling but meandering discussion of sex, love, marriage, fidelity).

Toughest questioning: In 1978 during a four-hour interrogation while under house arrest in a Buenos Aires hotel on suspicion of possessing 'subversive literature'.

Most famous sound-bite: 'Between the barbarity of capitalism, which censures itself much of the time, and the barbarity of socialism, which does not, I guess I would choose capitalism.'

View of fashion: The body must breathe.

View on battle of the sexes: I am a product of feminism . . .

Views on women and sex: They claim the right to orgasm in much the same way as they claim the right to social security.

Views on men and sex: Love is never platonic. One cannot love a woman without violently desiring her. (Has married for the third time, to actress Arielle Dombasle, who has been seen wearing shoes with a heart and an inscribed BH on heels.)

Views on battle in Balkans: Regular visitor to Sarajevo, introduced President Mitterrand to Alija Izetbegovic – 'Because I am an intellectual I have a duty to Bosnia.'

Views on everything else: Available on request.

Not to be confused with: Levi Strauss (jeans maker); Lévi-Strauss (French social anthropologist); Bernard Levin.

Passions: Black, white and grey ('When I find a new subtle shade of grey, I feel ecstatic'); shirts (made by Christian Dior Monsieur, inspired by Cocteau); cashmere; silk.

Advice to British philosophers: Never button shirt right up to collar.

Most likely to say: 'J'accuse . . . ' (please fill space with name of any misguided genius).

Least likely to say: 'Oh, I get my underpants at M&S.'

Lennox Lewis

Age: 27.

Appearance: Very tall (6ft 5in). Very heavy (16st 4lb). Very frightening.

Appearance in tabloid press: Permanently draped in Union Jack.

Other vital statistics: Inside leg 38in, shoe size 15, neck 18in, biceps 18½in, reach 83in.

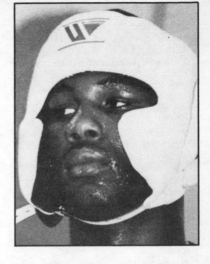

Nationality: Questionable. Weighed in in the East End of London. Emigrated to Canada as a boy and was teased about his accent. Took up boxing, teased less about his accent, won Olympic gold medal for adopted country in 1988, proclaiming that 'Canada needed that.' Turned professional after being offered the chance to base himself in either the USA or UK. Considered where the money was and returned to his roots.

Title: Became World Boxing Council heavyweight champion after previous holder, Riddick Bowe, threw his belt in the bin at a London press conference.

Private life: Not much known. The only woman so far discovered to have a claim on his affections is his mother, Violet. 'I'm a mother's boy,' he says.

Other disturbing psychological traits: Enjoys beating people up and hugging them afterwards. Like Mrs Thatcher and Arthur Scargill speaks of himself in third person: 'Lennox Lewis is in charge of his own destiny.'

Rate of pay for his job: Earned £322,000 for 226 seconds' work in beating Razor Ruddock. That is £1,424 per second. Turned down £3 million to face Bowe, describing it as 'slap-in-the-face money'. Subsequently offered to meet him for nothing with all the proceeds going to Africa.

Is he more intelligent than Frank Bruno? Almost certainly. 'I'm a deep thinker, very deep. My friends call me 'chemist' or 'scientist' 'cause I'm always thinkin' and always one step ahead.'

Relationship with 'arry Carpenter: Yet to develop one. His management signed a three-fight deal with BSkyB which means BBC has been granted only news access to his recent fights.

Miscellaneous likes: *Dr Who* – claims to have seen every episode; West Ham United, chess, pet miniature poodle.

Least likely to say: 'Spare us some change, guv, I'm boracic.'

Martyn Lewis

Age: 48.

Appearance: Tambourine-wielding rural vicar, who's just heard that he's the apple of his Bishop's eye.

Position: Presenter of BBC Nine O'Clock News, along with Michael Buerk who used to wink at the end of bulletins.

Background: A portly child known as 'fatty', at school in Wales and later Ireland he was soundly bullied (though not quite soundly enough), and developed a stammer. After a degree at Trinity, joined BBC in Belfast, reaching the dizzying heights of ITN newscaster in 1981. His departure for a reputed £100,000 BBC salary in 1986 earned from a producer the tribute: 'This is the best thing that has happened to ITN in years.'

Earliest public appearance: As an infant, his chubby, golden-haired winsomeness was used to advertise Cow & Gate baby food.

Why is he in the news? He has made a speech attacking broadcast news media for concentrating on nasty horrid things like Bosnia at the expense of nice, cheery stories about British economic success and cute pussycats.

How does Jeremy Paxman rate this argument? 'Nonsense.' And Trevor McDonald? 'Absolute nonsense.'

Talents:

Is he a serious journalist? So he insists.

But really? Well, he is a member of Annabel's; his publications include *Cats in the News*, *Dogs in the News* and *And Finally*, a collection of end-of-bulletin funnies; oh yes, and he's appeared in *Hello!* magazine.

Commonest tabloid epithets? Housewives' favourite; ambitious; gallant.

Gallant? Most certainly. When his 76-year-old mother visits, so he boasts, he makes her go into the garden when she wants a cigarette.

Passion: Cats.

Interests: Photography; eating (he once described a favourite delicatessen as 'a delicious kaleidoscope of smells'); tennis; appearing in tabloid 'at home with' features, showing off his delightfully genteel Kensington house.

Is there anything interesting about him at all? Certainly. His wife Liz is the daughter of Duncan Carse, who played Dick Barton on the radio.

Fair enough, but at least he doesn't present *Songs of Praise*: Er, sorry. He's been an occasional presenter for three years.

Preferred introduction to Nine O'Clock News: 'Good evening. Radovan Karadzic, leader of the Bosnian Serbs, has announced tonight that his tabby Tiddlic has had a litter of seven adorable kittens.'

Least likely to say: 'Who am I, a humble newsreader, to patronise the public with half-baked piffle about good news?'

And finally: . . . A BBC newsroom joke. What's the difference between Michael Buerk and Martyn Lewis? Michael Buerk is a winker.

30 April 1993. In July 1993 Lewis was moved – some said demoted – to the Six O'Clock News.

Peter Lilley

Age: 49; looks 39¾.
Appearance: Fair-haired,
vulnerable, boyish. Must have
looked angelic at school. Said to have
been compared to Robert Redford by
women civil servants at the DTI, a
notoriously ill-lit department.
Distinguishing traits: Few. Winner
of the *Daily Telegraph*/Gallup award
for the most invisible cabinet
minister three years running, his
recognition factor climbing last year
to a dizzy 5 per cent. Michael
Heseltine once referred to him as
Peter Willey.
**Very well then, any semi-
distinguishing traits?** Dryness;
Thatcherism – founder member of
the No Turning Back group of Tory
MPs. One of the cabinet's Euro-
sceptics and ERM doubters.
Early career: Dulwich College;
Cambridge. Economic consultant, specialising in overseas aid: has denied this
indicates idealism 'unless you count six months in Bali studying the money
supply as idealism'.
Do people who want to study the money supply usually go to Bali? Not
in any great numbers. Perhaps someone told him it was a place where you
might get head-hunted.
How did he get into politics? Via the Bow Group, or as newspapers usually
call it, the influential Bow Group. Conservative Research Department
1979–83, just after Chris Patten left. Elected for St Albans 1983; Trade and
Industry Secretary under Thatcher, 1990; second of the '83 intake to make
the cabinet. Became Social Security Secretary.
Is it true he was once in the SS? No, only the DSS, though *Spitting Image*
cast him as an SS officer because of his reputed views on cutting benefits.
Was this entirely fair? Not really. Some cabinet colleagues felt it was a
shade exaggerated. His record – so far – looks tougher on rhetorical cuts than
on real ones.
Is he a noted wit? That depends on whether you go for Gilbert & Sullivan
parodies. Also, when Donald Dewar became his Labour opposite number,
Lilley said: 'His only claim to fame is that he is even less well known than I
am.'
Is he seen at Westminster as a future Conservative leader? Not widely,
though he's been so depicted by sources as varied as the *Evening Standard*
(by columnist Simon Heffer) and the *Spectator* (by deputy editor Simon
Heffer).
So why is he in the doghouse? Because of his disgusting eating habits. In
the most doom-laden act of communal mastication since Neil Kinnock took
the press to Luigi's, he and his right-wing colleague Michael Portillo recently
supped with the *Mxrgxrxt Thxtchxr*. The *Mail on Sunday* spilled, as it were, the
beans. John Major is said to be not inconsiderably vexed.
Double acts he doesn't belong to: Lilley and Skinner (Lab., Bolsover).
Lillee and Thomson (Australia). Lillian Gish.
Least likely to say: 'I daren't go out there, they'll mob me.'

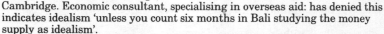

Viscount Linley

Age: 31.
Full name: David Albert Charles Armstrong-Jones.
Position: Son of Lord Snowdon and Princess Margaret; 12th in line to the throne.
Appearance: Cocktail barman at overpriced West End hotel.

Background: Victim of parents' failed marriage, he soldiered on through school but didn't make university, going instead to carpentry college. Left home at 20 for one-bedroom flat above fish and chip shop in Dorking, but interests in a furniture shop and two hamburger joints have improved his fortunes. After a succession of blonde, long-legged girlfriends, his engagement to blonde, long-legged Serena Stanhope was announced on Monday.

Why did the announcement surprise royal watchers? Because Nigel Dempster had *not* written a story in Monday's *Daily Mail* stating categorically that the romance was over.
Is Serena a Sloane paradigm? Yes, she went from finishing school to Sotheby's, and now works in fashion PR.
Is it a Marriage Made in Heaven or a Fairy-tale Romance? Both.
So when will it end? Don't be cynical. (Give it five years.)
Likes: Old cameras; vehicles; blondes; holidays; money; speeding (he was once banned from driving for four months).
Dislikes: Traffic police; any suggestion that royal status has helped his business; lack of readies.
On macro-economics: 'The recession is over. It was only in the mind anyway' (October 1991).
On micro-economics: 'Being who I am is a disadvantage in the furniture business. I keep hearing I don't need the money. I do. I work for a living.'
Rewards for surmounting the handicap of royal birth: Six holidays last year: Mustique (twice), Austria (skiing), Monte Carlo, Ibiza, Barbados.
And vehicles? A Range Rover, a souped-up black Morris Minor and a silver Aston Martin DB5; two mountain bikes; BMW and BSA motorbikes.
Linley and the Art of Motorcycle Riding: 'You know it's amazing what a motorbike can do for your personality.'
Money worries: 'The way I've been brought up and the way I would like to live requires substantial finance, so there is a need to earn some money.'
But won't things be even harder with a wife to support? Not really, Serena's father, Viscount Petersham, owns South Kensington, and she's worth about £5 million in her own right.
Other income: He was awarded £35,000 from *Today* newspaper in 1990, after a mistaken report that he'd been barred from a Chelsea pub for hooray hooliganism.
Least likely to say: 'I'm afraid it's Skegness for the honeymoon, darling.'

5 May 1993. Viscount Linley and Ms Stanhope were married in October 1993.

Loch Ness Monster

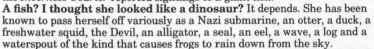

Age: Between 60 and 1,500.

Appearance: Long, with a giraffe-like head, a fishy sort of back, a tail like a dinosaur and a sinister glint in her eye.

Her? Despite the lack of concrete evidence, Nessie is always female.

Occupation: To terrify locals, fascinate ecologists, but most of all to bring £15 million worth of tourism to Scotland a year.

They come to the loch? In their thousands. From March they will be able to take a submarine trip in the loch to try to spot her.

And will they see her? They might. Lots of people have.

Who? All kinds of people. One of St Colomba's followers was attacked by her 1,500 years ago and he obviously terrified the life out of poor Nessie, who didn't reappear until 1868 when the *Inverness Courier* reported sightings of a giant fish.

A fish? I thought she looked like a dinosaur? It depends. She has been known to pass herself off variously as a Nazi submarine, an otter, a duck, a freshwater squid, the Devil, an alligator, a seal, an eel, a wave, a log and a waterspout of the kind that causes frogs to rain down from the sky.

Apart from lots of fuzzy pictures, is there any proof that she exists? In 1987 a £1 million project called Operation Deepscan traced a large unidentified object 600ft beneath the surface of the loch. The 300-strong flotilla of journalists following the search was ecstatic.

But what if she doesn't exist? She must exist: our love of mystery, a hefty chunk of the Scottish economy and quite a few authors depend on it. Nine books have been written on the subject, including one by Nicholas Witchell.

Tell us about the loch – that must be the key: It's 780ft deep and 23 miles long. It's ridiculously cold and you could fit the entire population of the world into it three times over, should you so desire.

How can we be sure she's not a dinosaur? It would be too cold for a dinosaur and anyway she couldn't have survived the Ice Age.

So, what sort of a fish is she? The latest theory is that she is a navigationally challenged Baltic sturgeon which blundered into Loch Ness in search of a mate and stayed. Sturgeons can live in cold water, reach three metres in length and live for 300 years.

Pretending to be a monster must help pass the centuries? It certainly amused 86-year-old H. Lambert Wilson, who recently admitted that in the thirties he used to swim in the loch in a Nessie disguise.

Not to be confused with: Skegness; Elliot Ness; 'Nessun Dorma' (Pavarotti is bigger).

Most likely to say: 'Oh no, not another sonar . . . '

Least likely to say: 'Blobby Blobby Blobby' (but the Scottish Tourist Board is working on it).

29 December 1993

Louis XVI

Age: 239 (born 1754).
Occupation: King (deceased), inherited the family business from his grandfather, Louis XV, who acceded to the throne against considerable odds on the deaths in swift succession of his grandfather, father and elder brothers; Marie-Antoinette's husband.

Why is he in the news now? French magazine cover star. A poll shows only 9 per cent of the French support his execution by guillotine in the Place de la Révolution after he was found guilty of treason.

Biggest mistakes: Calling the Assembly of the Notables in 1787, providing a focus for the 'aristocratic reaction' which resisted social and economic reforms set in train by his predecessor; getting caught as he tried to flee France; not finding a better hiding place for secret letters revealing he was negotiating with Austria, discovered in a palace cupboard.

Likely to be confused with: Louis XIV (the Sun King with the big palace), Charles I of England (similar wig, same fate – Napoleon observed that 'Charles I perished for resisting, Louis XVI for not resisting'), the Romanovs and Nicolae Ceausescu, fellow victims of revolutionary zeal.

Not likely to be confused with: Louis Jordan; Lois Lane; Joe Louis; Louis Armstrong; François Mitterrand.

Biggest successes: PR man for Monsieur Guillotine's wonderful invention; the Bourbon biscuit.

Biggest challenges: The guillotine; steering France from feudalism to constitutionalism (failed).

What they said about him: 'It's not a matter of judging him, but killing him' – Danton; 'The public assassination of a weak and good man is a repugnant scandal' – Albert Camus.

What they say about him: 'The execution of Louis XVI was an error committed thanks either to an excess of passion or an excess of reason . . . It stained the great achievements of the revolution with blood and uncertainty' – Jean-Marie Rouart, *Le Figaro*.

What he said: 'My people, I die innocent! I pardon the authors of my death. I beg God that my blood should not fall on France.'

Most likely to say: 'I'm not putting my head in there.'

Least likely to say: 'Oh all right then, let them have the cake.'

21 January 1993, the 200th anniversary of his execution.

Joanna Lumley

Age: 47.
Appearance: Barbie on HRT.
Occupation: Actress. Best
remembered as Purdey in *The New
Avengers* ('You've got to be grateful
that they remember you at all').
Recently she has starred as Patsy in
the comedy *Absolutely Fabulous*,
written by Jennifer Saunders who
also stars in it, and ads for cider, gas
and washing-up liquid. Notable for
her absence in the Cellnet ad with
John Cleese and Ronnie Corbett.
She's the posh one? That's her. In
fact she plays a down-at-heel
aristocrat in ITV's new series *Class
Act*.
What's she done now? Nothing as
such, but *Absolutely Fabulous* has
won an Emmy – one of five British
Emmy successes this year.
***Absolutely Fabulous* is going
down well then?** Yes. Its viewing figures are 8 million, a new series is in the
pipeline and Lumley won a BAFTA for it.
Isn't she famous for glamorous fast living? Up to a point. Born to a
British major in India in 1946, she went to private school in England where
she had her position as prefect revoked when she was caught smoking. She
has a 25-year-old son by a man she won't name and has been romantically
linked with various men she will name, including Rod Stewart, Lord
Snowdon, Michael Kitchen, her ex-husband Jeremy Lloyd and her current
husband Stephen Barlow.
Barlow . . . Barlow . . . that's a familiar name: Indeed. She once played
Ken Barlow's love interest: 'I often seem to have been cast as someone's
glamorous girlfriend.'
But Ken? Too gorgeous for him, surely? An interviewer once dubbed her
'as beautiful as Diana and quite as sharp'.
And when she's no longer beautiful? 'I wouldn't hesitate to have plastic
surgery.'
Hasn't she already had some? Emphatically, no. She was dogged by
controversy in the seventies over whether or not she'd had a bum lift (she
hadn't) and for a while she received letters addressed to it.
But back to her mind: She votes Conservative.
Yes, but . . . She is the first to admit that people simply expect actresses to
be stupid and if they find one that can string a coherent sentence together
they 'ask her to judge the Booker Prize or something'. In fact she has written
a book called *Forces Sweethearts*.
Not to be confused with: Joanna Trollope.
Least likely to say: 'I suffer for my art.'
Most likely to say: 'I'll do it!'

Lord Mackay

Age: 65.

Appearance: Upright gait, rosy cheeks, bristling white hair, head slightly large for his body.

Full name: James Peter Hymers Mackay, Baron Mackay of Clashfern, of Eddrachillis in the district of Sutherland.

What's he like? Twinkly and friendly; good but not goody-goody.

So why do lawyers hate him? Solicitors because he's cut their legal-aid fees; barristers because he's cut their legal-aid fees and opened the higher courts to solicitors.

Background: Son of a Scottish railway worker; took maths degrees at Edinburgh and Cambridge before changing to law. Practised at the Scottish Bar, specialising in rating.

Job: Lord High Chancellor of Great Britain, since 1987.

Salary: Around £110,000 a year – higher than anyone else in the cabinet, including the Prime Minister, over whom he takes precedence (after the Archbishop of Canterbury).

Why so much? Because he has more jobs than anyone else. He heads the judiciary and appoints the judges, runs the courts and the legal system, and serves as Speaker of the House of Lords.

Constitutional position: Usually politely described as 'anomalous' or 'unique'. You know how the government, the executive and the judiciary are supposed to be separate? Well, the government and the judiciary come together in the Lord Chancellor. He is both the top judge, head of the judiciary and a politician, whose job is up for grabs if the government goes.

But is Lord Mackay really a politician? By background, no. Unique among Lord Chancellors, he was a Scottish lawyer who became a Scottish judge and went to the House of Lords as a law lord, whence he was plucked by Margaret Thatcher, whose nonconformist creed of thrift and hard work he shares.

Was it 'bizarre', as Labour says, for him to go to Northern Cyprus to try to extract Asil Nadir? As a cabinet member, no. As a judge, arguably. But the chance that he would ever have to sit on a case involving Nadir is remote. He occasionally sits on cases in the House of Lords, but there are nine full-time law lords. And he was already in Southern Cyprus, so the fare was cheap.

Religion: Former member of the 'wee wee frees', the Free Presbyterian Church of Scotland, a tiny sect which regards the Catholic mass as idolatrous. Resigned after a row over his attendance at requiem masses for two Catholic judges. Now attends various churches. Still a strict sabbath observer; will not read Sunday newspapers or be interviewed for TV or radio programmes broadcast on Sunday.

Not to be confused with: Peter McKay; Whyte & Mackay; the real McKoy.

Least likely to be caught doing: Stocking up at Sainsbury's on Sunday.

Madonna

Age: Past it.

Appearance: Over-made-up trollop or ringletted girly, depending on mood.

Lookalike: Increasingly, Myra Hindley experimenting with lipstick and curling tongs.

Background: As a pudgy, adenoidal pop star, Madonna made her name by parading her belly button a lot and indulging in fairly innocent sartorial quirks like wearing her bra on the outside. Around 1987, the breasts got pointier and the gaze icier in direct proportion to the amount of loot, attitude and Jean-Paul Gaultier corsetry she amassed.

Biggest hit: 'Like a Virgin', which sold 7 million nine years ago.

Stunts to date: Simulated masturbation, dry-humping members of her dance troupe, toe-sucking, filling up men's navels with hot candle wax, fellating mineral-water bottles.

Has it paid off? Yes, she's the third richest woman in the world.

But now her popularity's plummeting, right? It would seem so. Her album *Erotica* notched up blushingly modest sales of 650,000, whereas *Immaculate Conception* achieved British sales of 2 million in 1990. Her film *Body of Evidence* was a box-office flop, and *Sex*, the bondage and lesbianism coffee-table book, provoked widespread criticism that she was overexposed, literally and metaphorically. Martin Amis was moved to call it 'the desperate confection of an ageing scandal-addict'.

Any fresh evidence that the material girl is becoming immaterial? Yes. Only three people turned up to fawn outside her hotel when she arrived in London for the start of her much-hyped Girlie Show tour.

Headlines Madonna has shared with editors of national newspapers: Andrew Neil interviewed her for the *Sunday Times Magazine* ('Madonna's Cherish flowed from my Walkman as the jumbo jet banked south over Malibu . . . '); Donald Trelford, former *Observer* editor, was criticised for paying £15,000 for exclusive pictures from *Sex*. The *News of the World* called him 'Dirty Don' and 'a mucky toff'.

Madonna on sex: 'I don't want to be a virgin any more, f*** my brains out.'

Madonna on God: 'I find the crucifix very sexy because it has a naked man on it.'

Madonna on Jesus and Mary Magdalene: 'They probably got it on.'

The *New York Post* on Madonna: 'Where Monroe was subtle, Madonna is coarse. Monroe enticed, Madonna bludgeons. Monroe was fun, Madonna embarrasses. Monroe winked a sexy innocence, Madonna is crude and lewd.'

Fans on Madonna: 'People just don't understand her.'

Most likely to say: 'Come and get me, big boy.'

Least likely to say: 'Sorry, I don't kiss on the first date.'

Nigel Mansell

Age: 40.
Appearance: Mr Ordinary.
But does that belie a fascinating personality? Sadly not.
So why's he in the news? He has just added the US Indycar motor racing championship to the Formula One world championship he won last year. He's the first Brit to win both, the first driver to hold the two championships simultaneously, and the first to take the Indycar title in his debut season.
What does that make him? The boldest, fastest driver in the world, and hugely wealthy.
And happy? Yes, amazingly. For the past decade he has been winning races and then complaining bitterly about them: when he won the 1991 British Grand Prix at Silverstone, his post-race press conference centred on his supposed gear-change problems. He became better known for whingeing than winning, but in the USA he has put all that behind him.
Did his rhetoric rise to the occasion? No, but it never does: 'I just love racing and I like this kind of racing. It's just pure racing.'
But the achievement is extraordinary? Little short of miraculous, and it was appropriate that he won the Indycar title in Nazareth . . . Pennsylvania.
But what is Indycar racing? It's the US version of grand prix racing, but with one crucial difference: half the races take place on oval circuits flanked by concrete walls. Which means that if you crash you're in big trouble, as Mansell discovered in Phoenix when he injured his back in a smash.
Why did he leave the more glamorous (and better-paid) world of Formula One? It's a long story, but he would argue it left him. He had just won the world title with the Williams–Renault team when it announced its intention to hire ex-world champion Alain Prost. Mansell refused to accept Prost as his team-mate and flounced out.
Do the UK fans miss him? Desperately, and attendances at grands prix have dropped in his absence. The *aficionados* at Brands Hatch and Silverstone used to be middle-aged men with handlebar moustaches. During the 12 years he spent trying to win the title – and invariably coming a cropper in the vital race – he attracted hordes of young, flag-waving fans loathed by the traditionalists. Lager louts had invaded a G&T world.
What do they think of him outside the UK? Italians love him and christened him Il Leone (the Lion). Americans adore him.
Not to be confused with: The much more charismatic Nigel Short.
Most likely to say: 'Five million pounds! You must be joking. It would take more than that to get me out of bed in the morning.'
Least likely to say: 'Fancy a weekend at my house in Florida, Alain?'

21 September 1993. Mansell returned to Formula 1 to race for Williams at the end of the 1994 season following Ayrton Senna's death.

Diego Maradona

Age: 33.
Childhood: Brief. Argentinos Juniors signed him aged 15, selected for national side at 16 . . .
Earnings: £30 million in five years at Napoli.
Did they get good value? Definitely. Won Italian League for the first time in 1987; again in 1990; won the UEFA Cup in 1989.
Famous for: Being the former greatest footballer in the world.
And? Punching the ball into the England net, thus depriving Bobby Robson's side of a World Cup semi-final place in 1986. Later described the goal as 'the hand of God'.
What about his superb individual run for the second goal? OK, so maybe England wouldn't have got to the semi-final anyway.

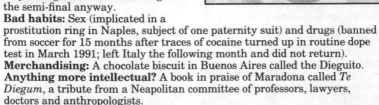

Bad habits: Sex (implicated in a prostitution ring in Naples, subject of one paternity suit) and drugs (banned from soccer for 15 months after traces of cocaine turned up in routine dope test in March 1991; left Italy the following month and did not return).
Merchandising: A chocolate biscuit in Buenos Aires called the Dieguito.
Anything more intellectual? A book in praise of Maradona called *Te Diegum*, a tribute from a Neapolitan committee of professors, lawyers, doctors and anthropologists.
So there is a revisionist approach to Diego? Certainly. From the book: 'His goal scored with the hand, the famous hand of God, reminds one of Ulysses for its deception and cunning.'
Who can afford him? For $250,000, he's yours for an afternoon. Played in kickaround with sheikh's son from the United Arab Emirates for that. Offered $600,000 at 16 to endorse Coca-Cola. Subject of wildly optimistic transfer rumours linking him with Birmingham City – have they got that sort of cash?
The other drug problem: Cortisone has become a way of life. The sediment from the drug has to be surgically removed from his knees each season.
Any connection between Napoli and Birmingham City? Napoli play in blue in the best league in the world, in a great stadium, where the weather is warm, they have a fabulously wealthy chairman, can afford the best players in the world and have won the Italian League twice as well as European trophies. Birmingham City play in blue, too.
Is there a Spurs angle? Yes. Maradona was sold by Terry Venables as his first act on taking over as manager of Barcelona in 1984. He is also a very good friend of Osvaldo Ardiles, the new Spurs supremo, and appeared in a Spurs shirt for the Ardiles testimonial at White Hart Lane.
Was Maradona happy in Spain? No. Got hepatitis. Had his leg broken by Andoni Goicoechea, 'the butcher of Bilbao'. Maradona has three steel support pins in his leg; 'the Butcher' has the boot that did the damage under glass in his living room. Fought Bilbao players in Spanish Cup Final.

25 June 1993. Maradona captained Argentina in the 1994 world cup but was banned from the competition after testing positive for the drug Ephedrine.

Rik Mayall

Age: 35.
Occupation: Comic actor.
Appearance: Beatnik intellectual.
Background: Born in a village with
the unlikely name of Matching Tye;
went to public school and only just
managed to get into Manchester
University ('I was too busy
snogging'). Awarded the Boris
Karloff award for Most Outrageous
Ham at a student drama festival.
Met Adrian Edmondson and went
around with him shouting 'We're
going to be stars!'
Why? Apparently to irritate the
'right-on worthies'. Alexei Sayle
thinks he's 'an empty-headed bimbo'.
Has he won any awards lately?
Funny you should ask. He won the
British Comedy Awards prize for
best TV comic actor, but may have to
return it amid allegations that the
ballot was rigged because the other contenders – David Jason, Richard
Wilson, Chris Barrie, Michael Williams and Neil Pearson – were not
considered good enough.
Does he have the comic qualifications to win? He does. He was part of the
original Comic Strip team with Alexei Sayle, Dawn French and Jennifer
Saunders, starred in the cult series *The Young Ones* (based, apparently, on
student life at Manchester), appeared in *The Government Inspector* and
Waiting for Godot, and played odious Tory MP Alan B'Stard in *The New
Statesman*.
Did he have anyone particular in mind? He and Ade Edmondson
interviewed Michael Portillo as part of the research.
Wasn't he quite good-looking in *The New Statesman*? 'I didn't realise
Rik Mayall was so attractive,' wrote one critic. 'There are some people who
think Michael Heseltine attractive,' Mayall replied cryptically.
Didn't the series prompt a scandal? Mayall incited national outrage when
he suggested that Prince Charles might be having an affair with Camilla
Parker-Bowles. Perish the thought . . .
So what's with the serious stage stuff? He felt the need to prove he could
do it – 'Oh! I can cry. I'm brilliant . . . but I don't want to belittle waving your
bottom about on stage.'
That, after all, is what he's famous for? True. 'Really, I'm not trying to do
anything spectacular except to change the fabric of our society and bring
down the government.'
Not to be confused with: Royal Mail.
Most likely to say: 'Bum, fart, toilet, bollocks, tits, ****, ****, ****.'
Least likely to say: 'For in that sleep of death what dreams may come /
When we have shuffled off this mortal coil, / Must give us pause . . . '

16 December 1993

Sir Patrick Mayhew

Age: 63.
Appearance: Overweight owl.
Position: Northern Ireland
Secretary.
Background: Tonbridge, Balliol
(president of Oxford Union).
National service in Irish regiment.
Decided to take Silk before becoming
MP for Tunbridge Wells at 45 – 'too
late to scale the heights'. Definitely
'not one of us', but appointed
Solicitor-General and Attorney-
General by Mrs Thatcher, despite
standing up to her over the Westland
affair. Supported Douglas Hurd in
leadership contest. He has been
described as the last grandee in the
cabinet and 'the only proper Tory
we've got left'.

Hanging fudge: Voted for capital
punishment in July 1979. Now says
that was an aberration.
Parliamentary career: Took some time adjusting to politics after lifetime in
law. 'It took me two years to make a speech anyone would listen to because
every time I spoke I made a Court of Appeal speech, as if I had a bad smell
under my nose.' Spent much of eighties embroiled in Spycatcher saga and
dealing with Irish cases – particularly the aftermath to the Stalker inquiry.
Fiercely criticised for not prosecuting 11 RUC officers for alleged shoot-to-kill
offences.
Attitude to Irish: Genuinely likes them, with an almost romantic passion.
But despairs of their memories 'which make elephants seem amnesiac'.
Almost certainly first Ulster Secretary to have asked for the job. Told deputy,
Michael Mates, on first day: 'We'll have some fun.' Anglo-Irish ancestry
confuses local politicians about his real attitude to North.
Adjectives to use when writing about Mayhew: Urbane, upright, suave,
brusque, unruffled, patrician, droll, relaxed, polite, clubbish, faintly pedantic,
Brylcreemed, haughty, plummy, intellectually impatient, aloof, elegantly
weary, witty, lofty, ambitious, combative and calm. 'He approaches the
dispatch box with the air of a man struggling to retain his dignity while
swallowing a bad oyster' (*Times*).
In what respect is he different from his predecessor, Peter Brooke?
Peter Brooke knows more about cricket.
Mayhew on Mayhew: 'I am not a particularly patient man. I can be patient
with a horse, but it doesn't come easily.'
Ideology: Not really. More of a pragmatist. Most pleased with himself when
'doing a Willie'. This is a political trick named after his mentor, Lord
Whitelaw. It involves using bluff image of faint buffoonery to conceal sharp
mind and neat political footwork.
Family: Wife teaches RE in London school. Four children, two in Royal
Dragoon Guards.
Hobbies: Horses and dogs.
Least likely to say: 'Would you like a few bars of "Oh My Darling
Clementine"?'

18 December 1992

Peter Mayle

Name: Peter Mayle.
Nom de plume: Wicked Willie.
Colour of hair: Tan.
Colour of eyes: Tan.
Colour of skin: Tan.
Colour of wallet: Tan.
Appearance: Cross between Ian McEwan asleep and Peter O'Toole in pebble glasses acting Hamlet.
Profession: Failed novelist.
Marital status: Between divorces.
Most lasting achievement: Single-handedly destroying the serenity of the whole Luberon area of the Vaucluse.
Longest work of fiction: *A Year in Provence*.
Shortest work of fiction: 'Why didn't you have BO when you were her age?' – advertisement for Bud deodorant (1968).
Greatest fictional achievement: Changing the name of his wife from Jennie to Annie for the BBC-TV serialisation of his longest work of fiction. At a stroke, this removed the only vestige of resemblance between her and the character on screen.
Most realistic line of dialogue: 'Nice one, Cyril' – written for 30-second commercial for WonderLoaf in 1970s.
Last known job: Part-time chairman of microscopic London advertising agency, Peter Mead & Partner. Mr Mead never recovered from the association and went on to become a director of Millwall FC.
Most unselfish act: Donating his endorsement fee for the two outrageously overpriced red and white wines on sale at Sainsbury's labelled 'A Year in Provence 1991' to the Catastrophe Vaison fund which helped victims of the local 1992 flood. This does not include the victims of the flood of British tourists trampling over peasants in an attempt to find the reclusive author's house to take away a piece of souvenir plaster.
Other Mayles: Son Simon, 31, is shortly publishing his own autobiography, *Bum Jobs*, telling how he was expelled from school and was twice arrested for drunk-and-disorderly behaviour in California.
Not to be confused with: Rick Mayall; Royal Mail; Norman Mailer.
Least likely to say: 'Donnez-moi un autre verre d'eau, si'l vous plaît.'
Most likely to say: 'Si l'on est intéressant soi-même, on rencontre toujours des gens intéressants.'

Paul McCartney

Age: 51.

Appearance: Bad as ever. Hair looks like Davy Crockett's hat.

Career: From mop top to crock rock.

Reminiscent of: Wise without Morecambe.

Voice: According to Lennon, 'like Engelbert Humperdinck'.

Millstone around neck: He lived, John died.

Marital status: Paul is to Linda what Branagh is to Thompson.

Odd habit: Buys lobsters, and puts them back in the sea.

Old school friend: Peter Sissons.

Title: MBE, in 1965.

Shouldn't it be Sir by now? It would be, except for that dope bust in Japan.

Other awards: Numerous, including the Royal Swedish Academy of Music's Polar Award for 'creativity and imagination'.

Meaning what? Everything pre-Wings.

The Beatles, they were quite a successful band. He must be rich. To the tune of £400 million.

Who's richer? In Britain? Eighteen people . . . one of whom is the Queen, and it's not really her money.

In his favour: Still not a tax exile; sent children to state school.

If he doesn't need the money, why does he carry on touring? Because he loves to play live.

But his concerts are crap, aren't they? More boring than crap. Great songs, nothing to look at.

So who goes? Dentist-type people. And accountants.

Are there a lot of them? In Rio, 184,368 in one night.

So is there anything to be thankful for, tour-wise? On his 1989 world tour, a French businessman offered to sell his sweat at £8 a can.

He's the world's most famous . . . Vegetarian.

He's the world's least famous . . . Cousin of a crossword compiler.

Is any other ageing pop star as embarrassing? Only David Bowie springs to mind.

Owns: The rights to 'Happy Birthday' – 'Right! Blow those candles out. That's 10 quid you owe me' – but not his own Beatles songs.

Who does? Michael Jackson.

Aren't you going to do any 'Mull of Kintyre' jokes? No.

What about *Give My Regards to Broad Street*? We haven't seen it. Even on telly. And as far as we know, nobody else has. Except Linda, probably.

Least likely to say: 'Medium rare, thanks.'

Least likely to sing: 'Yesterday, all my chequebooks seemed so far away . . .'

Victor Meldrew

Age: Geriatric.

Appearance: Bald codger with a grimace the size of the Arc de Triomphe.

Most frequently described as: A grump.

Record breaker: Britain's most-watched (if not best-loved) sitcom character ever. An episode of *One Foot in the Grave* amassed 17.3 million viewers, more even than Del Boy attracted to *Only Fools and Horses*.

Early setback: The first series, in January 1990, averaged a paltry 8.9 million viewers per show. Then again, it was scheduled against the Gulf War.

Stroke of luck no. 1: Saddam gave up in time for the second series.

Stroke of luck no. 2: The recession bit, making grumps of us all.

Sitcom least likely to appear in: *Terry and June*.

The men behind the myth: He's played by Richard Wilson, a booming baritone luvvie, and was invented by David Renwick, who has written for Spike Milligan and Alexei Sayle and adapted the odd episode of *Poirot*.

Pop culture assessment: He's a middle-class Alf Garnett.

Posh culture assessment: He's a hero for our age of spite – cantankerous, dystopian, gloomy. Samuel Beckett for the masses.

Things TV critics like about his show: Clever references to David Cronenberg, *The African Queen*, Anne Diamond, etc.

Things audiences like about his show: His weak bladder, and he says 'Bollocks!' and 'Bastard!' at peak viewing time.

Tabloid fascination: Sudden, and in spades.

Tabloid justification for crude, lavatorial jokes: 'When he dumps manure on his enemies, he dumps it in style' (*Today*).

No stone unturned: The *Sun* has invited readers to fax its 'Victor Meldrew hotline' with pictures of men who look grumpy. It has also requested anyone called Victor Meldrew to call in.

What the *Sun* should know: There are no Meldrews in any British phonebook.

Hobbies: Coach trips; collecting money-off coupons; pub lunches; bowls; cheating the cashier at the five-items-or-less checkout.

Likes: None of the above.

Objects he always carries: A string shopping bag, prejudices.

Least likely to sing: Anything, but especially 'The sun has got his hat on, Hip, hip, hip, hooray!'

Least likely to say: 'Enjoy!'

Carlos Menem

Age: 64 (though he claims to be 58).
Appearance: Nightclub singer.
Occupation: President of Argentina.
Preoccupation: Getting Lady Thatcher to come to South America.
What, for a lecture tour? Not exactly. He thinks she should be extradited for war crimes over the sinking of the *Belgrano*.
He can't be serious? Apparently he is. He even compared her with a former SS officer responsible for a massacre of Italian resistance fighters in the Second World War.
British officials must be incendiary. The Argies can't get away with saying that about the Iron Lady. This means war! Calm down. Stiff upper lips have never been stiffer. The MoD, in an Exocet of understatement, said: 'This comes as a tremendous surprise.'
Will no one stand up for our lost leader? Step forward Tam Dalyell, MP for Belgrano Central, who described the idea of extradition as far-fetched.
So why is carping Carlos saying these things? Does he hate Maggie? Of course not. He made a point of saying that he respects her. But he already has his eye on the 1995 presidential election and hopes a bit of Malvinas mischief-making will attract the veterans' vote.
But I thought Argentinian Presidents couldn't run for two consecutive terms? That's remarkably well informed of you: the *Economist* subscription is obviously paying off. But you forget that he has just changed the constitution to allow himself to do precisely that.
Ah, so Señor Menem is fond of power? When elected in 1989, he declared: 'I'm not coming in for six years and then going home. I am here to stay.'
Has his first term been a success? Bankers, industrialists and the US government think it has been a triumph, with inflation cut from 5,000 per cent to 5 per cent.
That's fantastic. Any downside? Not really, apart from the endemic corruption, growing poverty, occasional riots and the fact that his sister-in-law has been charged with laundering drug money.
Oh well, you can't have everything. Isn't he a bit of a ladies' man? His wife, Zulema, stormed out of the presidential home alleging infidelity. But he says he is a seducer, not a philanderer.
What's the difference? No one has ever dared to ask.
Claim to fame: Only world leader whose name is a palindrome.
Key presidential aides: Tennis coach and two personal hairdressers.
Useful headlines: Menem the Megalomaniac. The Playboy President.
Not to be confused with: Carlos the Jackal; Eva Peron.
Most likely to say: 'Hija de puta, le vamos a dar una ostia . . . ' (translation too rude to print).
Least likely to say: 'Gotcha, Maggie.'

Paul Merton

Age: 36.

Appearance: Peeled potato; a pig (courtesy of Mrs Merton).

Trademark: Bemused vocal surrealism.

Background: Merton boy (his real name's Paul Martin – he had to change it because of Equity rules) goes from gags to riches in one night of early eighties glory at the Comedy Store. At least that's what he tells interviewers. Got two A-levels and worked in Tooting employment office.

Occupation: Funniest man on TV (*Whose Line Is It Anyway?*; *Have I Got News for You*), funniest man on radio (*Sorry, I Haven't a Clue*; *Just a Minute*; *The News Quiz*), would-be funniest man in commercials (Cussons Imperial Leather).

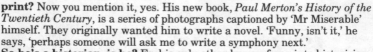

But is he the funniest man in print? Now you mention it, yes. His new book, *Paul Merton's History of the Twentieth Century*, is a series of photographs captioned by 'Mr Miserable' himself. They originally wanted him to write a novel. 'Funny, isn't it,' he says, 'perhaps someone will ask me to write a symphony next.'

So he's a historian, is he? Er, his only other known foray into historicism was a sketch based on Vinny Jones's previously unknown role in the assassination of Kennedy.

That sounds a bit far-fetched: That's not what m'learned friends said. The sketch never saw the light of day due to its alleged libellous content.

So why is he so miserable if he's so successful? All part of the persona, although breaking his leg the day after a newspaper review was published with the headline 'Go and see this man' did depress him.

He's not as sexy as Angus Deayton, is he? Suffers from 'cryptozoic pallor' but 'I've got a pulse and I appear on a prime-time slot, which by definition gives me sex appeal.' Sorry girls, he married actress Caroline Quentin in 1991, having proposed under Eros.

So is the professional cynic a romantic at heart? Gets dewy-eyed when talking about his family: says he wants his children (as yet imaginary) 'to believe in Santa Claus until they are 25'.

Sounds a bit of a joker: Professes to be 'serious'. Other guests on *Have I Got News for You* claim he is very serious – about winning.

What's the big joke then? He is the joke, dummy.

What keeps him awake at night? He claims to lie awake at night trying to guess the combined weight of the cast of *Upstairs Downstairs*.

Not to be confused with: Angus Deayton; Clive Anderson; Willie Rushton; etc., etc.

Least likely to say: 'My mother-in-law is so ugly . . .'

Most likely to say: 'But what does it all mean?'

George Michael

Real name: Yorgios Kyriacos Panayiotou. 'Yog' to his friends.
Age: 30.
Appearance: Leather, denim, shades, stubble – mummy's boy meets James Dean. Mummy won.
Occupation: Multi-platinum-selling pop singer. Does a lot of work for AIDS charities. Businessman – 'Human nature is capitalist.'
Previous occupations: Lead singer with pop duo Wham!, Andrew Ridgeley's social worker.
Andrew Who? Precisely.
Most famous for: Being Andrew Ridgeley's mate, hiring supermodels to appear in his videos, shoving shuttlecocks down his shorts for the titillation of Wham! fans.
Michael on Michael: 'I know I've tried to make everybody think I am sexy for the last 10 years but that's not what I really set out to do.'

What others say about Michael: Calculated, efficient, well-blended confection, hard-working, Thatcherite rocker, Lloyd Webber with a beard, Manilow without the nose.
The secret of his success: OK looks, the occasional good tune, the occasional good line – 'Guilty feet have got no rhythm.' You must remember, we live in an age when John Major can become Prime Minister and George Carey is Archbishop of Canterbury.
Current gig: M'lud, ladies and gentlemen, today, live at the High Court, London, England, the one, the only . . . yes, I think we get the picture.
Are there any support acts? Yes. Mr Justice Parker. Some of the best legal brains in London, half of Fleet Street, a plethora of screaming teenies and the Sony Corporation.
The Sony Corporation? George's record company. It is contesting the singer's attempt to be released from his contract with Sony. 'I have seen the great American music company I proudly signed to become a small part of a production line for a giant electronics company,' he says.
Sounds interesting, when's the live album? There won't be any albums if George loses the case. 'He will stop being a recording artist,' promises his biographer Tony Parsons.
Is that such a big loss? It will be to Sony. Michael's debut solo album *Faith* sold 14 million worldwide. The company got £3.38 for every record sold, Michael got 69p.
Not to be confused with: George Gershwin; Boy George; Michael Ignatieff.
Most likely to say: 'Wake Me Up before You Go-Go. It was a pop tune m'lud.'
Least likely to say: 'Listen Andrew, I think I've made a terrible mistake. Let's dust down our shuttlecocks and reform Wham!'

19 October 1993. Michael lost his case and was saddled with £3 million in legal costs. He plans to appeal.

Milk Tray Man

Age: 26.
Also known as: The Man in Black (MIB); Jonathan Cake, a classically trained Shakespearean actor. Previous incarnations include an actor, beach bum, miner-turned-model, and ex-art school student.
Appearance: Details are vague. Tendency to wear black, possible Gothic fashion victim. In his latest embodiment he appears as a kiss-curled, pasty-faced Vauxhall Astra owner-lookalike.
Occupation: Changing. Previously a straightforward, do-or-die deliverer of boxes of chocolates. Now redesigned (they have the technology) from rugged, macho delivery man, to younger, more approachable, modern-day romantic hero. At least that's what Cadbury's says.
Explain: In his new, more caring role, he delivers the choccies and exits via billowing net curtains. Mission accomplished, MIB arrives home to find a package waiting for him. He opens it to discover a (white) Aran jumper.
Doesn't he like chocolates then? That's not the point. The Aran jumper signifies a yearning to reject the culturally stagnant 'rebel' label imposed on him by sixties advertising executives trying to excoriate their own *alter ego*'s 'Why didn't I go to Woodstock?' guilt trips. Instead MIB wants to settle down, find a steady mate and dump his synthetic black poloneck.
We're heading for Nescafé Gold Blend's caring relationship territory? Cadbury's say they see him as a 'younger, spirited, contemporary hero paired with a successful, attractive, independent woman'.
So jumping on any more trains is out of the question then? Definitely.
But he's had an interesting bachelor life, hasn't he? Not wishing to intrude on his privacy, any comments about an alleged relationship with the Cadbury's Flake girl resulting in the disputed parentage of the Milky Bar kid cannot be printed in this newspaper.
Not to be confused with: Michael Ignatieff; Action Man; James Bond.
James Bond? His creator said of him that 'All the mums with nobody and all the girls who wanted somebody could fall for this mysterious good-looking man. In many ways, it was James Bond.'
Assignments: Leapt on to his first moving train in 1967. Went on to hang from a helicopter, dive into Malta's Blue Grotto, setting a world record . . .
Hang on. What sort of world record? Er, for Blue Grotto jumping.
What else? Swinging across city skylines suspended from crane, parachuting out of a helicopter, jumping on to a plane's undercarriage.
Did he always accomplish his mission? Er, not quite. The undercarriage stunt saw the chocolates fall into the sea.
Least likely to say: 'Who knows the secret of the Black Magic box?'
Most likely to say? 'Da-daah, da-da-da-da' (plunges into ravine).

General Ratko Mladic

Age: 51.

Appearance: Butcher.

Current job: Butcher-in-chief. He is the driving force behind the Serb military campaign in Bosnia.

Previous job: As commander of the local Yugoslav army corps, he was the driving force behind the Serb military campaign in Krajina, Croatia.

Born: Kalnovik, a Serb stronghold south of Sarajevo, in 1943.

Early experiences: His father was killed by Croatian fascists shortly before the end of the Second World War, and he spent his childhood in a region where clashes between the Croats and the Serbs were at their most brutal.

Did this affect his outlook? He has hated both Croats and Germans ever since. Believes passionately in Greater Serbia, at whatever price, and regards himself as the paramount defender of Orthodox Christianity.

What else makes him what he is? He claims that his brother's entire family were massacred last year in Sarajevo by Muslims.

Upbringing: He attended military academy in Belgrade, graduating first in his class with an average grade of 9.57.

Does that make him a brilliant military strategist? Some people just think he's mad.

Mladic on the Vance–Owen plan: 'A monstrosity with about as much chance of survival as Siamese twins.'

Is he thought to have expressed sensible views on any other subject? No.

Described by his followers as: Saviour of the Bosnian Serbs.

Described by himself as: The Napoleon of Bosnia.

Described by others as: A war criminal.

How does he plead? Not guilty. Adamantly denies the systematic abuse of the Bosnian population.

What about the Serb-run detention camps? 'Propaganda arranged by the Bush administration.'

And the systematic rape of Muslim women? 'The product of a sick mind and paid propaganda. There has never been a Muslim woman in any prison.'

Most likely to say: 'You have my word on it.'

Least likely to say: 'Allah be praised.'

11 August 1993

President Moi

Full name: Daniel T arap Moi.
Age: 68.
Position: President, since 1978, of
Kenya.
Background: A former headmaster,
he entered politics in 1957 and for 11
years was Vice-President to Jomo
Kenyatta. Initially acclaimed as a
modest, serious leader who refined
Kenyatta's autocratic grip while
managing to maintain high levels of
foreign aid. Kenya was widely
portrayed as a model for the rest of
Africa.
What went wrong? Moi became
increasingly paranoid and
autocratic. Introduced one-party rule
in 1982. Survived bloody coup
attempt same year, brought in
detention without trial and
abolished secret ballot. Re-election
in 1983 may have been helped by

absence of any opposing candidate. Once re-elected he surrounded himself
with thugs who encouraged corruption on massive scale. Amnesty
International has repeatedly criticised Moi's regime for widespread use of
torture and for killing opponents. By 1987 most leading dissidents either had
fled abroad or were locked up.
Mystery of Moi's presidency (1): Who killed the Foreign Minister, Robert
Ouko, when he threatened to blow the whistle on corruption? Ouko was shot
in the head, his body partially burned and dumped by a river bank. His death
left Moi without any obvious rival.
Mystery of Moi's presidency (2): Was the death of Bishop Alexander Muge
– another prominent critic of Moi – a genuine traffic accident or was it a
political assassination?
Who does Moi blame for the mess? 'Marxists, the rich, hooligans, drug-
pushers and tribalists.'
Friends: (1) Margaret Thatcher. Moi shared her anti-sanctions policy on
South Africa. On a visit to Kenya in 1988 she praised his 'strong and decisive
leadership within a constitutional framework . . . We admire your country's
peace and stability.' (2) Robert Maxwell. He had a major stake in the *Kenyan
Times*, which was always slavishly loyal to Moi. (3) Nelson Mandela. He
defended Moi in 1990: 'What right have whites anywhere to teach us about
democracy?'
The writing on the wall: Western donors, no longer tolerant of anti-
communist autocrats, finally pulled the plug. Moi initially branded US
Ambassador as 'a racist with a slave-owner mentality'. He soon agreed to lift
ban on opposition parties and agreed to elections.
Useful headlines when writing about Kenya: Après Moi le déluge; L'état,
c'est Moi; Paramoia.

19 November 1992. Moi won the elections in December 1992 amid allegations of
ballot-rigging.

John Monks

Age: 47.

Appearance: Boyish Third Division football manager with a sideline in cut-price insurance and cheap holidays.

Background: Unremittingly dull – son of Mancunian parks superintendent; economic history graduate from Manchester University; management trainee with Plessey; full-time TUC apparatchik since 1969; a bureaucrat's bureaucrat.

Occupation: Newly appointed TUC general secretary – not a job to be taken on lightly. Some might say not to be taken on at all.

Why so? Would you want to run an organisation with 52 disputatious bosses (the TUC General Council) which has lost 90 per cent of its influence and 40 per cent of its membership since 1979?

Was the competition for the job tough? Not unduly. Monks was the only candidate.

He must be quite something then? Not necessarily. The TUC has always conducted Soviet-style elections for its general secretary.

What are his main strengths? (1) Not being Norman Willis, widely seen as a disaster. (2) A self-effacing competence which makes John Major seem colourful and convinced the trade union barons he wouldn't steal their thunder.

Doesn't he have an alarmingly low profile for organised labour's chief of staff? Exactly. The barons want a TUC which provides a bit of training and research and leaves the serious stuff – the embassy cocktail round, TV interviews, lunches with captains of industry – to them.

What does the TUC actually do? Bit sensitive, that. It once bestrid the corridors of Whitehall like a colossus. Nowadays it tries to stop its affiliates stealing each others' members (a role the Tories have declared illegal), goes on day trips to Brussels and discourages strikes wherever possible.

But aren't strikes a good part of what trade unions are about? You must be joking! That's Jurassic Park talk. John Monks is a modern man.

Will we ever hear of him again? Certainly. 'Monks to lead TUC into 21st century' doesn't necessarily presage a Trappist takeover.

Not to be confused with: Benedictine monks, General Monk, Thelonius Monk, Bob Monkhouse.

Most likely to say: 'Steady as she goes.'

Least likely to say: 'Down tools, brothers and sisters, it's the only language the bosses understand.'

David Montgomery

Age: 44.

Appearance: Trainee undertaker.

Nickname: Used to be the Cabin Boy, because he was such a sycophant. Now Monty, though the general was thought to be a better listener.

Background: Grew up in Bangor, Co. Down, in a working-class Protestant family. Read history and politics at Queen's University, Belfast. Mirror sub-editor in Manchester; moved to the *Sun* in 1980, and then to the *People*. Edited *News of the World* and *Today*. Resigned from latter in 1991 after the paper's chaotic relaunch.

Characteristics: Workaholic, hates delegating, cool and calculating, temper always under control.

Position: Chief executive of Mirror Group Newspapers. Appointed in October 1992 to save group from post-Maxwell wreckage.

Who appointed him? The banks which hold a controlling interest in MGN.

Did the staff see him as a saviour? Not exactly. The *Mirror*'s journalists stopped production and only went back to work after a plea from editor Richard Stott (sacked two weeks later). Paul Foot described the appointment as 'one of the most shocking in newspaper history'.

What did they object to? He was too right-wing; as editor of *Today*, he called for a boycott of the *Mirror* because of its 'troops out' policy; same hire-and-fire mentality as his mentor Rupert Murdoch.

What the saviour said: 'Anyone would think I bite the heads off babies.'

Hide those babies: Said when he took over that he had no plans for editorial job cuts, that the editors of all titles would remain, and that union recognition would continue. In the following six months, more than 100 regular casuals were dismissed, scores of staff members were made redundant, *Mirror* chapel FoC Trevor Davies went, two of the three MGN editors were replaced, and most of the key editorial jobs on the *Mirror* were filled by old colleagues from *Today*.

Greatest achievement at the *Mirror*: Sales dropped 6 per cent year on year.

What people say about that: He's helped Rupert Murdoch more since he left News International than he ever did when he worked there.

Qualities he shares with the other Monty: Skinny and sharp-faced; ruthless; unremitting will; messianic vision; difficult to work with; arrogant; stubborn; cocksure.

So what's the battle plan, Monty? Attack: the group is now poised to benefit from its drive for 'quality and efficiency'.

Not to be confused with: Gay film, *David, Montgomery and I*.

Least likely to say: 'Great column today, Paul.'

6 April 1993. In April 1994 Montgomery's MGN assumed effective control of the *Independent* and the *Independent on Sunday*, provoking further cries of anguish about job losses and editorial freedom.

Sir Alastair Morton

Age: 55.

Position: Chairman of Eurotunnel.

Appearance (relaxed): Mixture of 'goody' character from 1950s Ealing comedy and Our Man in Anywhere-in-the-world from same era.

Appearance (when talking about Eurotunnel): Messianic fundamentalist, zeroing in on anyone who does not share his belief that the Channel Tunnel is the Greatest Project of the Twentieth Century.

When is he relaxed? When asleep, but has been known to talk about Eurotunnel in his slumbers.

Lineage: Born Johannesburg, the son of a Scots oil engineer father and Afrikaner aristocrat mother. Left South Africa and went to Worcester College, Oxford, as De Beers scholar. Spells working for Oppenheimer organisation and World Bank.

Politics (1): Joined the Industrial Reorganisation Council set up by the Wilson government to handle, among others, the loss-making steel industry. Fell out with the powers-that-be.

Other great fallings out: Over denationalisation of British National Oil Corporation. Said Britoil would be a disaster (correct). Over takeover of Guinness Peat by Equiticorp. Said it would be a disaster (correct), but still recommended the bid to shareholders.

Politics (2): Advised David Owen on finances of nascent SDP.

The great tunneller: Took over as head of Eurotunnel in 1986, and has since been locked in a non-stop war against Trans-Manche Link, the five British and five French contractors building it. TML has demanded £1.4 billion extra for equipping the tunnel; he says he is being ripped off. The cost of building the tunnel, meanwhile, has doubled to nearly £10 billion, and he will have to ask for another £850 million to see it through.

What his friends say about him: A visionary, intellectually honest, a great negotiator, 'the only man who can get the Channel Tunnel built'.

What his enemies say about him: Arrogant, confrontational, combative, 'the greatest single obstacle to the Channel Tunnel being built'.

Hobbies: Sailing (presumably not across the Channel); walking (with wife Sarah around Thailand); the opera (probably not the *Beggar's*); writing (to journalists who he believes have got it wrong on Eurotunnel).

Least likely to say: 'I'll leave the cheque open so you can fill in the amount.'

Kate Moss

Age: 19.
Appearance: 12.
Occupation: Model.
Tall, curvaceous, big hair? No.
Moss is 5ft 7in with bandy legs,
concave chest and split ends.
**So what are her credentials for
the job?** A bankable pout, the most
endearing lazy eye since Piggy's in
Lord of the Flies, and an ability to
look good in mimsy florals.
Background: Born in south London
(aren't they all?), spotted in a local
shopping centre looking like a
heavily sedated fawn – or as her
agent put it 'a gawky, wispy,
refreshing looking girl with
staggering cheekbones'.
Subsequently marketed as the
embodiment of fashion's New Age of
Innocence.

Old age: Shoulder pads, breast
implants, Chanel handbags, power suits, designer labels.
New age: Flares, filmy grungewear, striped tanktops, centre partings.
Career advice: Keep your kit on.
Why? Isn't nudity part of the job these days? Yes, but not when the
model has the physique of a 9-year-old. Controversy surrounds a fashion
spread in *Vogue*, featuring a childlike, passive Moss posing semi-naked in
grown-up's bras and panties. Critics accused *Vogue* of serving up a
paedophile's picnic, and presenting Moss as a role model for anorexics.
How does *Vogue* justify the photographs? 'They capture the spirit of the
moment, the move away from the work ethic to a new way of dressing.'
***Cosmopolitan* on *Vogue*:** 'The pictures are hideous and tragic. If I had a
daughter who looked like that I would take her to see a doctor.'
***Harper's & Queen* on *Vogue*:** 'When the pictures were shot, maybe they
summed up how the young felt: bleak, broke, sleeping baggy.'
Moss is certainly bleak and baggy, but is she broke? Not likely. She got
£650,000 for a Calvin Klein jeans ad, and £500,000 as YSL's Opium girl.
Products she ought to promote: Pampers, Kellogg's Pop Tarts, Nesquik.
Products she will never promote: Gossard Wonderbra, Wash 'n' Go.
Advice her parents failed to deliver: Eat your greens; cabbage makes your
hair shine; for God's sake, go outside and get some colour in your cheeks.
Likes: 'Chilling out', 'vegging out' and 'getting it together' with boyfriend
Mario Sorrenti.
Anyone we should know about? Yes. He was the gorgeous but dim one
who took his trousers off in a snooker hall for Levi Strauss.
Natural habitat: Back-to-school department at John Lewis; Thorpe Park.
Most likely bedside reading: Anything by Angela Brazil; *Bunty*.
Least likely bedside reading: *The Change – Ageing and the Menopause* by
Germaine Greer; *Fat Is a Feminist Issue*.

Mr Motivator

Age: 41.

Appearance: A Gladiator on holiday, equipped with baseball cap, bum bag and loud lycra leotards.

Occupation: GMTV's wake-up-and-dance king. Wakes up the nation from Monday to Friday with short sharp slots of grunting, grinning and general gyration.

Also known as: Mr M (to the *cognoscenti*); Derrick Evans (to his mum and dad).

Why is he in the news? His new fitness video has lunged its way to number one. Shot in Jamaica (that's the video, not Mr Motivator), *The BLT Workout* has sold 60,000 copies.

BLT? Bums, Legs and Thighs, although critics have suggested the alternative of Bloody Lousy Television.

Background: Not the clean, lean fighting machine he portrays to the nation. He left Jamaica at 10, left school at 16, and three years ago left his wife Jewel for javelin thrower Tessa Sanderson.

Is this love? Apparently not. The athletic romance finished last September.

So how did he manage to get the prestigious slot on GMTV? By breaking another woman's heart. When Tonia Czerniawskyi decided to take a well-earned holiday, Mr M was hired to fill in. He caused women round the nation to sprint to their phones pledging devotion, and the rest is hysteria. By the time Tonia returned, Mr M's £60,000-a-year feet were well and truly under the GMTV coffee table.

The fact that Mr M is personal trainer to director of programmes Peter McHugh must have helped? We couldn't possibly comment.

But surely everyone does fitness videos these days, don't they? The flow is unending. Jane Fonda is still asking the world to 'feel the burn'; Cher has launched her Step Challenge; Cindy Crawford is working out on the beach; Barry McGuigan (ex-boxer) and Sam Fox (ex-page-three girl) are boxing their way to fitness; the Calvin Klein-clad Marky Mark has challenged Britain's motivating mogul with a video and a spot on *The Big Breakfast*; and Zsa Zsa Gabor has released the only no-sweat workout.

People unlikely to make a fitness video: Luciano Pavarotti, Cyril Smith, Mr Blobby.

But Mr Blobby has already made a fitness video: Oh God, don't tell Luciano and Cyril.

Mr M's only known social comment: 'Being black was important when I was younger, but it isn't an issue for me any more.'

Not to be confused with: The Terminator.

Most likely to say: 'It's seven o'clock and I need your body.'

Least likely to say: 'I think I'll have a lie-in this morning.'

Mo Mowlam

Age: 44.
Temperament: Funny, lively,
extrovert, occasionally raucous,
popular, gabby.
Employment: Shadow Heritage
Secretary.
**Who's she expected to back in the
Labour leadership race?** No doubt
about that: Tony Blair. Some think
(or thought till yesterday) that she
might be his campaign manager.
So why are there doubts? She
admits to having shared a
conversation and coffee in a first-
class compartment on the way to the
Eastleigh by-election with John
Patten.
Is that seen as improper?
Certainly not. It's what they
discussed as the train thundered
southwards that is causing trouble.

Which was? She says it was a
general chat, nothing to do with the leadership, between Winchester and
Eastleigh – a journey which BR, or whatever it's called nowadays, times at 10
minutes. He told the morning campaign press conference that *en route* from
Waterloo to Eastleigh, Mo had told him that Blair and Cherie (Blair's missus)
were worried about whether Number 10 was big enough for themselves and
their children.
What have Mo's Labour colleagues been saying? They think Patten's a
dirty sneak. That's unanimous. But some, according to yesterday's *Times*,
'will also question whether Ms Mowlam was wise to give a political opponent
the chance to suggest that Mr Blair is so presumptuous as to be thinking
already about life inside No 10'.
And what are the Tories saying? A lot of them think that Patten's a bit of
a sneak as well.
**This Patten: isn't he the one who's always boring on about high moral
standards?** No, that's Michael Winner.
Has Mo's sportive tongue got her into hot water before? Less often than
you might think, considering she's so friendly and open. When she got the
Heritage job, she feared it meant reading the arty-sporty bits of the Sunday
papers which she'd previously thrown away. The odd aesthete shuddered.
Do I take it she doesn't spend much of her time at the Garden?
Apparently not, but she thinks that doesn't matter: the party transport
spokesman doesn't have to have form as a train spotter. Her tastes aren't
exactly grand. She supported Middlesbrough pre-Bryan Robson.
How can she ensure that such embarrassments do not happen again?
For long train journeys, she once told the *Guardian*, she likes to pick up
Cosmo, Hello! or *Prima*. From now on she'd be well advised to spend the
whole journey cowering behind them.
Least likely to say from now on: 'John! Great to see you. Sit down.
Amazing story to tell you about Tony Blair . . . '

James Naughtie

Age: 42.

Appearance: Senior chorister who has just remembered a dirty joke.

Why's he in the news? Has just had his first 3.30 a.m. wake-up call as presenter of *Today*, replacing another ex-*Guardian* journalist, the late Brian Redhead. Previously he anchored *The World at One* for five years.

I can't quite place that accent? He hails from a village in God-fearing rural Banffshire, north-east Scotland.

But he's put all that Dr Finlay stuff behind him, like all good Scotsmen gone south? On the contrary, he's an elder of the kirk, worshipping weekly *en famille* in a church conveniently close to the Royal Opera House.

How will he get on with John Humphrys, his new *Today* partner? The BBC pooh-poohs talk of rivalry but Humphrys clearly sees himself as Redhead's heir, whereas Naughtie believes 'there's no lead presenter'. Humphrys says: 'I hardly know Jim'; Naughtie says: 'I know John well.' Hands were rubbed at the prospect of *Broadcast News*-style tensions between the 'Welsh terrier' and the 'Scottish kebab cook'.

Kebab cook? Yup. In 1989 Neil Kinnock interrupted an interview with Jim about trade figures, refusing to be 'bloody kebabbed' into specifying Labour's economic strategy. The row was not broadcast, but bootleg versions circulated and Naughtie acquired a reputation as an inquisitor.

A potential radio Paxman then? No chance. Remember he spent 11 years in the lobby (for the *Scotsman* and the *Guardian*): like John Cole, and unlike Paxman and Humphrys, he actually seems to see politicians as basically decent chaps. He's tenacious but elaborately courteous; better known for long-winded, complicated questions à la Peter Jay than for going for the kill.

What about his style on Radio 3's *Opera News*? About as testing as *The Merry Widow*. Put an obese tenor or a bejewelled diva in front of him, and his critical faculties shrivel. Pavarotti fell asleep during one interview.

What to mention if asked about your close friend Jim: Sings Naughtie Scottish songs at parties; so absent-minded and disorganised his wife keeps all train and opera tickets; legendary expenses on *Guardian* resulting from fondness for lunching cabinet ministers.

Parliamo Naughtie: *The Worruld at One*; *Wooman's Hour*; *Thocht for the Day*.

Not to be confused with: Tommy Docherty; John Naughton; Richard Baker; My Naughty Little Sister.

Least likely to say: 'Just answer the sodding question, Dame Kiri!'

Most likely to say: 'I have to put the suggestion to you, Mr Humphrys, and I must ask you to be succinct, and indeed affirmative and monosyllabic, that it might be for the best, in view of all the relevant circumstances, if I were to interview the Prime Minister on this occasion, rather than, as it were, and with all due respect, yourself.'

Steven Norris

Age: 48.
Appearance: The cat who got the cream and lashings of it.
Day job: Minister for Transport in London and Tory MP for Epping Forest. Lately to be found moonlighting as Minister for Mistresses.
Background: Born in Liverpool, went to same school as Paul McCartney, built a lucrative business in second-hand cars. Voted the *Guardian*'s backbencher of the year in 1986. Has lent strong support to hanging, the poll tax, student loans and football identity cards. Passionate about animals, London's Travelcard and, it now transpires, women.

Alleged number of mistresses at time of going to press: Five.
Five? Yes. Where randy MPs normally find a single extramarital dalliance complicated enough, Naughty Nozza has exercised a plate-spinner's dexterity in keeping two mistresses and a wife on the go at the same time. Another two were dumped in quick succession for newer models (it's the car salesman in him). The fifth dumped him.
Family man? Not entirely. His wife of 24 years, an admiral's daughter and devout Catholic, Vicky Cecil-Gibson, left the family home with the couple's two sons after the revelation of his affair with mistress number 3.
Those mistresses in full: Mistress 1 – political reporter for a cut-price national paper; Mistress 2 – magazine promotions director and Norris's current main squeeze; Mistress 3 – House of Commons secretary; Mistress 4 – sales executive; Mistress 5 – knee surgeon.
Is any woman safe? According to the sales executive, he is a 'serial sex cheat. He feels he has to pull every woman he fancies.'
So he's a bit of a looker? Hardly. Six parts Jocelyn Stevens, four parts Roy Hattersley. Tom Cruise need lose no sleep.
But he must have something that women want: He drives a vulgar green Rolls-Royce, if you like that sort of thing, and all his schmoozing is conducted with a slight but alluring Liverpudlian accent.
What's his seduction technique? Corny textbook stuff involving candlelit dinners, Valentine cards, letters, flowers, outings to Annabel's, the Carlton Club and the House of Commons Churchill dining room.
Is he, as a friend of Mistress 1 put it, a total shit? No, apparently he has a caring side. Founded Crime Concern, is big on preventing alcohol and drug addiction, and was selfless enough to find time to date Edwina Currie when they were at school together.
Uses for Steven Norris should he resign in disgrace: Walk-on part as a randy fat person in *Brookside*; quiz-show host on *Come On Down (My Trousers)*; 0898 heavy breather (special responsibility, five in a bed).
Most likely to say: 'My wife doesn't understand me.'
Least likely to say: 'Back off lady, I'm a married man.'

John Osborne

Age: 63.

Appearance: Retired bank manager from Ewell.

Occupation: For the last 40 years Angry Young Man; previously actor, stagehand and reporter on *Gas World*.

Qualifications: In 1956 he wrote a famous play about ironing called *Look Back in Anger* whose anti-hero, Jimmy Porter, was furious about everything. The play was produced at the Royal Court and caused a sensation, propelling postwar British theatre out of the drawing room and into the kitchen sink.

Who liked it? Domestic appliance manufacturers and Kenneth Tynan, who declared: 'I doubt I could love anyone who did not wish to see *Look Back in Anger*. It is the best young play of its decade.'

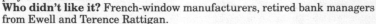

Who didn't like it? French-window manufacturers, retired bank managers from Ewell and Terence Rattigan.

What happened next? Osborne wrote *The Entertainer, Luther, Inadmissible Evidence, A Patriot for Me* and a string of flops. He made a comeback in 1992 with *Déjà Vu*, the sequel to *Look Back in Anger*.

Is Osborne Jimmy Porter? No, Jimmy Porter is Osborne.

What is Osborne angry about? Critics – 'nearly all cripples, suffering from some terrible disease'; the Irish – 'what an ugly, unpoetic, charmless, humourless, coldhearted and cowardly race they are'; the suburban-dwelling lower-middle classes – 'everything I detest'; Gays – 'fairies'; and, of course, women.

Which women? All women, but particularly his mother – 'hypocritical, self-absorbed, calculating and indifferent'; his daughter – 'a very unpleasant girl'; and his ex-wives.

On wife number three, the film critic Penelope Gilliatt: 'She was the grotesque adult embodiment of that properly despised schoolboy creature of fretful, continent ambition: a swot.'

On wife number four, Jill Bennett: 'She was the most evil woman I've ever come across – she was a bitch.'

What did Bennett think of Osborne? 'Poor old John. He's a bit potty.'

Why is he in the news? He's not, but he'd like to be. However, his 1964 play *Inadmissible Evidence* is being revived at the National Theatre.

Isn't this a bit politically incorrect for such a liberal organisation? Undoubtedly, but they're getting an avowed feminist, Di Trevis, to direct it.

Most memorable unscripted moment: Speech at the Writers' Guild awards in 1992 when he berated the British theatre as 'this horrible profession which has never been held in more contempt' before collapsing and being gently led away. Osborne's 'extensive dental work' was later held to blame.

Least likely to say: 'I'm organising a surprise party for the family at Ewell Community Centre next Saturday.'

Camille Paglia

Age: 45.

Sex: Varies. As a child, wondered if she was male or female, later discovered she was attracted to men but plumped for lesbianism. 'Officially bisexual' but only rarely in practice.

Appearance: Grumpy frump with a taste for fancy dress. 'I'm a small, rather nondescript-looking woman.' Recently presented her cleavage to readers of *Vanity Fair* – 'No one even knew I had a bosom!'

Star sign: Aries.

So what? 'I am an Aries woman like Joan Crawford and Bette Davis, we are aggressive, competitive, ready to murder the father.'

Occupation: Professor of Humanities at the University of the Arts, Philadelphia, unpaid PR for Madonna, media manipulatrix.

CV: Daughter of a professor of Romance languages, an Italian immigrant, Paglia developed her own brand of 'radical, Amazon feminism' in puberty. A militant student at Yale, she later taught for eight years at Bennington, a private college, but was asked to leave after a punch-up with a male undergraduate. During five years of exile she wrote the 700-page *Sexual Personae*, which made her internationally notorious and, once again, employable.

What's it about? Culture as a sexual battleground, in which men, struggling against nature, have created the whole of Western civilisation. To summarise: 'There is no female Mozart because there is no female Jack the Ripper.'

Whose side is she on? Men's. Particularly Aeschylus, De Sade, Nietzsche.

And against? Sloppy academics and whingeing feminists.

Such as? Foucault, Lacan, Derrida. Anita Hill, Susan Sontag, Germaine Greer, Kate Millett ('that imploding beanbag of poisonous self-pity'), Naomi Wolf ('teacher-pleasing little kiss-ass'), Susan Faludi, Gloria Steinem, Marilyn French; all women who want men to be weeds.

Politics: 'Radical sixties activist libertarian'.

Unique selling points: The only woman in the world with a good word for gang rape. Being ruder about feminists than any man has ever dared to be.

Constant companions: A knife, two black male bodyguards.

The Paglia fan club: Lauren Hutton, Norman Mailer, Nick Nolte, Annette Bening.

British equivalents: Julie Burchill? Fiona Pitt-Kethley? Er, that's it.

What she wants on her tombstone: 'She served no man.'

What she should add: 'And no women either.'

Most likely to say: 'Puh-leeese!'

Least likely to say: 'Thank you.'

Ian Paisley

Born: Armagh, 67 years ago, son of a preacher man.

Jobs: MP for North Antrim, Euro-MP for Northern Ireland, heads the Democratic Unionist Party and the Free Presbyterian Church.

Appearance: Belligerent cattle baron.

Why is he in the news? He's not, really. But he is meeting John Major for talks about talks. Unusual only for the fact that he, given more to walk-outs than walk-ins, asked for the audience.

Pet name: Wife Eileen calls him Honeybunch or My Sunshine. Others have their own ideas. He calls her The Boss.

Where did he acquire his way with words? South Wales Bible College.

What did he do with it? Launched the *Protestant Telegraph*. Published works including *No Pope Here, Mr Protestant, Paisley's Pocket Preacher*. Called Margaret Thatcher 'Jezebel' and a former Roman Catholic bishop 'the black pope of the republican movement'. The real Pope was 'the Antichrist, the enemy of Christ'.

Does he really mean it? Well, he has a sense of humour. Once called journalists 'whirring multitudes of pestiferous scribbling rodents'.

What does the family make of it? Daughter Rhonda, former mayoress of Belfast, said of boyfriends: 'They tend to rush you home by 8.30 and decline an offer to come in.'

How long has he been at it? He's been Moderator (pardon?) of his Church since 1951 and a Westminster MP for 19 years.

So he's put some time in? Yes. Six weeks in gaol in 1968 for unlawful assembly. Failed bid for incarceration five years earlier when he said he'd rather be banged up than pay £10 fine for illegal march. But anonymous admirer or member of anti-martyr tendency coughed up.

Party policies: Save Ulster from sodomy. The Treaty of Rome is the treaty with Rome. No surrender.

How long can he last? Demise predicted for years but DUP deputy leader Peter Robinson is still waiting behind cold eyes and tinted specs.

So what's his secret? Eileen's cider vinegar and honey mixed with warm water keeps the legendary larynx lubricated.

Has he ever been silenced? He went quiet for a minute or two after proposing to Eileen. Hasn't stopped buying her flowers and perfume since.

What his opponents say about him: He's an intransigent obstacle on the road to a settlement in Northern Ireland.

What his supporters say: Much the same.

Not to be confused with: Bob Paisley; Roman Catholic Bishop of Paisley.

Most likely to say: 'No', very loudly.

Least likely to say: 'Pass the port, John Paul.'

17 September 1993. The benevolence was short-lived. He attacked the government's overtures to Sinn Fein and in June 1994 described John Major as 'a fool who has allowed himself to be strung along by thugs and murderers'.

Andrew Parker-Bowles

Age: 53.

Appearance: Decent cove.

Job: Formerly Silver Stick in Waiting. Now a brigadier and head of the army veterinary service. His appointment brought about the resignation of the corps' Colonel Commandant, who thought it odd that a non-vet should be put in charge of the corps.

Background: Educated Ampleforth and Sandhurst. Commissioned into father's regiment, Royal Horse Guards. Became close to the Queen, who extended his tenure as Commander-in-Chief of the Household Cavalry from three years to five.

What does being Silver Stick in Waiting entail? Holding a silver stick at the state opening of Parliament.

Why? To guard against Popish plots. Even though he is a Roman Catholic.

Relationships: He is reported to have been 'passionately close' to Princess Anne in the early seventies.

Marriage: Married Camilla Shand, former girlfriend of Charles, 19 years ago in Guards' Chapel at Wellington Barracks. They have a son, Thomas, 18, and daughter, Rose, 14. Charles is godfather to Tom.

Nicknames: 'Barker' Bowles. 'Ernest Simpson', after husband of Wallis.

Friends: The late Lord Soames. His daughter, Charlotte Hambro. Louise Gubb, a Zimbabwean-American photographer with the Associated Press.

Obsessions: He is crazy about horses. Until recently he was more generally written about on the racing pages than in the scandal sheets. In 1991 he chaired a committee into going, watering and racing surfaces.

What does he say about his wife and Charles? His last words on the subject were last November, when he told reporters: 'It is not true. It's fiction.'

Friends say: 'He's from a bygone age – an old-fashioned soldier for whom honour is everything. You can genuinely look up to him – he's that decent.'

How does Camilla refer to Andrew in the taped conversations between her and Charles? As 'A'. Or 'It'.

Why doesn't he horsewhip Charles? Friends say he is a 'courtier in a sense that has become almost lost. His position as a favourite of the Queen carries with it a sense of duty.'

How is he taking things at the moment? 'He is feeling pretty low,' say friends. 'But his soldiers are being very supportive.' Divorce from Camilla is said to be out of the question.

Homes: A 500-acre estate 15 miles from Charles's home at Highgrove. Also has a flat in Kensington.

Car: Peugeot 405.

Clothes: Favours check shirts, cravats, waterproof trousers and Barbours.

Least likely to say: 'Just my luck to come back as a Tampax!'

Camilla Parker-Bowles

Age: 45.

Appearance: No Diana, but sexy in a knowing sort of a way.

Nicknames: The King's Mistress (among courtiers); Gladys (to Prince Charles); Soapy (at her former hairdressing salon 'because she looked like she needed a good wash').

Could do with a haircut, too? Her former hairdresser, Daniel Galvin, reportedly asked her to take her custom elsewhere because staff feared a meeting with another patron – the Princess of Wales.

Why would that be problematic? Something to do with Camilla's 23-year illicit relationship with Prince Charles perhaps.

If it's illicit how come Diana knows? She may have read extracts from a telephone call allegedly between Charles and Camilla, in which the two repeatedly proclaim their high esteem for one another and the heir declares his desire to live inside Camilla's trousers.

Presumably now the Waleses have separated, Camilla and Charles can continue their affair in peace? Not according to the Prince's friends. They say he has ended the relationship to clear his path to the throne.

How does Camilla feel about that? Gutted.

Isn't she married to Andrew Parker-Bowles, former Silver Stick in Waiting to the Queen? She is.

He must be delighted by the severance? On the contrary, the pair were said to have enjoyed 'an understanding'.

Any history of royal adultery? Camilla's maternal great-great-grandmother, Alice Keppel, was the long-time mistress of Prince Charles's great-great-grandfather, Edward VII.

Where did Camilla meet HRH? At the polo, of course.

Her chat-up line? My great-great-grandmother was your great-great-grandfather's mistress. How about it?

What does Charles see in her? 'She's great fun, oozes sexuality and has a dry and wicked sense of humour' (a friend).

Who are these friends constantly quoted in the tabloids? Good question.

Camilla's greatest achievement: 'To love me' (Charles).

Is that difficult? 'Easier than falling off a chair' (Camilla).

Other things which have their own 'gate': Water, Squidgy, Bastard.

What they say about Camilla: 'A child born with not one silver spoon in her mouth – but a whole canteen of cutlery' (biographer, Caroline Graham). 'A Sloane Ranger before Sloane Rangers were invented' (schoolfriend).

Don't say: 'I prefer Lillets actually.'

Most likely to say: 'Can I have a copy of the speech you gave today, darling?'

Least likely to say: 'Don't be such a bore.'

John Patten

Age: 47.

Silly middle name? Yes. Haggitt.

Appearance: Donnish, monk-like but faintly maniacal badger.

Background: Paradigm of self-made Tory, he is the son of a Guildford gardener. Went to Wimbledon College, then a grammar school run by Jesuits, and on to Sidney Sussex, Cambridge, to read geography. Took a PhD and fulfilled ambition of becoming an academic, spending 10 years as a geography don in Oxford. Thought that was lifetime career until decided to run for council out of a 'sense of minor public duty'. Caught the bug and entered Parliament as MP for Oxford West and Abingdon in 1983. Had ministerial spells at Northern Ireland and the Home Office but progress to cabinet slowed by his failure as crimebuster. Joined cabinet in April 1992 as Education Secretary.

Politics: Dripping wet, with occasional lurches to right over law and order and educational standards.

Is he related to Chris? No, though the two are friends, fellow Catholics and political blood brothers on the left of the Tory Party.

Family: Wife Louise is a £250,000-per-annum city management consultant who was once voted the prettiest of all Tory MPs' wives. The couple have a London flat, a house in Oxfordshire, several cats and one daughter.

Is he a hands-on father? Most certainly. He attended the birth of Mary-Claire, now a precocious, photogenic 6-year-old, and loves to be photographed walking her to her London state school. The two spend quality time at the weekends discussing theology.

How religious is he? Very. Caused concern in Tory circles in April 1992 when he argued for greater fear of hell and damnation as a tool for keeping down the crime figures.

So is he a killjoy? Far from it. He's a bit of a dandy (once spotted in the House sporting yellow socks) and a bon viveur.

Likes: Cats, good food, flashy vintage cars, 'talking with my wife' (his only stated interest in *Who's Who*).

Dislikes: Satan, in any of his myriad guises.

Has he made any major contribution to the English language? Indeed yes. He coined the phrase 'lager louts'.

Ambitious? Deeply, though hidden under jokey, self-deprecating façade.

Least likely to say: 'Put your homework down, Mary-Claire, *Gladiators* is about to start.'

20 November 1992. Now has even more time for his family, having been sacked as Education Secretary in July 1994.

Jeremy Paxman

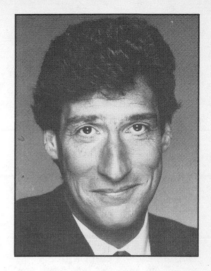

Age: 43.

Appearance: Lopsided leer and sartorial colour coordination make him classic *GQ* Man and 'thinking woman's crumpet'. Although married with one child, he still conveys smooth eligibility. Looks made for a Range Rover, but travels by bicycle.

Reputation: Languid *Newsnight* interviewer with heretical disrespect for politicians but exaggerated respect for J. Paxman.

Is he irresistible to women? Apparently not. 'He seems very pleased with himself and appears to use hairspray,' commented one non-admirer.

Does Paxman break the ice at parties? No. 'He is socially awkward – he doesn't try very hard in company. He is very shy,' said a 'friend'.

Achilles heel: Melancholy streak. Went into analysis following gruelling experiences in El Salvador and Beirut while working for *Panorama*. Complained of a 'sinking heart'.

Views: By his own admission, 'liberal, Christian and middle England'.

Why apply for membership of the Garrick Club then? Perhaps, at 43, Paxman feels a yearning for sober respectability and hopes to study Sir Robin Day at close quarters. Image of Young Iconoclast of Current Affairs TV has limited lifespan.

But surely the Garrick is stuffed with actors and elderly curmudgeons? Sir Michael Hordern says it is full of businessmen.

Why was Paxman denied admission? Hard to say. Garrick members are being frugal with the *actualité*.

Why is Paxman rude to politicians? He says: 'It's frustrating having to listen to people talk unutterable crap.'

Prominent figures upset by Paxman: Norman Lamont (asked if he would miss being Chancellor, before he'd resigned); Gerald Kaufman ('never again', he said after interview); Mrs Thatcher (deplored *Panorama* filming an IRA roadblock and giving terrorists publicity. The reporter? Paxman).

Finest riposte delivered to Paxman: 'You're full of crap, you are' (from Linda, cashier in BBC canteen, responding to Paxo's romantic overture).

Paxman's ambitions: Long term – angling and sheep farming. Possibly more books along the lines of *Friends in High Places – Who Runs Britain?*. Short term – our hero's future is cloudy in Birtist climate of BBC. The unruly Paxman is known not to be the apple of the director-general's eye.

Not to be confused with: Jeremy Beadle; Pac-Man; Trevor McDonald.

Most likely to say: 'Yesssssssss . . . , welllllllllllll . . . '

Least likely to say: 'Hello, good evening and welcome.'

8 November 1993. Shortly after being blackballed by the Garrick Club, Paxman was made an honorary member of the Garrick pub in Stockton-on-Tees. 'My life is now complete,' he said.

Pablo Picasso

Age: Lived 1881–1973.
Appearance: Haughty waiter ageing into lecherous Costa Brava deckchair attendant.
Occupation: Both painter *and* sculptor, as the new Tate exhibition shows; hailed as the greatest artist of the twentieth century.
Any dissenters? Quite a few. Evelyn Waugh and Philip Larkin thought he was mad. Winston Churchill said he would 'kick him in the something something arse' if he ever saw him. Clive James called him 'a titanically gifted child, always finding new ways of avoiding maturity'. Arianna Stassinopoulos Huffington's biography portrays him as a serial sex pest whose art was powered by a rage to destroy.
Didn't he say 'I paint with my cock'? No, that was Renoir. But one of his lovers described his idea of the happy life as 'first rape, then work'.
How can I get his wives and lovers in the right order? Try the useful mnemonic 'FElOny MaDe FiJi': Fernande, Eva, Olga, Marie-Thérèse, Dora, François, Jacqueline.
Which mistress is top of the pops? Schoolgirl Marie-Thérèse Walter has her slightly dodgy supporters, but François Gilot was intelligent, a painter in her own right and the only one to dump him. She also pioneered the thinking woman's kiss-and-tell book with *Life with Picasso*.
So what was his chat-up technique? Seeing the 15-year-old Walter emerging from the Métro, he said: 'I am Picasso! You and I are going to do great things together!' He gave the virginal Gilot a book by de Sade, and cupped her breasts while asking her to look at a huge phallic graffito. With Sylvette Davide he limited himself to 'sitting on his bed and bouncing'.
Contribution to fashion: Anticipated Elvis's tropical shirt and Jean-Paul Gaultier's matelot top; posed in his underwear 40 years before Madonna.
Contribution to feminism: I'll get back to you.
Best joke: To a German soldier, looking at a print of *Guernica*, who asked: 'Did you do this?' 'No, you did.'
Best Thought for the Day: 'A green parrot is also a green salad and a green parrot. He who makes it only a green parrot diminishes its reality.'
Record saleroom price: $51.6 million in 1989 for *Les Noces de Pierrette*, bought on the phone by a Japanese businessman while he was throwing a party in Tokyo.
Not to be confused with: Pablo Casals; Camille Pissarro; Francis Picabia; Georges Braque.
Least likely to say: 'I just can't seem to get her nose right.'
Most likely to say: 'A quick bite of Catalan sausage and beans and then back to my place?'

Mary Pierce

Age: 19.

Occupation: Saviour of women's tennis circuit hitherto boringly dominated by Steffi Graf.

Nationality: Franco-Amero-Canadian; born in Montreal, brought up in a Florida trailer park but registered four years ago to play for her mother's country (France) rather than her estranged father's (US). Hence huge support in French Championships, where she lost to Arantxa Sanchez-Vicario in the final but slaughtered Graf in the semi.

Appearance: Before: Miss Tallahassee High. Now: Eric Rohmer heroine *en fleur*.

War-cry: Before: 'Way to go, Mary Lou!' Now: 'Allez, Marie!'

French nickname: The Body.

Could you explain, monsieur?

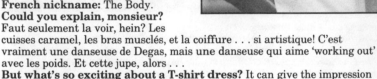

Faut seulement la voir, hein? Les cuisses caramel, les bras musclés, et la coiffure . . . si artistique! C'est vraiment une danseuse de Degas, mais une danseuse qui aime 'working out' avec les poids. Et cette jupe, alors . . .

But what's so exciting about a T-shirt dress? It can give the impression that she's forgotten to put her real skirt on.

So what's Mary's forte? She just biffs it very hard.

Harder than Gaby? Much.

Harder than Steffi? Yes.

Not harder than Monica? Even Monica.

Why is she so aggressive? The Freudian view is that her father is the unconscious target of every smashed forehand.

He's not a sweetie then? Jim Pierce has spent a total of five years in gaol for offences including armed robbery and grand larceny. From the age of 10, his daughter was hit whenever she lost. Last year he was banned from tournaments at her behest after shouting during matches ('Kill the bitch, Mary!'), fighting with her bodyguards and leaving visible bruises on her arms and shoulders.

Someone should write a novel about her: Maybe someone already has. Audrey Armat, the tennis-star heroine of *The Total Zone*, the forthcoming debut by the Czech emigré writer Martina Navratilova, is 'a combination of sugar and steel' who is brutally beaten by her father after every defeat.

Wimbledon prospects? Good; grass will favour her power game. But the Paris final suggested temperamental weaknesses.

How's Steffi reacting to her new rival? Regally. She implied that her victory was a fluke: 'You will have to give her some more time before we can talk of a Graf–Pierce rivalry.'

Not to be confused with: Gareth Peirce; Stuart Pearce; Edward Pearce.

Most likely to say: 'I'm just putting you on hold, Papa . . . Security!!'

Least likely to say: 'Come back soon, Monica, we all miss you like crazy.'

6 June 1994. Ten days later Pierce announced her withdrawal from Wimbledon 'for reasons beyond my control', widely interpreted as a reference to her father's intention to attend the tournament.

Harold Pinter

Age: Angry young 62.
Appearance: Retired prop-forward now in debt-collecting business.
Likes: Black rollnecks, cricket, behaving badly at dinner parties (typical opening gambit 'What have you done to prevent nuclear war?').
Dislikes: Americans, journalists.
Background: Born in east London, the son of a Jewish tailor. Faked a nervous breakdown in order to bunk off RADA. Aged 18, he faced two tribunals and two civil trials for conscientious objection; fined £80.
First performed play: *The Birthday Party*. Opened in April 1958. Closed after a week, but not before Harold Hobson wrote: 'I am willing to risk whatever reputation I have as a judge of plays by saying that Mr Pinter, on the evidence of this work, possesses the most original, disturbing and arresting talent in theatrical London.'
Assessment: Once a mighty and original talent famous for short angry plays (*The Caretaker*, *The Birthday Party*), he has let ranting about politics spoil his eloquence. Now a half-decent writer of screenplays.
First big payday: £5,000 in 1961 for the screenplay to *The Servant*.
Biggest ever payday: £250,000 for the screenplay for *The Comfort of Strangers*.
Recurrent themes: Nameless menace, erotic fantasy, obsession, jealousy, family hatreds, mental disturbance, the inadequacies of everyday speech, interminable pauses.
Record number of pauses: 240 in *The Homecoming*.
What people say about him: Irascible, belligerent, explosive.
What they really mean: Foul-tempered.
What people say about his plays: Haunting, enigmatic, cryptic.
What they really mean: Impenetrable tosh.
Three obsessions he should give up: (1) Writing boring celebrity letters for good causes. (2) Right-on poetry (on the Gulf War: 'We blew the **** out of them / we blew the **** right back up their own *** . . . they suffocated in their own **** . . . we blew them into ****ing **** etc.'). (3). Giving bad phone, as to Francis Bacon, who, ringing for a chat after meeting Pinter at a party, was told 'whoever you are, you can **** off'.
What he should never do: Become a Samaritan.
What he's good at: Taking the piss out of ordinary folk.
What he's bad at: Taking a joke.

4 November 1992. In September 1993, *Moonlight*, Pinter's first full-length play for 15 years, opened.

Raymond Plant

Also known as: Lord Plant,
Professor Plant, Baron Plant of
Highfield of Weelsby in the county of
Humberside.
Rarely referred to as: Ray, Prof,
Plant.
Age: 48.
Appearance: Frank Dobsonesque.
Tall, tubby, bespectacled; a bit like a
swotty yeti.
**Is that all he has in common with
Frank Dobson?** No. Both have
three children, got married in 1967
and were born in March. Neither is
keen on rave music.
Occupation: Professor of Politics at
Southampton University, *Times*
columnist, head of Labour Party
commission which has been
examining the case for electoral
reform for the past two and a half
years.
Why so long? He said: 'The fundamental issue is not so much the timetable
but trying to achieve the broadest possible consensus we can.'
So have they reached a broad consensus? No. The commission is split,
with nine in favour of a form of proportional representation and seven
supporting first-past-the-post.
How many different forms of PR are there? Almost as many as there are
countries, although the most popular ones are single transferable vote (STV),
additional member system (AMS) and the list system.
Which one did the Plant commission favour? Supplementary vote
system.
Background: 'Born and bred in Grimsby', he joined the Labour Party 31
years ago and studied at King's College, London, and Hull University. He
nearly became an Anglican priest but decided to go to Manchester to teach
philosophy instead. He has lectured at universities of Oxford, Cambridge,
Glasgow and Dublin.
Not to be confused with: Ray Charles; 'Sugar' Ray Leonard; Robert Plant;
cheese plant; egg plant.
Interests: Opera, thinking about the garden, listening to his wife play the
piano.
His colleagues say: 'A very practical man' with 'an outstanding brain', who
'never gave any indication of what his personal political views are'.
Others say: Electorally challenged.
Plant on Plant: 'I think it was possibly felt by the leadership that my
relative degree of ignorance actually assured a certain amount of
impartiality.'
Some political commentators said in 1992: The inquiry is a cynical
method of delaying any decision on proportional representation and averting
a possible internal row until after the election.
Now they think: Right first time. It was a PR job all along.
Least likely to say: 'I can't talk to you now. I'm working to a tight deadline.'

David Platt

Age: 27.

Occupation: Soccer star.

Appearance: Roy of the Rovers but more clean-cut.

Why's he in the news? Named as captain for Terry Venables's first game in charge of England, against Denmark.

Competition for the job: A convicted drunk driver (Tony Adams); a punk-rock *aficionado* who once appeared on the cover of a Lurkers album (Stuart Pearce); and a man conditionally discharged after admitting assaulting someone in the street who had insulted his sister (Paul Gascoigne).

More exotically named England captains from history: Tinsley Lindley (1888), Cuthbert Ottoway (1872), B. C. A. Patchitt (1923), Vivian Woodward (1903).

Flaw in personality: OK, it's not much, but some say he is addicted to fast food. Allegedly.

No occult or Devil-worshipping angle? None, though his match-day superstitions include wearing a horseshoe pin bought by his wife and putting his right boot on first.

Drugs? Said to have lit a patchouli joss stick in his bedroom in 1979, but didn't inhale.

Dislikes: At a wild guess, smoking and insincere people.

Other claims to fame: He is the world's most paid-for footballer, having moved from Crewe to Aston Villa (£200,000) to Bari (£5.5 million) to Juventus (£6.5m) to Sampdoria (£5.2m).

So a lot of clubs have made a lot of money? Yes. All except Manchester United (then manager: Ron Atkinson), who gave him a free transfer to Crewe after 18 months as an Old Trafford trainee.

Is he rich? Said to have accumulated £10 million from signing-on fees and endorsements. Oh, and there's his £25,000-a-week salary at Sampdoria.

Early career moves: Pondered a future in Rugby League and then wanted to be a jockey, but too fat (fast food again).

Discovered by: Graham Taylor, who took his wife on a Christmas treat to Crewe v. Newport County and was impressed. Wife left early.

Career turning point: In 1990, as an England squad player at the World Cup in Italy, he came on as a substitute against Belgium and scored in the dying seconds of extra time to see England through to the quarter-final.

How many David Platts could you get for the price of the Pergau dam? 43 (or 44 if you don't pay any backhanders).

Not to be confused with: Plato; Sylvia Plath; Paul Gascoigne.

Least likely to say: 'Thanks for the offer but I'm happy where I am.'

9 March 1994

Pontius Pilate

Appearance: Well-scrubbed hands.
Background: Upper-class twit – old school toga; married well.
Position: Governor of Judaea, AD 26–36.
Was he well qualified for the job? Eminently. His pal was Sejanus, who happened to know the Emperor Tiberius rather well. After Sejanus fell (AD 31) he was on his own in one of the most difficult Roman provinces.
Performance: Hopelessly out of touch, but clung to his job for 10 years, through good connections in Rome and a tough stance on law and order which is not entirely reflected in the Gospels. Succeeded in annoying just about everybody. Hung imperial votive images throughout Jerusalem and minted coins with classical religious devices which offended Jewish law, etc., etc.
Gospel truth? Pilate authorised the execution of Christ but the Gospels go out of their way to find excuses for him, arguing that he believed him innocent and only gave way because of mob pressure. Matthew offers staunchest defence: 'When Pilate saw a riot was beginning, he took water and washed his hands before the crowd, saying "I am innocent of this man's blood." And all the people answered "His blood be on us and on our children." '
Wide of the mark? Reliability of the accounts in the Gospels is now questioned, and it is likely that Pilate did have blood on his hands.
But didn't he do anything worthwhile? Improved hand-washing facilities by building a new aqueduct. But he used Temple funds, which caused a riot.
The last straw: Sent troops to attack the Samaritans (stroppy local sect) on Mount Gerizim in AD 36. Characteristically, they whinged to the Legate of Syria, and Rome recalled him for an early bath. Tried on charges of cruelty, oppression and, curiously enough, executing people without proper trial. Reputedly committed suicide on the Emperor Caligula's orders in AD 39.
How others see him: Regarded as a saint by the Ethiopian Church (his day is 25 June); his wife Procla (or Procula) is a Greek Orthodox saint.
Webber feat: Had all the best lines in *Jesus Christ Superstar*: 'Show to me that you're no fool, walk across my swimming pool. If you do this for me, then I'll let you go free.'
Not to be confused with: Skypilot; autopilot; Judge Jeffreys.
Most likely to say: 'Er, sorry, I'm planning to be away this Easter.'
Least likely to say: 'The buck stops here.'

Pooh

Age: 5.

Appearance: Tan and white, four legs, floppy ears, wet nose.

Sounds suspiciously like a dog. I thought Pooh was a rather stupid bear with a honey fixation: Forget A. A. Milne, we're talking serious news here. Pooh is a Jack Russell which disappeared a week ago. He has still not been found and hopes are beginning to fade.

That's terribly sad. But, compared with the carnage in Gorazde, the slaughter in Rwanda and the epoch-making elections in South Africa, it doesn't exactly set the pulses racing: The dog lovers of the press would beg to differ and have devoted acres of newsprint to the search. The *Sun* put up a reward of £500 and established a Hot Dog Line for readers to report sightings; the *Mail* is offering £1,000 for information on the dog's whereabouts.

Any leads? I hope that's not a joke.

No, sorry, inadvertent pun. Any sightings so far? The *Mail* reported one in Maida Vale.

Sounds promising: Not necessarily. The dog was lost in a forest in the middle of Scotland.

I know we're animal mad, but isn't this sort of attention a little excessive? Losing a pet is a traumatic experience. As Jilly Cooper wrote on the *Mirror*'s 'Comment' page: 'No one but a dog lover could ever understand the heartbreak and anguish you feel when your pet goes missing.'

I think you may be hiding something. Does the dog belong to somebody famous? Smart guess.

Nelson Mandela? No, not Nelson Mandela.

Michael Portillo? I think he favours Rottweilers.

Bill Clinton? He has Socks.

Dull sort of pet . . . OK, I give up. Who is it? Prince Charles. His beloved Pooh vanished during a walk at Balmoral and, despite the efforts of a pack of presshounds, hasn't been seen since.

Sounds like a job for a level-headed, experienced troubleshooter: They couldn't get anyone, but Vladimir Zhirinovsky has offered his services. A senior aide to the Russian ultra-nationalist got round a table with some prominent psychics in an attempt to track down the missing pooch.

How has Charles taken the loss of another close companion? He is mortified, according to royal watcher James Whitaker. 'Charles has bonded with Pooh, there can be no replacement,' says a reliable palace source.

How not to describe the Prince: 'One dog short of a full litter.'

Charles most likely to say: 'One's dog is missing.'

Charles least likely to say: 'Pooh, I've got a bone to pick with you.'

25 April 1994. Despite herculean efforts by legions of royal retainers, Pooh has never been found.

Michael Portillo

Age: At 39, the baby of the cabinet.
Appearance: Castilian hit man.
Background: Born in neat three-bedroom semi in suburban Stanmore cul-de-sac. Father Luis was a poet and law professor who came to England to escape Franco; mother Cora came from a Scottish Calvinist background and was a left-wing schoolteacher. A star of local hothouse Harrow County School for Boys (nickname: Polly), he went on to Peterhouse, Cambridge, where he came under the influence of Thatcherite guru Maurice Cowling. Took a first in modern history. Worked as adviser to various ministers. Won 1984 by-election and joined government as DHSS minister in 1987. Joined cabinet as Chief Secretary.
Politics: Staunch, ultra-dry, Thatcherite monetarist.
First public appearance: As the Ribena boy in a TV commercial when an adorably cute 8-year-old.
Ever made a U-turn? Yes. As an A-level student he had posters of Harold Wilson on his bedroom wall.
Family: Married to Carolyn Eadie, a high-powered City head-hunter reputed to earn upwards of £200,000 p.a. They live in Westminster; no children.
Most frequent newspaper confusion: That he went to Harrow, the posh school at the top of the hill.
Most convincing theatrical performance: The corpse in school production of *The Real Inspector Hound*.
Second most convincing theatrical performance: Explaining why ditching the poll tax was quite consistent with previous government policy.
Likes: Europe (holidays therein), 19th-century English literature, low-spending councils, good food.
Dislikes: Europe (closer links therewith), lunching, prying journalists, taking the popular line.
Ever had a proper job? Sort of. After Cambridge spent several months on graduate trainee scheme for a freight company at Heathrow. Hated it.
Manners: Overwhelmingly correct in the style of a 16th-century Spanish courtier. At Cambridge, just before starting relationship with Carolyn Eadie, travelled to Oxford to ask permission of a friend who had stopped going out with her a full year before.
Mistakes: As local government minister told party conference that poll tax would be election winner. New bouffant hairdo is in questionable taste.
Ambitious? Not 'arf.
Least likely to say: 'You know, Dad was right about Franco . . . '

12 November 1992. Given the unlikely post of Employment Secretary in July 1994. Remains the hope of the Right but gaffe quotient is increasing.

Marjorie Proops

Age: No reader or interviewer dare ask, but the charitable estimate is mid-70s. The uncharitable, like Virginia Ironside, whom she has replaced at the *Sunday Mirror*, reckon she's over 80.

Appearance: Glam granny posing as executive in a secretary's wig and Sunny Mann specs.

Position: Doyenne of agony aunts, in the *Daily Mirror* (since 1954) and now in the *Sunday Mirror* too.

Latest project: Her biography, *The Guilt and the Gingerbread*, which she authorised Angela Patmore to write.

Background: Father was a publican in Hoxton, east London. She became a fashion journalist who stayed and rose with the *Mirror*. Married (after checking that he was a Labour voter) for 53 years to Sidney Proops. One son.

Described late spouse as: Good, tolerant, patient, intelligent and sensitive. Prepared to make sacrifices, share chores, share worries, give support and encouragement.

Image: Sensible, unshockable exorciser of skeletons in the closets of the 500 to 600 people (a third of them men) who write to her every week.

Reality: Skeleton she has just chosen to reveal in her own closet is that her own marriage was such a sexual disaster that, although she decided to stay with her husband ('I couldn't bear him to kiss me: I was revolted by him'), she had a secret affair for 20 years with bachelor and *Mirror* lawyer Phillip Levy. He was an older man who died in the same year as Sidney.

What she decided to do: Keep it from the readers, even in her autobiography.

Who the doyenne of AAs could have turned to for advice: Barbara Cartland, unquestionably: she would have told Marje how to turn on her hubby by flouncing round in a pink negligée.

Achilles (high) heel: Couldn't spot a swindling, seducing, ego-bloated conman even when she was his valued colleague: completely taken in by Robert Maxwell.

What she says to a woman abandoned by her married lover: 'The other woman knows, but rarely admits, that she's an endangered species. The wife, in pole position, almost always holds the winning cards.'

Does she have a sense of humour? Apparently. Recently she told a middle-aged woman abandoned by her lover: 'And yes, toy-boys and pottery classes could be a good idea.'

What she'll never say: To teenage lads – 'Masturbation will turn the palms of your hands hairy, you little sniveller.' To bored wives – 'Always wear a see-through nightie and no knickers when you open the door to the milkman.'

Paul Raymond

Age: Old enough to know better.
Appearance: Barry Gibb in 30 years' time.
Profession: 'Tasteful adult entertainment.'
Alternative reading: Puerile smut for sexually retarded schoolboys.
Motto: 'Tits, bums and a few laughs.'
Real name: Geoffrey Quinn.
Bank balance: £1.5 billion, according to *Business Age* survey.
People he's wealthier than: Everyone in Britain.
Credit-card rating: Gold, with knobs on.
Possible alternative career: Chancellor of the Exchequer.
Background: Comes from an Irish Catholic family in Liverpool. Grandfather was a superintendent in the Liverpool police, his brother is a doctor and his mother was 'a terrible

snob' who banned the *News of the World* from the house. She wanted him to be a British Rail booking clerk but instead he spent two weeks down a mine as a Bevin Boy before joining the RAF. He swallowed vast amounts of saccharin and sliced bread before his medical, hoping to feign a temporary heart murmur, but was passed A1 fit and served two years as an RAF bandsman in Glossop. In 1952 he opened the Raymond Revue Bar. Now owns vast girlie magazine empire and most of Soho, including restaurants, nightclubs, office blocks and a cinema.
West End plays he's produced: *Pyjama Tops, Let's Get Laid, Anyone for Denis?*
Previous incarnations: One-half of a clairvoyant act called Mr and Miss Tree (mystery – geddit?). Ran market stall selling combs, nylons and hairnets.
Nicknames: Sexploiter, Skin Merchant, Smut Merchant, Sex King, Strip King, King of Tease, King of Sleaze.
Most imaginative and expensive sexploit: Trained a dolphin to strip Miss Nude International of her bikini ('You put a piece of fish on the bra hooks').
What did it cost? Onstage swimming pool, £45,000; dolphin's offstage dressing-room pool, £7,000; a lift to move it about, £15,000.
Philosophy: 'I buy birds rather like buying goods in a shop. Shoes if you like.'
Favourite birds: Trixie Kent, Mika Mingo, Bonnie Bell, the Ding Dong Girl, Tempest Storm, Cheri Thunder, Melody Bubbles.
Sex: 'There'll always be sex – always, always, always.'
Lies: 'I have a lot of respect for women.'
Videotape: You want 'em? He's got 'em.
Least likely to say: 'I respect you as a woman.'

John Redwood

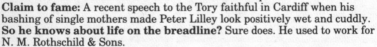

Age: 42.

Appearance: Mr Spock with surgically corrected ears. Some say a Dalek, minus the long front bit, in a well-cut suit. Anyway, genuinely scary eyes with a voice to match.

Occupation: MP for Wokingham, doubling as Secretary of State for Wales. Continues the long tradition of English Tory placemen running Wales, following in the footsteps of David Hunt, MP for Wirral West, and Peter (now Lord) Walker, formerly MP for Worcester.

Background: A former fellow of All Souls. Loyal Thatcherite who headed the Downing Street policy unit in the mid-eighties.

Qualifications for the Welsh job: Has spent holidays in Wales and claims to have legged it up a few mountains. Luckily, he has a streetwise team which can chauffeur him round the place.

Claim to fame: A recent speech to the Tory faithful in Cardiff when his bashing of single mothers made Peter Lilley look positively wet and cuddly.

So he knows about life on the breadline? Sure does. He used to work for N. M. Rothschild & Sons.

What provoked him: Observed to be grinding his teeth while visiting St Mellons housing estate near the Welsh capital when told of the high concentration of single-parent families.

He's not a one-parent family himself, is he? Certainly not, strongly nuclear: happily married with a son and a daughter.

Any other problems associated with the Welsh job? Numerous. Sorting out local government reorganisation, which has enraged the Taffia. Learning to pronounce names like Pwllheli and Ynysddu so that the locals don't fall about. Remembering to pop an AA handbook in his Red Box.

Any pluses? His experience as a banker could be useful – advising redundant miners how to charm a loan from Jones the Bank, for example.

And he loves the language: 'I'd like to learn a little Welsh but I have a very heavy workload.'

Will he get a welcome in the valleys? Most unlikely, since Tory votes are almost as scarce as Redwood smiles.

At least his colleagues like him: Arguable. When he was appointed to the cabinet, one was quoted as saying (off the record of course): 'We want fewer swivel-eyed ideologues, not more.'

And the press? Even the *Yorkshire Post* dubbed him 'the Pol Pot of privatisation'.

Least likely to say: 'The welfare state must look after people from the cradle to the grave.'

Most likely to say: 'Is this the road to Abertillery?'

Oliver Reed

Age: 55.
Appearance: Bill Sykes.
Occupation: 'Swashbuckling'
(euphemism for getting pissed a lot)
and acting.
Background: Born in Wimbledon,
the son of a racing correspondent;
expelled from various schools,
worked in a seed factory before doing
National Service; dyslexia prevented
him from staying in the forces. Was
a boxer, a bouncer and an extra
before his career took off in the
sixties, since when he has appeared
in more than 75 films. Big break was
appearing naked in *Women in Love*.
**Why is he in the nude, sorry
news?** He's just been cleared of
throwing his stunt double, Reg
Prince, over a balustrade in a
drunken rout during the filming of
Castaway in the Seychelles seven
years ago.

Was that in the script? No. They were in the middle of dinner, actually.
And there was an argument? The circumstance are a little hazy.
How come? According to the judge, Mr Justice Owen: 'The drunk may not
only remember poorly, he is also likely to remember selectively.'
Oliver's a bit of a lad then? You could say that.
And someone to avoid sitting next to in restaurants? At a *This Is Your
Life* dinner, he was sick over a table and had to be removed.
Does he have a drink problem? The only problem is deciding whether to
have a double or a treble.
Does he plan to stop drinking? He claims he would rather die. In fact, it is
surprising that he has not already done so, since the *Sun* reported that he
had only two years to live – in 1987.
Examples of his barmy behaviour please? Frequently appearing drunk
on television chat shows; encouraging like-minded pal Alex Higgins to down
a glass of Chanel No. 5; having bird claws tattooed on to his penis; smashing a
hotel window; appearing in Ken Russell films.
So he has his quirks? 'I accept I am a bizarre character.'
But he remains an optimist: He wants to be remembered 'with a smile'.
And his swashbuckling wows the women? Amanda Donohoe on *Castaway*
wasn't too impressed when he accused her of 'twittering' and bared himself on
the beach, but on the whole he's pretty popular.
Married? Yes, for the second time. Number two, Josephine, is a mere 28 – he
started seeing her while she was still at school.
Not to be confused with: Austin Reed (different sort of suits).
Most likely to say: Something slurred.
Least likely to say: 'Mere alcohol doesn't thrill me at all . . .'

Lord Rees-Mogg

Age: A smug 66.
Appearance: Smug prelate.
Personality: Smug.
God: Devout Roman Catholic.
Mammon: Monetarist convert.
Likes: Alexander Pope, *'Allo 'Allo*, money.
Dislikes: John Major, atheism, the *Guardian*'s 'shallow and sentimental' ideology.
Nickname: Moggadon Man.
Profession: 'I am a pillar of the Establishment, but I don't have a great deal of power.'
Meaning? 'I am merely an elderly crossbench peer who occasionally votes to amend government legislation.'
Interfering then? Just so. After preaching and soothsaying, interfering is what Lord Rees-Mogg loves most and does best. That's why he wants to take the government to court, to stop Maastricht.
Moggadon Man's qualifications for interfering: Exemplary. Charterhouse head boy, president of Oxford Union, editor of the *Times*, unsuccessful Tory candidate, High Sheriff of Somerset, vice-chairman of the BBC, chairman of the Arts Council, antiquarian bookseller, life peer, chairman of the Broadcasting Standards Council, author and now *Times* columnist.
What about the common touch? No problem. Once he met a 'black boy' who said: 'It must be grand to be a lord.'
Critics say: 'The authentic voice of the Patrician Tendency – pure snobbery.'
Fans say: Ditto.
Somerset wisdom: 'Anyone who wants to be a millionaire can be.' 'When you are a boy, cricket matters.' 'I think it is a good thing, the Establishment.' 'We need saints.'
But didn't he support Rupert Murdoch? Yes.
And Richard Nixon? Yes.
And mistrust Keynesianism because of Keynes's homosexuality? Yes.
And agree, in principle, to lend his name to a violent computer game called 'Mogg-Man'? Yes.
So why is he taken seriously? Because Rees-Mogg is a spiritual seer with unique historical vision. Looking back, he can even remember the ice cream cake he ate on the eve of the Second World War. Looking forward, he sees extinction: 'If we are lucky, mankind as it is has about 50 years left.'
Gloomy, huh? Not if we bathe, with Lord Rees-Mogg, in the blood of the Lamb: 'The only people who are really without hope are those who have cauterised their religious feeling.'
A note from Alexander Pope: 'Scarfs, garters, gold, amuse his riper stage, / And beads and pray'r-books are the toys of age: / Pleas'd with this bauble still, as that before; / Till tir'd, he sleeps, and life's poor play is o'er.'

19 July 1993. A month later Rees-Mogg dropped his legal action to block ratification of the Maastricht Treaty.

Sir Bob Reid

Age: 58.
Appearance: Scottish football manager after a difficult season.
Position: Chairman of British Rail since 1990.
Background: Born in Cupar, Fife, the son of a butcher. At the age of 9, he lost his right arm in an electric mincer at his father's shop while cutting a joint of beef. Within two weeks had learned to write with his left hand. Studied history and politics at St Andrew's, winning a golf blue and getting his handicap down to four. Joined Shell as a graduate trainee and stayed for 30 years, spending spells in Brunei, Nigeria, Thailand and Australia. Became chairman and chief executive of Shell UK in 1985.
Was he first choice for the BR job? No, Lord King and Colin Marshall were approached, but were put off by the paltry salary (£200,000).
Declared aim when he took over: 'I want to make the trains run on time.'
Key policy in meeting objective: Extending the timetabling hour on some lines to 66 minutes – immediate improvements.
Undeclared aim: Privatising BR in line with government policy.
But does he really want to do it? Of course not. He once described it as a pantomime, is convinced it will mean a worse service for passengers, and believes private companies will put profit before reliability and safety.
Bob's philosophy: 'The railway should meet social needs as well as economic needs.'
Bob's grouse: 'Give me the Italian subsidy and everyone could travel for free. And I would give the passengers a tenner at Christmas.'
So he agrees with Jimmy Knapp? Not exactly. They're on shouting rather than speaking terms, with Reid opting for a public demonstration of macho management. 'The union wanted jobs for life and they wanted to put unacceptable restrictions on the use of contractors. I decided it was time for some straight talking.'
At least that should please the government: It may be too late. After his attacks on privatisation, he was rubbished by 'sources close to the Department of Transport' who said he had gone native and was talking nonsense.
Commuter belters: A group of Conservative MPs in the South-east have led the attacks, arguing that privatisation will improve the quality of service. Such was the level of public hostility when Reid travelled on the Southend to Fenchurch Street route that he had to be accompanied by a bodyguard. This may have been because Sir Bernard Braine and Teresa Gorman were waiting for him at the end of the line.
Future prospects: Less time on platforms; more time on greens.
Not to be confused with: Sir Robert Reid, his predecessor at BR.
Least likely to say: 'Don't worry, you can always call a cab.'

16 April 1993

Albert Reynolds

Age: 61.
Appearance: Ageing country-and-western singer with sunbed.
Occupation: Prime Minister and leader of Fianna Fail (Soldiers of Destiny) party.
Isn't he called the Teashop? No Taoiseach, stupid. It's an old Gaelic title for a clan leader, adopted in the 1930s when such terms were briefly fashionable in European politics.
Previous occupation: Dancehall owner. First step up political ladder was a plan to fly wild salmon from Longford to restaurants in Dublin.
Why is he in the news? He's meeting John Major in Dublin to bring peace to Ireland after 900 years of strife. If all goes well they'll squeeze in a bit of golf after lunch and then go ceilidh dancing with Paisley and the Pope.

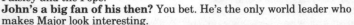

John's a big fan of his then? You bet. He's the only world leader who makes Major look interesting.
So his words aren't spoken by an actor on TV? No, but his handlers wish they were.
Surely being Irish he has a way with words? Straight from the Dan Quayle Speech School, I'm afraid. Surprised the Dail recently by saying that he would work for the 'cessation of peace in Northern Ireland'.
So how did he get where he is? By being a 'cute hoor'.
What, you mean he put on a short skirt and slept with Charles Haughey? No, that's what the breed of pragmatic parish-pump politicians who have run the South for the last 30 years are called.
You mean they promise heaven and earth to get elected and then don't deliver? You're getting the idea.
And the people keep electing them? Not any more, it seems. After a string of corruption scandals, Reynolds's party was forced into coalition earlier this year with Dick Spring's Labour Party, which had campaigned to clean up the corridors of power.
Political style: Back-slapper, the last man to leave the party.
He takes a drink then? No, he's a teetotaller.
Has the man no vices at all? He did once tell a journalist he personally tasted all his company's products before they left the factory. His firm makes dog food.
Secret of his political success: Staying sober in Irish politics.
Political philosophy: What would that be now?
Not to be confused with: Burt Reynolds.
Most likely to say: 'You finish that bottle of Jameson's first, John, and then we'll talk about peace.'
Least likely to say: 'I think we should re-examine this issue from a post-structuralist perspective.'

3 December 1993. On 15 December Reynolds and Major signed Joint Declaration on the future of Northern Ireland.

Sophie Rhys-Jones

Age: 28.
Appearance: Strong teeth, strong jawline, strawberry blonde, blue eyes, dimples, fresh-air complexion.
Occupation: Public relations consultant to small west London firm.
Prospects: Reportedly due to announce engagement to rookie theatre producer, aged 29, who's third in line to multi-billion-pound fortune but with poor prospects of succession. He has healthy elder brothers, long-lived mother and gran.
Wait a moment, he's that Prince Edward, isn't he? Afraid so.
What's he done to be worth another Pass Notes so soon? Getting spotted with a detective picking up Ms Rhys-Jones in his Rover from 'a dingy terrace block in west London' at 7.40 p.m.
So what? Well, they did arrive at Buckingham Palace at eight o'clock. They enjoyed a candlelit supper. The detective was given the rest of the night off.
And? 'At one in the morning the lights were still on in the corridor leading to Prince Edward's second-floor apartment at the palace.'
Does that mean hanky-panky? Judge for yourself. 'While I counted Sophie out of her west London flat, I did not count her back in again . . . Next morning at 8.32 a.m. a chauffeur-driven car drove Sophie to her offices.'
Doesn't Buckingham Palace have guest rooms? You shouldn't ask royal-watchers to raise that sort of point. But this one says this 'pattern was repeated throughout December. The conclusive evidence for me is what I saw with my own eyes.'
Who says this? The Diana book 'millionaire' Andrew Morton, in a *News of the World* three-page spread. The fact it's Morton, who gave us the 'truth' about the Princess of Wales, gives it more credence than most *NoW* stories.
Is there a tittle of substantiation? They met last summer when she helped him organise press coverage for the Prince's Summer Challenge, part of the Duke of Edinburgh Award scheme. He posed with her for a publicity picture, displaying the strong teeth.
What's the rest of the media think? The Press Association news agency, part of the media camp outside the house yesterday, reported: 'Any move to Buckingham Palace would be a huge step up for Miss Rhys-Jones.'
Isn't the Prince supposed to be gay? No solid reasons have emerged for supposing that and he's angrily denied it on the few occasions the question's been put. It's imprudent to believe all the gossip you hear.
Not to be confused with: Romy Aldington; Alison Beil; Eleanor Weightman; Ulrika Jonsson; Georgia May; Marsha Bland; Princess Elena of Spain; Astrid de Schooten Whettnall – or any other previous girlfriend.

Stella Rimington

Age: 57.

Appearance: Shirley Williamsish except when wearing false beard, when she resembles Rolf Harris.

Job: M.

Background: Born in South Norwood, London, only daughter of David Whitehouse. Educated at Crosslands convent in Barrow, where her father was a draughtsman at Stanton steelworks. Went on to fee-paying Nottingham High School for Girls, and to Edinburgh University, which listed her profession after she graduated (second-class honours in English) as 'archivist'.

OHMSS: Has worked for MI5 for the past 23 years. Earned her spurs as head of F2 branch, responsible for monitoring domestic 'subversives', including trade unions. According to Tam Dalyell she played an important role during the 1984 miners' strike which led to MI5's biggest telephone-tapping operation. She was promoted to direct counter-terrorist activities in the late 1980s when the agency began to shift resources from anti-subversion. Director-general since 25 February 1992. In charge of an estimated 2,000 full-time staff – more than half of whom are women – and an annual budget of over £300 million. Salary about £80,000.

Relationships: Married to, but separated from, John Rimington, director-general of the Health and Safety Executive. Two daughters, Sophie, studying anthropology, 21, and Harriet, 19.

What does her husband say about her? 'There is not the slightest prospect of Stella and I getting divorced. We are extremely good friends. She is a very kind and straight person and the country is fortunate in having her services.'

Manner: Down-to-earth charm which belies a taste for empire-building. Peter Wright, author of *Spycatcher*, said there were two types of women in MI5, the silly debutante and the matron. He saw Stella as the latter: a wearer of solid shoes and thick stockings who devotes her life to the service.

Shops: At M&S. Dresses at Jaeger.

Reputation: Shrewd, unpretentious, but bullish Whitehall infighter. Tireless analyser of files.

Not likely to be confused with: Mata Hari.

Biggest success so far: Taking over the Met's lead role in countering IRA activities on mainland Britain, a move which angered Scotland Yard.

Biggest challenge: Dragging MI5 into the real world, and opening it up to democratic scrutiny. Catching members of the IRA .

Most unbelievable initiative so far: Visit to Moscow in September 1992 to advise the Russian Ministry of Security on how to be more open.

Biggest fear: Being photographed.

Least likely to say: 'Tell Tina it's the cover story or nothing.'

Tim Robbins

Age: 33.

Appearance: Sacked Eurobond dealer turned wine bar proprietor. Fleshy-faced Tefal head on gangling 6ft 4in frame. So poor he wears suits from his films. No Warren Beatty.

Key facts: Currently Hollywood's Midas touch on the strength of two politically correct satirical classics inside six months: the first notable for cameo performances by 65 Hollywood stars and the second because he wrote, directed and acted in it. Compared to the young Orson Welles.

Key words: Integrity, compromise (no), sacred cows (no), irreverent, satire, iconoclastic, excoriating, *enfant terrible*, mokumentary, coruscating.

The films: *The Player*: coruscating satire on the ruthless politics and moral bankruptcy of show business in Hollywood. *Bob Roberts*: coruscating satire on the ruthless show business and moral bankruptcy of politics in Pennsylvania.

What the critics say: Oliver Stone with a sense of humour. The man of the moment. The man of the hour. The man. A puckish commanding presence.

What the audience say: Is that the end? Who did it then? Didn't you see his foot move? Do you know he even held the camera himself?

Better to say: 'I heard Warren Beatty was furious he wasn't asked to be in *The Player*.'

On no account say: 'Isn't he the Texan billionaire with the ears?'

Secret of his success: So unexceptional looking he must be a good actor. Drives a Volvo. Doesn't live in LA. Thank God it's not Kevin Costner again.

Tim's radical ideas: There are no heroes/happy endings/sacred cows.

Tim's friends: Robert Altman (director of *MASH* and *The Player*), Alan Rickman.

Tim's enemies: George Bush, Warren Beatty.

The trouble with Tim: Not enough space on cinema hoardings to fit all the eulogies. Liberal critique unfocused and occasionally crude. Wry, enigmatic look could just be vacuous. Firmly hitched (Susan Sarandon).

Upcoming projects: *The Plumber*: coruscating satire on the ruthless politics of the water business with Anthony Hopkins, Arnold Schwarzenegger and Madonna as extras. *George Bush*: satirical mokumentary on failed right-wing politician attempting to become a folksinging stock-market dealer.

Least likely to say: 'Hasta la vista, Baby.'

Katie Roiphe

Age: 25.

Appearance: Skinny, curly-haired Jewish-American princess.

Occupation: PhD student at Princeton who took time out to write a slim treatise on the non-existence of date rape, *The Morning After: Sex, Fear and Feminism*, in which she says women are making victims of themselves.

Date rape? That's the one where No means Yes and you ring your lawyer in the morning? No, it's the one where your date buys dinner and you're the pudding.

Any British examples? Yes, the case of the solicitor Angus Diggle, who spent £200 on his dancing partner then attempted to rape her while she was sleeping. He got three years in prison. A classic example.

What about Austen Donellan? I'm glad you mentioned him. He was the King's College student who had sex with a semi-comatose drunken female student. She attempted to have him punished by the university authorities, but he insisted the case went to court and was cleared. Caused a media storm.

So why all the fuss about an American book on date rape? Exactly. Roiphe's book is all but untranslatable to this country. She rants against feminist orthodoxy taking over the East Coast Ivy League campuses, citing the blue lights campaign (ever heard of it? Actually it's an emergency phone system on some American campuses) and take-back-the-night marches (which flopped for lack of interest in this country) as examples of anti-male paranoia.

What, another loud-mouthed American telling her British sisters how to do it for themselves? Yes, she joins the ranks of Camille Paglia, Naomi Wolf and Susan Faludi, backed up by second-wave figures like Gloria Steinem and Betty Friedan.

How did she go down on home territory then? Badly. The *New Yorker* said: 'The book is a careless and irresponsible performance, poorly argued and full of misrepresentations, slapdash research and gossip.'

Didn't anyone like it? Camille Paglia said: 'Here is a voice from inside saying all the things I had said. Suddenly I'm off the hook.'

If it's so limited in scope and was so badly received in the States, why was it even published here? It's the same old story. America throws up professional shit-stirrers like Roiphe all the time. British publishing companies latch on to such personalities for controversy value, which usually equals high sales. And the media fall in behind, because they love to see women tearing each other apart. British feminist writers never get the same treatment, more's the pity.

Least likely to say: 'All men are rapists.'

Most likely to say: 'Oh stop whingeing. The rugby team just wanted a bit of fun.'

Salman Rushdie

Age: 46.
Appearance: Overweight, balding with hooded eyes and a beard, which may or may not be false.
Pronounced: Salmaahn.
Early life: Born Bombay. Educated Rugby and Cambridge.
Early career: Started life as a copywriter for Ayer Barker, where he dreamed up 'Delectabubble' (Aero) and worked on the Burnley Building Society account. Responsible for the slogan 'Better Save than Sorry.' Also wrote the jingle: 'Dreamin' 'bout a pile of money / Dreamin' 'bout wedding rings / When you're saving with Burnley Building Society / That's where your dreams begin.' Shortly after this he decided to become a novelist instead.

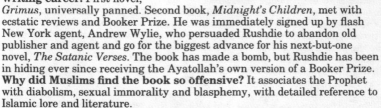

Writing career: First novel, *Grimus*, universally panned. Second book, *Midnight's Children*, met with ecstatic reviews and Booker Prize. He was immediately signed up by flash New York agent, Andrew Wylie, who persuaded Rushdie to abandon old publisher and agent and go for the biggest advance for his next-but-one novel, *The Satanic Verses*. The book has made a bomb, but Rushdie has been in hiding ever since receiving the Ayatollah's own version of a Booker Prize.
Why did Muslims find the book so offensive? It associates the Prophet with diabolism, sexual immorality and blasphemy, with detailed reference to Islamic lore and literature.
Friends of Rushdie: Bill Buford, Gillon Aitken (agent), Harold Pinter, Michael Ignatieff, Francis Wheen, Matthew Evans, James Fenton.
Enemies of Rushdie: President Rafsanjani, Edward Heath, Toby Jessel, Kalim Siddiqui, *Esquire* magazine, Marianne Wiggins, Norman Tebbit.
Luvvies for Rushdie: Norman Mailer, Mario Vargas Llosa, Nadine Gordimer, Peter Carey, Fay Weldon, Melvyn Bragg.
Golf club view of Rushdie: 'He knew damn well what he was doing . . . I find his books unreadable myself . . . He always used to slag off Britain, he should be bloody grateful for our bobbies now.'
Groucho Club view of Rushdie: 'His novels are a violent reaction against the littleness of English fiction . . . If he didn't have a foreign name the Tories would have been right behind him.'
So does he lead a life of solitude? Not exactly. He makes it to a fair sprinkling of dinner parties, book launches and book signings. He has travelled to America, Germany, Ireland and Denmark. He even appeared on *Wogan* and found time to become engaged to a former publisher.
Least likely sequel: *Buddha, You Fat Bastard.*
Least likely to say: 'I hear Mecca's very nice at this time of year.'

Ken Russell

Age: 65.

Appearance: Trainee Father Christmas with a drink problem.

Obsessions: Composers, sex, prostitutes, suspenders, death, masturbation, madness, nudity, D. H. Lawrence, Glenda Jackson, Oliver Reed, Alan Bates, English countryside, naked composers masturbating madly on misty mornings in rural settings.

Before discovering nudity: Served in the RAF, ballet dancer, actor, photographer, maker of sensitive films for the BBC.

Best films: *The Music Lovers*, *Women in Love*, everything he made for *Monitor*.

Worst films: *Whore*, *Valentino*, *Lair of the White Worm*.

Most famous scenes: Oliver Reed and Alan Bates grappling nude in

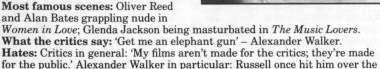

Women in Love; Glenda Jackson being masturbated in *The Music Lovers*.

What the critics say: 'Get me an elephant gun' – Alexander Walker.

Hates: Critics in general: 'My films aren't made for the critics; they're made for the public.' Alexander Walker in particular: Russell once hit him over the head with a rolled-up copy of the *Evening Standard*.

Other job: Was briefly opera critic of the *Evening Standard* but sacked for leaving at the interval of *William Tell*.

On actors: Meryl Streep: 'an android'. Harrison Ford: 'an extra in a big hat'. Richard Dreyfuss: 'more concerned with his hair than the story'. On producers: 'We're working for gangsters.'

What his second wife says: 'Ken is my anchor. I like to take my ship on wonderful stormy seas but I always come back to my mooring.'

What his third wife says: 'Ken is my anchor . . .'

Philosophy: 'I think most men would be liars if they said they didn't want to make love to an air hostess.'

How you'd recognise him: Red face, red fingernails, red toenails, striped trousers (red optional).

Hobbies: See obsessions.

Recent projects: *Princess Ida* ('a riotous romp' – ENO blurb). *Lady Chatterley's Lover* for the BBC (unexpurgated). *The Secret Life of Arnold Bax* for the *South Bank Show* (English composer, obsessed with sex, nudity, madness, countryside, etc.).

Future projects: Life of Scriabin ('He composed this great erotic symphony for a 250-piece orchestra, 300 dancing girls, 500 chorus . . . ').

Most overused description: 'The *enfant terrible* of British cinema'.

Jimmy Savile

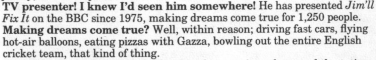

Age: 67.

Appearance: Zany Radio 1 DJ who went into the jungle 25 years ago and only came back last week. No one has told him the sixties are over.

Fab gear: Gold lamé tracksuits, trainers, improbably blond hair, chunky gold rings, cigar, spectacles retrieved from Elton John's dustbin.

Status: Roman Catholic, member of Mensa, confirmed bachelor. 'I quite envy people who have been in love and would be perfectly happy to fall in love today. But how could I, with my lifestyle?'

Occupations: Miner, wrestler (107 fights, won 7), professional cyclist, marathon runner, fund raiser for Stoke Mandeville Hospital (some £30 million over two decades).

Is that it? . . . part-time adviser to minor royalty (Duchess of York), chairman of the advisory committee at Broadmoor special hospital, disc jockey, television presenter.

TV presenter! I knew I'd seen him somewhere! He has presented *Jim'll Fix It* on the BBC since 1975, making dreams come true for 1,250 people.

Making dreams come true? Well, within reason; driving fast cars, flying hot-air balloons, eating pizzas with Gazza, bowling out the entire English cricket team, that kind of thing.

A winning formula? Indeed. The show has consistently topped the ratings and made him a national institution.

If it ain't broke don't fix it? Not in Sir James's case. He is stepping down as presenter at the end of the next series.

Not another victim of the new BBC regime's vendetta against elderly DJs? Perish the thought. We owe a great debt to him for all his BBC work and wish him well for the future. We trust we shall be his first port of call when he has new ideas to discuss, said BBC managing director Bill Wyatt.

Favourites to take over: Graham Taylor, Norman Lamont, Boutros Boutros-Ghali. Turnip'll fix it, Norm'll fix it, Boutros'll fix it? On second thoughts, perhaps not.

Jim's gongs for services rendered: OBE, knighthood, papal knighthood, gold and bronze medals (St John of Jerusalem), male jewellery wearer of the year award.

Future projects? Unclear but unlikely to involve *The Clothes Show* or *Newsnight*.

Not to be confused with: A Savile Row suit.

Most likely to say: 'Now then, now then. What have we 'ere then? Owowowowowow. How's about that then?' Any combination thereof.

Least likely to say: 'You want to do what? Sorry mate, can't help you there.'

Arthur Scargill

Age: 55.

Appearance: Ageing monarch of ancient English kingdom. Original carefully coiffured ginger hayrick now too thin to cover increasing bald pate. Has a noticeable twitch which, when he's animated, goes with a fanatical gleam in his eyes and thrusting rigid index finger. Only trade union leader who still gets standing ovations.

Background: Born in Worsbrough near Barnsley and started work at Woolley colliery when he left school. Mother died when he was 18. Joined the Young Communist League but, unlike his father, never joined the adult Communist Party.

Occupation: President of the National Union of Mineworkers. Legally he should have stood for office again in 1993, but nobody has

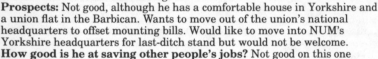

challenged him. Probably nobody cares. When the final pit closes, he will be the last one left to turn out the lights.

Prospects: Not good, although he has a comfortable house in Yorkshire and a union flat in the Barbican. Wants to move out of the union's national headquarters to offset mounting bills. Would like to move into NUM's Yorkshire headquarters for last-ditch stand but would not be welcome.

How good is he at saving other people's jobs? Not good on this one either. Since he became NUM president in 1982, 130,000 miners have lost their jobs.

Is he a good tactician? You must be joking. He was the man who called the 1984 miners' strike at the end of the winter when coal stocks were brimming over and the Nottinghamshire miners stayed at work. He has presided over a decline in NUM membership from 250,000 to under 25,000.

Most famous foreign contact: During the seven-month-long 1984–5 strike he dispatched an emissary to Libyan dictator Colonel Gaddafi.

Enemies: Michael Heseltine, moderate trade unionists and a litany of names too long to list.

Friends: The outraged middle class of middle England (in the winter of 1992, they took to the streets over pit closures; but they have gone a bit quiet now the pits are closing more slowly).

Nicknames: Expletive deleted; Our Arfur, King Arthur, That Man.

Greatest achievements: Retaining a place in the heart of the nation; forecasting pit closures accurately; outlasting Thatcher, Kinnock and Coal Board chairman Ian MacGregor.

Favourite pastimes: Having his portrait painted, slagging off the nuclear industry, baiting journalists and waiting for martyrdom.

Motto: 'I did it my way.'

Least likely to say: 'I'm sorry about the strike.'

Arnold Schwarzenegger

Age: 45.

Nickname: The Austrian Oak.

Background according to Arnie: Brought up in rural bliss in Austria where years of determination transformed him from sickly wimp to the youngest ever Mr Universe in 1967.

Background according to unofficial biography by Wendy Leigh: Son of a Nazi, he had a miserable childhood in East Germany and became a champion bodybuilder only because he took steroids from the age of 13.

Appearance: Concrete outbuilding with a policeman's haircut.

Accent: Despite 20 years of elocution lessons he still speaks the kind of joke German suggestive of Lurch strayed on to the set of *'Allo 'Allo*.

Political ambition: A modest one – to become President of the USA.

Bad political career move (1): Married John Kennedy's niece, Maria Shriver.

Bad political career move (2): Admitted smoking marijuana – and inhaling.

Awards to date: Mr Europe, Mr Olympia, Greatest Body in the Galaxy, Most Violent Actor of 1988 for 146 acts of brutality an hour in *The Running Man*.

Most obscene act: Delivering several speeches from Hamlet in his new film.

Best known for: Wearing bullet belts and murderous expressions like the rest of us wear M&S knickers; homicidal robotic roles (*Terminator*, etc.).

But isn't unrelenting violence a bit old hat? Yes, which is why Arnie's image has been readjusted to represent a gentler approach for the nineties with *The Last Action Hero*. After copious rewriting to edit out a plethora of violence and anal jokes, it tells the story of a young boy's adventures after he is magically transported through the cinema screen.

How has it gone down in the USA? Badly. 'A joyless, soulless, machine of a movie' (*Variety*); 'A noisy monstrosity that not even Arnold Schwarzenegger's star power can pump into life' (*Hollywood Reporter*); 'A movie reeking of tunnel vision, insularity, smugness, cynicism and virulent, self-serving commercialism' (*Montreal Gazette*).

Hobbies: Flexing, listening to Spanish language tapes in the toilet, collecting art by Chagall, Miró, Picasso ('I like a whole bunch of painters').

Alternative uses for Arnie, should his cinematic career take a nosedive: Bouncy castle, novelty hat stand, industrial skip.

Least likely to say: 'For me, acting is purely a kind of spiritual mechanics. If you add this element to that element, what do you want to get out of the combination and what do you want to distil? It's very complicated actually if you're going to do it interestingly.'

Selina Scott

Age: 41.

Appearance: Slightly cerebral version of Princess Di.

Background: The eldest of five children, she grew up in middle-class comfort in rural Yorkshire (she still professes to hate city life, begging a large question about career choice). After East Anglia University, became press officer for the Island of Bute, on which she lived alone but for her dog. Joined Grampian TV, and at 30 went to ITN as a newscaster. After a stint on the BBC's breakfast show, she went extraterrestrial, then briefly worked for CBS in the USA. Her CV also includes presenting the BBC's *Clothes Show*, bucolic documentaries and hilariously standing in for Wogan.

Private life: Famously private, to the frustration of the tabloids. No known lovers or even friends, though she lunches with Sir John Junor.

Current career: Presenter of BSkyB breakfast show thrice weekly. Has signed contract to present a showbiz show for the BBC.

Is she likely to suffer a breakdown through overwork? Not really. She provoked guffaws at a recent advertising awards ceremony when heard complaining to a colleague about her 20-hour week.

Earnings: £250,000 to £350,000, though she vaguely denies this.

She must be very bright? Some people say so.

Does she take herself seriously? Immensely. Maintains she's a serious journalist, and says it's only her looks that make people treat her as a bimbo. Doing TV commercials for Sainsbury's (her penne and mozzarella personality recipe won her an award at this week's BAFTA adverts ceremony) has done much to increase *gravitas*. Also 1991 winner of *Radio Times* 'Sexiest Woman on TV' award.

Likes: Appearing on TV, her huge salary, clothes, and building walls at her Perthshire farmhouse.

Dislikes: Being recognised by the public, any mention of her huge salary, and, unusually for a journalist, journalists.

Interview technique (1) with royals: Attempts to be endearing by pretending to be unimpressed and feisty.

Interview technique (2) with anyone else: Cursory attempt at interest often leading to emetic mateyness and lapses in concentration.

Example of (2): (To bibulous chef Keith Floyd) 'Well, well, well, what have we got here, as they say?'

Most famous TV cock-ups: Asking a Booker judge in an awestruck voice if she had read all the books; expletive on breakfast telly; asking a childless celebrity about his offspring; asking a monk about his sex life.

Least likely to say (to the TV studio crew): 'Well, that was a hard day's work, lads. Who's coming for a few bevvies?'

Will Self

Age: 32.
Occupation: Er, writer.
Best of Young British Novelists?
Yes, but for how long?
Looks like: Junkie going cold turkey.
Because he is a: Self-confessed junkie who went cold turkey.
What's the big deal about Self?
His new novel, *My Idea of Fun*, has been mauled by the critics, thus undermining glowing dustjacket quotes from literary toffs. He has been fêted as the saviour of the British novel, successor to Ian McEwan and Martin Amis.
Is he? He has the low-life obsessions of McEwan, but he writes like Amis going cold turkey with a thesaurus.
Previous work: The novellas *Cock* and *Bull*, and a book of short stories, *The Quantity Theory of Insanity*, which won the 1993 Geoffrey Faber Memorial Prize.
Self-publicity story. Chapter one: The literati swoon (over his short stories): 'If a manic J. G. Ballard and a depressive David Lodge got together, they might produce something like *The Quantity Theory of Insanity*' (Martin Amis); 'An unusually good writer' (Salman Rushdie); 'Black, macabre and relentless – also wildly funny' (Beryl Bainbridge).
Chapter two: The critics pounce (on his new novel): 'Nothing more than the literary equivalent of a splatter movie.'
What's his idea of fun? Tearing the head off a dosser on a Tube train and copulating with the severed neck. Disembowelling a pit bull terrier and fellating the severed penis. At least those are a couple of the things his narrator does in the novel, which is dedicated to his 3-year-old daughter . . .
Previous occupations? Road sweeper on the A101; running an adventure playground for the GLC; cartoonist for the *New Statesman* – sacked because the editor found his brand of 'humour' depressing.
Recurring verbal resonances? Motorways, masturbation and myself.
Self in slippers: Death and copulation may be his literary obsessions, but he lives in a nice house in Shepherd's Bush, with his wife and two children. Marriage to well-connected Kate Chancellor has led to lots of cutey-pie copy in the Sundays about how he likes playing with his kids, and how family life has reformed him.
Useful puns for headline writers: Self-image, Self-abuse, Heal thy Self, Do it your Self, a short Self-life.
Not to be confused with: Anita Brookner.
Most likely to say: 'Subcutaneous diapason of verbose spewage.' Not once but thrice in tedious, tripartite tautology.
Least likely to say: No comment.

16 September 1993

Vikram Seth

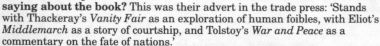

Age: 40.

Appearance: Unassuming, small, balding, not dressy.

Mannerisms: Plays with toes (his own) during interviews.

Famous as: This season's literary lion; biggest talent to come out of India since Salman Rushdie.

Tell me more: He's written the longest single-volume novel in the English language. Ever. It's called *A Suitable Boy*. It weighs almost as much as it costs – 20 pounds – and is 1,350 pages long. Publishers and interviewers have reached new levels of loopiness in comparing him to the greats of 19th-century literature.

How long was Mr Seth at his labours? 2,920 days to write, 365 days to cut.

What have his publishers been saying about the book? This was their advert in the trade press: 'Stands with Thackeray's *Vanity Fair* as an exploration of human foibles, with Eliot's *Middlemarch* as a story of courtship, and Tolstoy's *War and Peace* as a commentary on the fate of nations.'

And what of the special raptures of Nicholas Pearson, Seth's publisher? He said: 'It's a wonderful antidote to the small but perfectly formed little novels we're used to.'

How do they rate Seth in New Delhi, where he now lives? 'They say he is the new Jane Austen.' 'Sometimes he makes conversation in perfectly formed sonnets,' according to the *Independent*.

And how much did Phoenix House advance? £250,000, with a reported £400,000 from US publishers.

What's the book about? The whole Indian subcontinent really, starting in the fifties. But at its heart is the tale of a young virgin and the search for a husband who will meet her family's approval. A good old-fashioned soapy-saga, really.

What else of his am I likely to have missed? Well, there's *The Golden Gate*, a novel entirely in verse about California. That sold 150,000 worldwide.

Will success spoil Seth? Unlikely. Though he's already rich, he still lives with his ma and pa. He has no wife, no house, no car.

What Seth says about the likely sales of his blockbusteruski: 'The public has limited purses and weak wrists.'

Least likely to say: 'Never mind the remaindered copies, the advance is what counts.'

What we most fear he might say: 'Actually, that's just the first part of my quartet of Indian novels.'

Suitable uses for *A Suitable Boy* if you can't finish it: Dropping from a great height on the heads of publishers and their PR persons in revenge for their shameless hype.

22 March 1993. There was an unseemly literary squabble when *A Suitable Boy*, favourite to win the Booker Prize, was left off the shortlist. Lord Gowrie, chairman of the judges, described the book as 'unfinished and uncut'; Seth's publisher, Anthony Cheetham, called the jury 'a bunch of wankers'.

Brian Sewell

Occupation: Greatest living art historian, scourge of the effete, the pretentious, the second-rate and the intellectually slipshod. In other words, art critic of the London *Evening Standard*, and second-string motoring correspondent for that paper.

Looks like: Norman Scott, erstwhile companion of Jeremy Thorpe, but shorter and no Great Dane.

Sounds like: The English Loyd Grossman.

What does the art world think of him? Funny you should ask. After all these years, the worm has finally turned and the lash of the Sewell pen has provoked an uprising. Thirty-five of art's great and good, including Christopher Frayling, George Melly, Eduardo Paolozzi and Marina Warner have put their names to an unprecedented attack on a critic in the form of a letter to the *Standard*.

What's their beef? 'His virulent homophobia and misogyny are deeply offensive . . . in place of an informed critique, he serves up the same tedious menu of formulaic insults and predictable scurrility . . . a dire mix of sexual and class hypocrisy, intellectual posturing and artistic prejudice.'

Ouch! What did he do to deserve that? A vicious review of a Tate exhibition, for which women writers were asked to select favourite women painters and sculptors. 'A show defiled by feminist claptrap,' said Sewell.

Dislikes: Nicholas Serota (director of the Tate), bricks, video, photography, concrete houses, Waldemar Janusczack, Edward Lucie-Smith.

Edward Lucie-Smith on Sewell: 'A mixture of Lady Bracknell and the mannerisms of an offended llama.'

First career move: Spokesman for Anthony Blunt, Keeper of the Queen's Pictures and Russian spy.

Second career move: TV critic for *Mail on Sunday*. He resigned after a week when they cut the word 'phallalgia' from his copy.

Phallalgia? It's a medical term for a pain in the *membrum virile*.

First big break: Played *Loose Ends* with Robert Elms.

Next big break: Chief art critic for *The Big Breakfast*.

Universities: The Courtauld. Sotheby's cataloguing department. Life.

Doctoral thesis: The life and times of the Range Rover with particular reference to Italian mannerism, a comparative history. Never submitted.

Publications: Not so far as anybody knows.

Critical technique: Mastery of lordly connoisseurship. It sure impresses the subs' desk at the *Standard*, even if it is a trifle thin on footnotes.

Some of his favourite words: Absurd, posturing, elite, intellectually dishonest, panjandrum, irredeemably amateur.

Most likely to say: 'I'.

As in? 'I know what I like.'

Nigel Short

Age: 27.
Appearance: John Denver after an
Open University computing course.
Claim to fame: Britain's greatest
chess player. Locked in battle with
Jan Timman of the Netherlands in
the match that decides who plays the
holder, Garry Kasparov, for the
world title.
Is he famous? No. Chess's profile in
the UK comes somewhere between
fly fishing and goat throwing, so the
game is being played in Spain,
courtesy of a chess-mad Spanish
millionaire, and followed in a
desultory way by the media. When
Short went 6–4 up against Timman,
the BBC ignored the game. On the
plus side, he is enormously popular
in Iceland, recently coming second in
a poll of TV personalities, ahead of
Madonna.

Prodigy: Born in Leigh, Lancashire, he took up chess at the age of 6,
inspired by the Fischer–Spassky world championship match in Reykjavik. He
quickly beat his father, a good club player; at 10, beat Soviet grandmaster
Victor Korchnoi; at 12, beat 10-times British champion Dr Jonathan Penrose;
became an international master at 15, and a grandmaster at 19. His
academic progress was less spectacular: went to Bolton School but left at the
age of 16 with four O-levels.
Punk: At school he played bass in a pop group called the Urge, which had a
brief spot on *Blue Peter*. Still strums punk standards to relax.
Politician: Used to belong to the SDP, but one of the group of prominent
young Owenites who came out in support of John Major at the 1992 election.
Writes a chess column for the *Daily Telegraph* and is a close friend of
Spectator editor and chess buff Dominic Lawson. Short is said to have
political aspirations, though unlikely to become Minister of Fun.
Progress to final: Has beaten fellow Brit Jon Speelman, Bielorussian Boris
Gelfand and former world champion Anatoly Karpov.
Would-be millionaire: The winner of the Short–Timman game gets £80,000.
But the real prize comes in the final, where the players share $4 million. It is
unlikely that the odd million would affect Short's austere lifestyle: he lives in
a small first-floor flat in West Hampstead with his Greek wife Rea and 18-
month-old daughter Kyveli.
Critics call him: Boring, myopic, mechanical.
Fans call him: Disciplined, hungry for victory, ruthlessly methodical.
Useful headlines: Man Who Would be King; The West's White Knight;
Chairman of the Board.
Can he beat Kasparov? Kasparov is the highest-rated player of all time
(though Fischer at his peak was better) and on paper would beat Short
comfortably. But Short, at his nasty and brutish best, could run him close and
might be inspired by Kasparov's arrogance ('My opponent will be Short and
the game will be short').
Least likely to say: 'Nice move Garry.'

28 January 1993. Short went on to complete victory over Timman, but lost heavily to
Kasparov in the final.

Nicholas Soames

Age: 45.

Appearance: 'Circumferentially challenged'; 'someone for whom second helpings are second nature'; 'a Vesuvius of conviviality'.

Position: Appropriately enough, food minister.

Nicknames: Fatty, Bunter.

Status: Divorced ('Silliest thing I ever did') from Keswick heiress Cathrine Wetherall (she ran off with intellectually challenged ski instructor Piers von Westenholz); one son.

Background: Born into one of the great Tory families – his grandfather was Winston Churchill; father: Lord Soames of the Lancaster House Agreement and Our Man in Paris; educated at Eton ('Everyone hated me'); Mons Officer Cadets School; army (11th Hussars); Equerry to Prince Charles; a few years in business and banking during which he did not always show the soundest of judgment in choosing employers; entered Parliament as member for Crawley in June 1983.

At one time or another: Was assistant to US Congressman called Bonker; PA to Sir James Goldsmith.

Biggest career hiccup: Equerry to Prince Charles? PPS to Nicholas Ridley? Involvement with Consolidated Environmental Technologies? Claiming a new openness for Min. of Ag. at the same time as sitting on patulin report? Batting for government over toxic apples.

Political suiting: One-Nation Wetness.

Biggest hurdle to promotion under Thatcher: One-Nation Wetness; yellow socks; sense of humour.

Friends: Almost everybody except Margaret Thatcher.

Hon. Timothy Sainsbury on Soames's sartorial style: 'Going ratting, Soames?'

Soames on Sainsbury's sartorial style: 'I say, fancy being lectured about your gear by your grocer.'

Anonymous civil servant on Soames: 'He did not seem nakedly ambitious to get to grip with the issues.'

Soames on the issues: 'I've never worked so hard in my life.'

Soames on food: 'It should be fun and pleasure – a celebration of life.'

Soames on diet: 'I am trying to develop beach cred.'

Soames on club life: 'The bar at White's is full of people who talk to flowers.'

Soames on the Bishop of Durham: 'That Jenkins man by all accounts is a nuclear-powered berk.'

Soames on toxicology in apples: 'It is a problem which has been with us since Adam ate the apple, and thus made a career decision.'

The Great Soames Mystery: How much brain is behind the bonhomie?

Least likely to say: 'Just a small piece for me.'

12 February 1993. Married Serena Smith in December 1993; became Defence Minister in July 1994.

George Soros

Age: 62, but regular tennis means he looks depressingly young and fit.

Occupation: Billionaire gambler on the financial markets. (He describes himself as 'financial and philosophical speculator'.)

Most famous for: Betting $10 billion that the British government would be forced to devalue sterling in September 1992. Soros won. The Bank of England (and Norman Lamont) lost.

So what were his winnings? Around $2 billion.

But surely, all gamblers lose sometimes? In autumn 1987, he predicted (correctly) there was going to be a stock-market crash. But he picked the wrong part of the world: Soros thought the Japanese market would crash so he transferred a few billion into investments on Wall Street. In fact it was Wall Street that crashed. Soros lost $650 million.

Any other big mistakes? As a child, had an idea that he was God. Occasional messianic fantasies reappear: a journalist once suggested to Soros that he should be the Pope; Soros replied: 'Why? I'm the Pope's boss now.'

What does he do with his money? Makes even more money, lives well and gives it away: he ploughed $50 million of his Black Wednesday winnings into humanitarian aid for Bosnia. He has set up 'Soros foundations' across eastern Europe, given grants to dissident intellectuals, provided scholarships for black students at the University of Cape Town and set up the Central European University in Prague.

Why the particular interest in eastern Europe? He was born in Hungary.

And what did you do in the war, George? Kept very quiet about being Jewish. Soros posed as the godson of a Hungarian official until Budapest was liberated by the Red Army.

So the war was pretty rough? He says not: 'It was one of the happiest times of my life . . . We took our destiny in our hands. It was exciting.'

And after that? Escaped to Britain (1947), worked as farmhand, decorator and railway porter, became economics student at the LSE (1949), went to work in the City (1954), moved to New York (1956).

Was he rich by then? No. He started earning serious money only in the sixties, and set up business in his own right only in 1973.

Why is he in the news again? Because he's putting $250 million into a new company to buy UK property.

So does that mean the property market is on the mend? Soros clearly thinks so. And because Soros thinks so, other people think they should think so, too. The value of British property companies has shot up as a result.

Not to be confused with: HP Soros; Manon des Soros; soros of the Nile.

Least likely to say: 'Sorry, have to dash. Class War have asked me to speak at their Bash the Rich rally.'

Ronald Spark

Age: 63.
Appearance: Wears a beret and dark glasses, even in midwinter. Cross between onion seller and Mafia hit man.
Position: Former chief leader writer of the *Sun*. Sacked for writing personal letter to Lord King distancing himself from the *Sun*'s coverage of the BA–Virgin battle.
Biggest mistake: Getting secretary to type the letter.
Nickname: 'Bright'.
Background: Read history at Worcester College, Oxford, where he got a second. Worked for the *Sunday Express*. Sacked by John Junor over irregularities in his expenses. But Junor admired Spark's writing and recommended him to Larry Lamb as the man to move *Sun* editorials to the right. This met with approval from Rupert Murdoch, an Oxford contemporary.
Finest hour: During Falklands War he branded Peter Snow and the 'pygmy' *Guardian* as traitors. He told an NUJ disciplinary committee to get stuffed.
Likes: Lady Thatcher, Norman Tebbit, Lord King. Roast beef, Yorkshire pudding, etc., etc.
Dislikes: Foreigners, poofs, eggheads, unions, the *Guardian*, the *Independent*, Robert Runcie, Argies, Jacques Delors.
Admirers: (1) William Waldegrave, who praised Mr Spark's editorials as models of concise populist writing. 'If you read such truly demotic writing you will find a thousand echoes of the words and phrases which the Book of Common Prayer and the King James Bible have embedded in our language.' (2) William Rees-Mogg. He says: 'I have an almost unlimited admiration for *Sun* leaders, which I think are among the finest expressions of British popular journalism.'
Spark on Emperor Hirohito: 'When he goes, he will surely be guaranteed a special place in hell.'
Spark on Ken Livingstone: 'A little twit, the most hated man in Britain.'
Spark on Spanish air controllers: 'Why don't you quit and take up bull-fighting, bird-strangling or donkey-torturing?'
Spark on the *Guardian*: 'The *Guardian* represents much that is sick and rotten and perverted in our society. A good guide is to believe the exact opposite of what it says on everything.'
Home: Rottingdean, Brighton.
Hobbies: Writing vitriolic private letters to people in public life; complaining to the Press Council about the behaviour of the 'posh' papers.
Don't say: I loved *Jean Brodie*. Are you planning a sequel?'
Least likely to say: 'On the other hand . . . '

26 January 1993. After leaving the *Sun*, Spark became a *Mail on Sunday* columnist.

Sir Maxton Spencer MP

Age: 53, the same as his Major-threatening mate, Tony von Marlow.
Appearance: Upmarket estate agent whose wife has inherited money. Prettier than Marlow, doesn't wear striped Wellington School blazer. Less menacing.
That's not difficult: You have a point.
Sounds like an identikit Thatcherite? Exactly. Got elected on the Lady's coat-tails in 1979 on the strength of his famous 'Traitor Heath' attack at the Brighton conference in 1976. Beat 203 candidates, including J. Major, to plum Otley and Brownoze nomination. Strongly anti-European.
High-flyer then? Well, er, not quite. PPS to Marcus Fox, then got junior office in DTI under Cecil Parkinson in 1983 after 'Traitor Scargill' attack. Pledged government to privatise British Rail 'within a year'. Resigned mysteriously in 1985 to become pillar of influential Keep Turning Right group.
Sounds like an old rogue. Why's he in the news? Suddenly the name Maxy is on everyone's lips at Westminster as the man with just enough self-importance to challenge Major for the leadership.
What's wrong with Marlow? It's his idea: Don't be daft. Ken Livingstone could get more Tory votes than Marlow, who lacks Sir Anthony Meyer's *gravitas* as a challenger. Sir Maxton told George Gardiner that he now hates Major.
Good heavens, what's he got against him? Maxy and Daphne were chummy with John and Norma. Daphne thought Maxy deserved cabinet place after Gentler John succeeded the Boss. His 'Traitor Heseltine' attack was credited with swinging wavering rightists to Major. Got his K for it.
What went wrong? Friendship cooled after he was passed over and his 'third-rate bank clerk' jibe at PM was overheard in Commons smoking room. All hope extinguished by *News of the World* report about the Bangkok holiday which preceded his mysterious resignation. Maxy said he was staying at the hostel 'to save money'.
So he's a libertarian on gay sex then? Absolutely. It's his big battle with Marlow. Both pro-hanging, anti-immigration, but Maxy voted for what Marlow called 'the buggery of teenage boys' at 16. Favours uniform Euro-age for sex, despite anti-federalist views.
I still don't see what's in it for him, leadership-wise? Bags of publicity, old boy, memoirs, revenge. And all the serious candidates have promised him a peerage. Lord Brownoze.
Most likely to say: 'Of course, what I'm really concerned about is the good of the country. But if you really think I'm Home Secretary material I'm not going to quarrel with you, Michael.'
Least likely to say: 'It's good of you to offer, John, but I think the job should go to a younger man.'

April Fool's Day 1994. Apart from a spot of trouble with whips, Sir Maxton has been strangely quiet since.

Raine Spencer

Age: 63.
Appearance: Battered Barbie doll.
Occupation: Marrying up.
Achievements to date: Two English earls, one French count (reserved).
Best known for: Her mother, Dame Barbara Cartland; stepdaughter, Princess Diana; husbands (as above).
Awards: Deb of the Year (1947); Bride of the Year (1948).
Hobbies: Bossybooting at the GLC, do-gooding for the English Tourist Board, molesting historic interiors.
Raine by many other names: Miss McCorquodale, Mrs Gerald Legge, Viscountess Lewisham, Countess Dartmouth, Countess Spencer, Stepmother from Hell, Acid Raine.
How to greet her: Formal: Madam; social: Lady Spencer; employee status: My Lady or Your Ladyship; in a dark alley: Aaaargh!

Her Ladyship on Lord Dartmouth: 'He is the Rock of Gibraltar, and divine.' They divorced in 1976 on the grounds of her adultery.
Her Ladyship on Lord Spencer: 'I'm madly in love.' He died last year.
On her new consort, Count Chambrun: 'I am crazy about him.'
What is Madam's appeal? It's sex, so they say. And 4 million quid never goes amiss.
Her Ladyship approves of: Their Lordships, beating children, gold paint and red wallpaper, breakfast in bed, selling Van Dykes, vitamins.
Her Ladyship disapproves of: Working mothers, homosexuality, Joyce's *Ulysses* – 'the book is the most disgusting one I've ever read' – dirty cups.
Why is the Count so utterly suitable? He's in water filters.
Tips from the top drawer: 'I judge people by their bathrooms.' 'I know misery does exist, but we don't want it in our drawing rooms.' 'It does not matter if you live in a council house or a stately home – the problems are exactly the same.'
Further reading: *The Earl Rings a Belle*; *Love and the Marquis*; *The Cruel Count*; *The Duke Is Trapped*; *The Magnificent Marriage*; *The Man of Her Dreams*; *Again This Rapture*. All by Mummy.
Chin up, girls! When the supply of British aristocrats dries up, follow Raine's example and snaffle a European. Rarely as noble as our native model but better looking, less stupid and more impressed by Englishness.
Shakespeare is inspired: 'The quality of mercy is not strained. It droppeth as the gentle Raine from heaven upon the place beneath.'
Fancy a break? B&B at Madam's new château costs between £180 and £240; dinner's £50. Prices are sure to rise, so book now to avoid disappointment.
A hard rain's gonna fall: Please remember in your prayers Elizabeth and Ariane, Count Chambrun's daughters.
A private message for Count Chambrun: Plutôt vous que moi, squire.

12 May 1993. The couple were married two months later.

Serena Stanhope

Age: 23.

Appearance: Lady Helen Windsor lookalike; English rose.

Previous appearance: Porky Sloane Ranger.

Occupation: Something absolutely fabulous for Giorgio Armani.

Why is she in the news? She marries Viscount Linley, 12th in line to the throne, at St Margaret's Church, Westminster, today.

Oh dear, divorce in a few years then? No. This is love they say. The Honourable Serena is part of the new squeaky-clean royal dream ticket with Lady Helen Windsor. Together they are going to be promoted as the Fergie 'n' Di for the chastened nineties.

Big wedding, is it? Naturally. But several big-name royals will be absent. Prince Charles is in Istanbul on 'business'; Prince Philip is attending a carriage-driving competition in America; and Prince Andrew is being military in the Mediterranean. Fergie wasn't even invited. But Mick and Elton will be there.

What has she got? In a word: money. Daddy, that's Viscount Petersham, is worth megabucks. Also, there are no big scandals in her private life.

Key words: Bubbly, friendly, spontaneous, *pas de chichi* (which is French for heavy on breeding, light on brains).

So we're not talking Mensa material? Affirmative. One of those girls who has no shame about her lack of educational qualifications. The key is that she isn't a good-time girl.

What is she going to get? Richer. The wedding present list came in at a total cost of £180,000. That includes two candlesticks at £2,150, a £1,600 porcelain teapot and a £3,300 silver one, and three 17th-century rugs that will set some poor mug back £72,500.

One of the royals could buy that then? Er, no. Prince Edward went for a £52 cup-and-saucer set.

Sounds a bit mean: Not as mean as the bride and groom's families; guests at the celebration dinner in the evening have to chip in £30 each.

Any clues to character? Prefers wine bars to pubs. Went to the Riviera for her hen night, wore a white punk wig and sang 'I Will Survive' in a club.

Sounds confident: Well, yes. Given the state of most royal marriages, and her own parents' divorce when she was 13, it would have been unsurprising if she'd hopped into Daddy's 140ft yacht and headed for the open seas singing 'Let's Call the Whole Thing Off'.

And if she did? Well diddy David could marry any number of SS women: Selina Scott, Sharon Stone, Susan Sangster, Siouxie Sioux.

But they're all taller than him, aren't they? Yes, Serena has height – or rather the lack of it – on her side.

Most likely to say: 'Is that *Hello!*? I wonder if you'd like to see some honeymoon photographs?'

Least likely to say: 'Can I talk to Andrew Morton?'

Evan Steadman

Age: 55.

Appearance: Retired Australian lifeguard.

Occupation: Theatrical impresario.

Why is he in the news? The courts have banned his production of *Maxwell the Musical*, based on the life of Robert Maxwell, which was due to open in the West End on 21 February.

They didn't like the songs? They didn't express an opinion. They were more concerned that the show might prejudice the forthcoming trial for fraud of Maxwell's sons, Kevin and Ian.

So when can it be put on? After the trial.

And when will that be? The way the legal system deals with the complexities of fraud, probably sometime in the next millennium.

So the performers aren't holding their breath? No, they're holding their redundancy notices. More than 100 people have lost their jobs.

Steadman must be mortified: Losing £500,000 on the venture seems to have dulled his natural ebullience.

Any previous track record in the theatre? He backed the massively successful *Me and My Girl* and co-produced *Around the World in 80 Days*.

Was that equally successful? It went around the provinces in about 80 days and then disappeared, never reaching the West End.

Music wasn't Maxwell's forte, was it? Former *Mirror* editor Mike Molloy said Captain Bob's singing 'was about as melodic as a pair of juggernauts rumbling along the M25'.

So what was the appeal for Steadman? He thought Maxwell's life had comic-opera potential, having observed him at dangerously close quarters when the tyrannical tycoon bought his exhibition company for £16 million in the late eighties. He was chairman of Maxwell Business Communications when the ship went down.

You are speaking metaphorically? Of course.

Who supplied the lyrics for the show? Steadman himself, updating Gilbert and Sullivan favourites. He thought of 'I am the very model of a modern megalomaniac' and the rest is legal history.

And Pavarotti was booked to play Maxwell? Sadly not, too small for the part. Originally, Barry Cryer was the unlikely choice to play the role, but he was dropped in favour of former policeman John Savident, described as 'a large man'.

So where does Steadman go from here? Novel-writing apparently. He recently completed a book about the IRA, fetchingly titled *Next Year I'm Going to Kill the Queen of England*.

Not to be confused with: Cameron Macintosh.

Least likely to say: 'The critics went overboard.'

Gloria Steinem

Age: 58.
Position: High priestess of American feminism.
Appearance: First feminist with genuine sex appeal – Stephanie Beecham crossed with Felicity Kendal.
Latest project: The distribution of *Ms* magazine in Britain.
Background: Father was a 21-stone Jewish showbiz entrepreneur and travelling salesman. Mother was a journalist, who had a nervous breakdown when Steinem was 10 and was dosed with chloral hydrate 'which made her appear permanently drunk'. Steinem looked after her mother from 10 to 18 while living in a rat-infested farmhouse.
Education and formative experiences: She escaped and went to Smith College where she began to

identify with women's causes. Never felt the need to wear army boots and cut her hair off in order to avoid becoming a sex object. Discovered poverty and injustice while living in India for two years. Back in Manhattan she lived a double life, writing articles on Christmas presents for *Glamour!* magazine by day and mixing with radicals by night. In 1968, *New York Magazine* gave her a chance to do the serious political reporting she wanted, alongside Tom Wolfe and Jimmy Breslin.
Themes: Effect of patriarchal society on women's lack of self-esteem. Twenty years ago women had to be more like men: now men should be more like women. Body image and anorexia generation.
Why *Ms*? No magazines would publish her articles on the liberation of women and she felt like a 'mascot' at *NY Magazine*, so she started *Ms*, a feminist women's magazine, in January 1972. Attacked by hardline feminists for 'backsliding bourgeois feminism'.
Most famous article: 1963 piece on Hugh Hefner's Playboy Club, where Steinem worked as undercover bunny girl. *Playboy* brought a $1 million libel suit against her and repeatedly published her bunny girl photo alongside pornographic spreads to undermine her credibility.
Sayings: 'A woman needs a man like a fish needs a bicycle'; 'The only form of arms control is how we raise our children.'
Marriage? 'The inequity of marriage made me not get married.'
Sleeping with the enemy? Yes, several long-term lovers including Mort Zimmerman, New York property magnate, and film director Robert Benton.
Men who have been charmed by Steinem: Martin Amis, Clive James, Terry Wogan, Jimmy Breslin.
Achievement: 'Twenty years ago there were no phrases like "battered women", "sexual harassment" or "date rape". It was just called life.'
Work to be done: 'We spent the first hundred years gaining an identity. Now we are trying to get legal and social equality. That will take at least a century. And we're only about 20 years into it.'
Least likely to say: 'Tits out for the lads.'

24 November 1992

Jocelyn Stevens

Age: 60.

Status: Chairman of English Heritage.

Job: Rationalising our national ruins; polishing the stone jewels in the heritage crown, while palming the tacky ones off to local authorities.

Background: Scion of newspaper family, the Hultons of Manchester. Mother died shortly after his birth. Grandfather acquired the *Daily Sketch*, *Sunday Dispatch* and *Evening Standard*. Married one of Princess Margaret's ladies-in-waiting in 1956. Long-time companion is now Vivien Duffield, daughter of Charles Clore.

Previous job: Turning moribund Royal College of Art into fast-track design factory.

Why he's never been out of work: First job, nepotism. After that building a reputation as a sharp-shooting whirlwind who, with no initial specialist know-how, gets things done.

Has he put others out of work: Yes, 2,000 *Express* newspaper jobs in Glasgow. Will privatise and shrink English Heritage staff.

Principal vice: Legendary temper. Terrified one secretary by pitching filing cabinet out of Fleet Street window.

Principal virtue: Ditto.

Early success: Took control of *Queen* – the magazine, not the rock group – when it was flagging in the fifties; a backer of Caroline – the pirate radio ship, not the Princess of Monaco – in the sixties.

Style, sartorial: Sharp dresser with occasional lapses. Has recently favoured Victorian shepherd's smock for country attire.

Style, life: Playboy who goes the extra mile to get the daytime job done. Member of Princess Margaret's sixties set who's still a swinger at 60.

Nicknames: Piranha; the Terror of Lubianka (the old *Daily Express* building).

Award he's least proud of: Engraved blunderbuss, presented by the print unions at the end of his term as managing director of the London *Evening Standard*.

What others say about him: 'Not a breath, rather a gale of fresh air' – Lord St John of Fawsley. 'He's not noted for thinking five times before he speaks' – former *Standard* editor Charles Wintour.

What he sings in the bath: 'It's a Bit of a Ruin That Cromwell Knocked About a Bit'.

Rod Stewart

Age: Really old.
Giveaway: He's receiving a Lifetime Achievement Award from the British pop industry.
Appearance: Essex girl holidaying in Ibiza. Leopard-spot trousers, white cowboy boots, blonde highlights, shaggy perm.
Attempts at updating image: Seven haircuts too late, stopped backcombing fringe and affected a dusting of stubble. Has finally ceased rolling up the sleeves of suit jacket.
Achievements (professional): Born in Glasgow in 1945. Busked around Europe before joining Steampacket, then the Jeff Beck Group. Formed the Faces in 1969. In 1971, 'Maggie May' was number one here and in the USA. By 1976, he was a tax exile in LA.

Services to the pop industry:
Made 21 bestselling albums and seven number one singles. Specialises in providing mawkish background schmoozery for a thousand dance-floor gropes. 'You Wear It Well', 'You're in My Heart', 'Sailing', 'Hot Legs', 'Do Ya Think I'm Sexy?', etc. . . .
Things they said about him: 'An ugly wimp covered in mascara' (Marcy Hanson); 'No class' (Joanna Lumley); 'He had a penchant for ladies' underwear' (Britt Ekland); 'Emotionally retarded' (Alana Hamilton).
Joy through hardship: On first wife, Alana Hamilton: 'Alana is tall, Alana is blonde. For the first time in my life I found it was possible to be happy with a flat-chested woman.'
Likes: Football, his mother, Double Diamond, Scotland.
Appendage of which he's proud: Wife number two, Rachel Hunter.
Appendage that embarrasses him: His nose. Had operation to slim it down.
Post-op disappointment: It's still enormous.
People whose noses are bigger than his: Barry Manilow, Cyrano de Bergerac, Jeremy Paxman, Desert Orchid, Oprah Winfrey.
Businesses which have profited from Rod: Sealink, Sun-In hair lightener, Scotties man-size.
Businesses which have made sweet FA out of him: Dunn & Co., Encyclopaedia Britannica, Ovaltine.
Other famous Rods: Rod Steiger, Rod Hull, Dyno-Rod.
Rod on Joanna Lumley: 'I'm desperately serious.'
Rod on Dee Harrington: 'I wouldn't want to marry anyone else.'
Rod on Kelly Emberg: 'All I want is Kelly.'
Rod on Britt Ekland: 'She's the only woman in the world who has made me want to be faithful.'
Rod on Rachel Hunter: 'For the first time in my life I would see my c**k cut off before being unfaithful to this woman.'
Least likely to say: 'God, I feel old.'

Sting

Age: A svelte 41.

Appearance: Personal physical education trainer to the Beverly Hills elite, with philosophical pretensions.

Early life: Born Gordon Sumner, Wallsend. Trained as a teacher, and while educating the under-9s at St Paul's School, Cramlington, joined Newcastle Big Band. Nicknamed Sting because his yellow-and-black striped shirt was reminiscent of a bee. Joined the Police in 1977 and began churning out string of indelible hits, e.g. 'Roxanne', 'Message in a Bottle', 'Can't Stand Losing You'. Doubts begin to creep in when Sting starts singing about invisible suns and being 'the king of pain'. Sure enough, a solo career is not long in coming.

Rumble in the jungle: Has fallen out with Chief Raoni, supremo of the Kayapo tribe of the Amazon rainforests, on whose behalf Sting has waged a highly visible eco-consciousness campaign. (Raoni is the man with the CD stuck in his lower lip.)

Chief Raoni says: 'The Brazilian Indians do not need Sting. It would be better if we forgot him.'

Sting says: 'I was very naive and thought I could save the world selling T-shirts for the Indian cause.' For once, the critics agree with him.

Most annoying trait: Displays of erudition worn on sleeve (or on sickeningly bronzed forearm). His hit album *Ten Summoner's Tales* is further grist to critical mill. Title a pun on Gordon's surname wedded to Chaucerian name-dropping. *The Dream of the Blue Turtles* comes complete with full load of dream-psychology references.

Alternative most annoying trait: Eagerness to barge to front of Good Causes queue. Has protested about almost everything – General Pinochet, global ecology, imprisonment of Nelson Mandela, plight of Kurdish refugees, people standing too close to him.

Another very annoying thing about Sting: His acting. Appearances by our hero in the likes of *Dune* or *Plenty* required him only to brood and display muscles and jawline.

Sting's fans say: Critics are only jealous. They resent Sting's rugged good looks, his money, his musical talent, his selflessness in endorsing thoroughly admirable causes and his self-evident acting ability.

Hopeful signs: Glimmers of humour in recent appearances and interviews. Dawning realisation that rock megastars are not, after all, at the epicentre of the universe. Maybe he got it all off his chest with his vastly overblown wedding to Trudy Styler.

Least likely to say: 'F*** art, let's dance.'

Oliver Stone

Age: 47.

Appearance: Post-Weight Watchers John Prescott.

Family background: Vague, as befits Hollywood's greatest rewriter of history. Father was a Wall Street stockbroker and Second World War veteran.

Mother was . . . actually, Oliver is too macho to remember much about his mother. Diligent research has revealed she was interested in 'arts and cinema'.

Early career: Dropped out of Yale and volunteered for Vietnam under impression he was Hemingway. Earned Bronze Star, Purple Heart and Bullet in Neck. Was busted for marijuana in Mexico, lived low-life existence in New York, then enrolled in New York University Film School. Martin Scorsese taught him to 'funnel my rage into movies'.

Such as? *Salvador, Platoon, Wall Street, JFK, Home Alone 2* . . . just kidding.

Reputation: Crusading polemicist fond of big, political issues. Vietnam, Kennedy, Reaganomics et al.

So he's a liberal – Hollywood's Harold Pinter? Not exactly. He also worked on the sexist, racist, reactionary, ultra-violent screenplays for *Year of the Dragon, Scarface, Midnight Express* and *Conan the Barbarian.*

***Conan the Barb* . . . that's the one where Arnold Schwarzenegger runs around covered in Ambre Solaire with Andre Agassi's haircut, shouting things like 'Die murderous hell spawn, son of Sogroth!'** Yep, that's the one.

What's he done now? He's executive producer of the BBC2 series *Wild Palms.*

A gardening programme? Sadly, no. It's set in Los Angeles in the year 2007 and ropes in sex, drugs, religion, virtual reality, holograms and rhinos.

Rhinos? It's that kind of show. *Twin Peaks* meets *Doctor Who.*

Is it any good? Yes, then no. It starts brilliantly but gets dull and confusing after a couple of episodes. The ending is an enormous cop-out. But Angie Dickinson is fab.

Secret of his success: Turns complex issues into melodrama.

Typical hero: American male confronting divided loyalties and/or oppressive father figure seeks redemption through armed combat or equivalent surge of adrenalin.

Typical heroine: See cutting-room floor.

Not to be confused with: Norman Stone; Sharon Stone; Fred Flintstone.

Most likely to say: 'Lights! Camera! Re-action-ary!'

Least likely to say: 'Hmmm, don't you think it's just a little bit, you know, too . . . controversial?'

Sharon Stone

Age: 35.

Appearance: Off-screen, extremely pleasing. On-screen, like a blonde fishfinger with appalling taste in clothes.

Career: Began as Woody Allen's fantasy girl in *Stardust Memories* (1980), then downhill all the way.

She's been in some bad films then? *Deadly Blessing, The Vegas Strip Wars, King Solomon's Mines, Police Academy 4, Action Jackson, Blood and Sand, Scissors* – we rest our case.

So why's she so famous? She started making bad but profitable films: *Total Recall, Basic Instinct* and now *Sliver* . . . although the latter, despite looking like a surefire winner – sex! voyeurism! murder! – is so bad it's struggling to recoup its costs.

She used to be: The new Marilyn Monroe.

She's becoming: The new Kim Basinger.

What she says of Hollywood: 'If you have a vagina and an attitude in this town, then that's a lethal combination.'

What she could have said: 'If you have a vagina and a miniskirt in *Basic Instinct*, then that's a lucrative combination.'

How lucrative? For *Sliver*, $2.5 million plus 10 per cent of the gross. For *Basic Instinct 2*, $7 million.

But is she any good at acting? The jury's still out. None of her roles has yet required her to do anything more than simper, pout, scream, shed her clothes and jerk about a bit – that's 'have an orgasm' in Hollywood shorthand.

However, Camille Paglia did call *Basic Instinct* 'one of the great performances by a woman in screen history'.

It's not, is it? No.

But: Naomi Wolf called Stone's character 'a complex, compelling, Nietzschean *Uberfräulein*'.

What does that mean? She bonks men and women. Then kills them.

With all that practice, is she a good kisser? 'Thin lips, OK breath,' opines her *Sliver* co-star Billy Baldwin.

Pass Notes thinks: Vagina, balls and attitude – whatta gal!

Scandal: She appeared 'at home' in *Hello!* magazine – in someone else's house.

Literary footnote: In *Basic Instinct*, she plays an author. In *Sliver*, she plays a literary agent. In her next film, a Booker Prize winner?

Like who? Sharon Stone is Anita Brookner . . .

And the film? Hotel du Lick.

Least likely to say: 'Get me the script for *Police Academy 6*. Now!'

Barbra Streisand

Age: 51.

Appearance: Megalomaniac trying to disguise herself as funny girl in pin-stripes and silly hats.

A trifle cruel, perhaps? *Au contraire*. La Streisand is good buddies with Bill Clinton, and has become legendary for seizing complete control of everything. For example, a 10-year contract with CBS she signed early in her career gave her complete artistic licence to produce and star in TV specials. The same goes for her movies.

What did the critics say? They took umbrage. They vented their spleen on *A Star Is Born* (1976) and had much sport with the farcical *Yentl* (1983). They were unable to stop *Prince of Tides* winning seven Oscar nominations in 1991, but poor Barbra ended up gong-free on the night. Heh heh.

Has she mellowed in middle age? Divas never mellow, they just become paranoid. For her four concerts at Wembley Arena, Babs has insisted that large areas should be carpeted to counteract draughts.

Chilblains? Her manager isn't saying.

Is this carpet business why she's in the news? No. It's the ticket prices.

Which are? £260, £105, £48.50.

What, each? Amazingly, yes.

Crikey. Even Pavarotti lets you keep your underpants. How can she justify this? Apparently she hates performing live, but concert promoters keep dangling zeppelins full of money in front of her until she agrees. Harvey 'Suave' Goldsmith and Barry 'Rich' Clayman stumped up a willpower-sapping £5 million for Babs's four Wembley dates.

Perhaps she's a bit skint: Unlikely. Estimates put her personal wealth at about £80 million, not counting the £3.8 million she earned recently by auctioning 534 lots of artworks and ornaments at Christie's in New York.

Why is she selling the family heirlooms? She says it's because 'I want only two houses rather than seven.'

When did she last sing live in Britain? In 1966, when she appeared on the West End stage in *Funny Girl*.

How much were the tickets then? A very reasonable two pounds five shillings.

Not to be confused with: Hillary Clinton.

Not to be romantically linked (any more) with: Andre Agassi, Don Johnson, Omar Sharif, Richard Gere, Ryan O'Neal.

Most likely to say: 'No interviews.'

Least likely to say: 'People in the cheaper seats please clap, the rest of you just rattle your jewellery.'

Alan Sugar

Age: 45.
Appearance: Essex crime-squad detective, complete with wide tie.
Became famous for: Making dodgy hi-fis in the 1970s.
Stayed famous for: Making less dodgy word processors in 1980s.
Currently famous for: Making extremely generous £114 million offer to relieve Amstrad shareholders of their stakes.
Considered infamous by: Certain of the above-mentioned shareholders, who may tell him to sugar off.
What they said about Amstrad 20 years ago: 'That's crap gear, it'll ruin your albums.'
What the same people said 10 years ago: 'It's marvellous, I mean, you can actually move paragraphs around.'
What they say about Amstrad now: '30p a share is a total insult.'
Best business decision: Steering well clear of BSB satellite company.
Most popular day on earth: 3 March 1988 (shares hit 232p).
Least popular day on earth: 9 September 1992 (shares hit 20p).
High point of 1992: His second company, Spurs, went back in the black.
Low point of 1992: His first company, Amstrad, went £75 million in the red.
Other Amstrad innovations: Super-cheap answerphone/fax combo (where user has to sit on floor to record answerphone message); super-cheap double-deck video recorder (allowing humblest citizen to breach Berne copyright convention); super-cheap computer/personal organiser (allowing humblest citizen to look silly on trains).
Big ones for the future: Consumer videophones (bringing a new dimension to 0898 services).
Biggest spin-off industry: Alternative, easy-to-read manuals for Amstrad word processors (the company's own being unintelligible).
Sugar on politics: 'That bloke [Kinnock], he's out to lunch.'
Sugar on Sugar: 'I have got a terrible temper, violent, wild, I bang the table and scream and shout.'
Sugar (according to his supporters): Single-minded, a street fighter, a survivor.
Sugar (according to his detractors): Another eighties hero with feet of clay, product of phoney boom, indictment of Anglo-Saxon economic system.
Tough sugar: 'I am your receiver, I am your liquidator . . . I'm the one to shrink this company down' (to shareholders).
Salty sugar: 'You can piss off. I've had enough of you today' (to his own PR officer).
Sugary sugar: Happily married for 24 years, three children.
Sugar on his forefathers: 'They're from Poland. Or Russia. Gawd knows.'
Loves: The old dosherooni. Spurs.
Hates: City analysts; photographers.
Least likely to say: 'Do you want me standing by the window?'

9 December 1992. Sugar's attempts to buy back Amstrad were rebuffed, but he had more success in holding on to Spurs in a battle with the then manager, Terry Venables.

The Sultan of Brunei

Full name: His Majesty Paduka Seri Baginda Sultan and Yang Di-Pertuan, Sultan Hassanal Bolkiah Mu'izzaddin Waddaulah Ibni Al-Marhum Sultan Haji Omar Ali Saifuddien Sa'adul Khairi Waddien.
A.k.a. Sultan of Brunei.
Age: 47.
Educated: Sandhurst.
Wives: Married cousin when he was 19, she 16. Is also married to air hostess named Mariam Bell. Room in life for two more under Islamic law.
What is he worth? Around $25 billion. Earns £70 a second and is therefore the richest man on earth.
His kingdom: Tiny patch of jungle in Borneo, about the size of Norfolk, but not so flat. Population of 220,000 is very loyal on account of free education, free health, almost-free housing and no taxes.
Etiquette when meeting Sultan: Imperative to approach him on knees. Must at all times remain lower than Sultan. On no account sneeze in his presence.
Raison d'être: None till discovery of oil put Brunei on map in early part of the century. Independence from UK in 1984 (self-governing since the Second World War). Bolkiah family have ruled pointlessly for 400 years.
Modus operandi: Benevolent dictatorship. Runs Brunei as a family business – he is Prime Minister, Home Secretary and Finance Minister; his father (Sir Omar, who abdicated in his favour in 1967) is Defence Minister; and his brother is Foreign Minister.
Home: Giant palace resembling Stansted Airport, with 564 chandeliers and 51,490 bulbs. Can seat 4,000 for dinner; 257 toilets. Five swimming pools, one Olympic size.
Other appointments: Financial adviser: Mahommed Al-Fayed (according to Tiny Rowland). Spiritual adviser: the mysterious Indian guru Shri Chandra Swamji, who also advised Richard Nixon and Elizabeth Taylor.
Friends: Adnan Khashoggi, from whom he bought his £25 million yacht. The Fayed brothers also helped him in negotiations to buy the Dorchester, and the SOB was suspected of providing the money to buy House of Fraser. Prince Charles. Lord Brammall (on board of Dorchester). Lord Fanshawe. Lord Chalfont.
Enemies: Tiny Rowland.
Other cranky deeds: Hired Cliff Thorburn and Dennis Taylor to teach his son Prince Mohammed to play snooker.
Drawbacks to job: Having to meet Alan Whicker.
Least likely to say: 'Can you spare a fiver, guv?'

John Tavener

Age: 49.

Appearance: Visigoth after a hard night's pillaging.

Background: Born in London. Educated at Highgate School and the Royal Academy of Music. His early compositions were avant-garde pieces heavily influenced by Stravinsky. First success was *The Whale*, written for loudhailer, metronome and orchestra, which the Beatles liked so much they had it recorded on their Apple label. Growing interest in Christianity led to his conversion to the Orthodox faith in 1977, since when all his music has been simple and devotional, using repetition and long-held chords to create a mood of ecstatic contemplation.

Friends say: Icon.

Critics say: Con.

Who are his friends? Mainly the public, who buy CDs of his music in their thousands. *The Protecting Veil* topped the classical charts for aeons until Gorecki filled our spiritual void with his *Symphony of Sorrowful Songs*.

Who are his enemies? Nicholas Kenyon, head of Radio 3, and modernist critics everywhere.

What do they object to? They say his work is substitute religion, simple music for simple desires and very, very boring.

Opinion the *Telegraph's* Michael Kennedy might now regret: 'I shall be surprised if his easy-chair brand of minimalism sprinkled with holy water is anything more than a passing fad.'

Do such remarks bother Tavener? No. 'The best criticism I can imagine would be if you were to dig up a 6th-century man and ask him what he thought of my music.'

His problem: Most current critics were born in the 20th century.

What he thinks of 20th-century music: 'I dislike the way that angst got into music through psychology at the turn of the century.'

But surely music has to develop? 'Art should have nothing to do with innovation. I want to go back to its primordial roots.'

An island unto himself: Likes to retreat to monasteries for spiritual renewal and relax in Greece, where he attends 24-hour services of Byzantine singing. Is close to Mother Thekla of the Orthodox Monestery of the Assumption in Yorkshire.

Not to be confused with: His distant relative John Taverner, a 16th-century English composer of sacred music. Much more avant-garde than Tavener.

Most likely to say: 'Chants would be a fine thing.'

Graham Taylor

Age: 48.

Appearance: Previously: imagine Herbert Lom in the Pink Panther films before he met Inspector Clouseau. Currently: imagine Herbert Lom in the Pink Panther films after he met Inspector Clouseau.

Background: Born into a football family (his father was soccer correspondent for the *Scunthorpe Evening Telegraph*), he played as a full back for Grimsby Town and finally Lincoln City before becoming the youngest manager in the League in 1975/6. After losing his first nine games, he eventually led them out of the Fourth Division. He repeated the feat with Watford, taking them into Division One and, briefly, Europe. Restored Aston Villa to the First Division before accepting current post.

Occupation: No one is sure exactly, though he is often found sat on a bench by the touchline when England play.

Qualifications for the England job: National service haircut. Must be prepared to wear a blazer.

Reputation as a club manager: Honest, hard-working, keen to talk to the press, disciple of Commander Charles Reep's Position of Maximum Opportunity Theory (a.k.a. the Long Ball). Widely admired by people in the game.

Reputation as an international manager: Honest, hard-working, hates the press. Widely admired by tabloid headline writers.

What exactly are the expectations of an England manager? He must win the World Cup or he will be classed a failure. Sir Alf Ramsey won the World Cup in 1966 and was then sacked in 1973. He was classed a failure.

Is he in a no-win situation then? Yes.

So why would anyone want the job in the first place? How do we know?

Is he a vegetarian? Highly unlikely. After the debacle in the European Championships in 1992, he was compared to a turnip (thanks to the headline: Swedes 2, Turnips 1). Before the World Cup qualifier with Norway at Wembley, he asked: 'What vegetables do they grow in Norway?' This question prompted much debate in the tabloid press, with carrots being the apparent answer. There were no references to pumpkins after the US match.

Most famous gaffe: Before the start of the European Championships he said: 'Sit back, put your feet up, turn on the TV and enjoy it. I expect to win it.' England were eliminated in the first round without winning a match.

Not to be confused with: Elizabeth Taylor; Lord Justice Taylor; Tim Brooke-Taylor; Burton the Tailors.

Least likely to say: 'Sit back, put your feet up, turn on the TV and enjoy it. I expect to win it.'

11 June 1993. England failed to qualify for the 1994 World Cup. Taylor resigned and took the rather less pressurised post of manager of **Wolverhampton** Wanderers.

Norman Tebbit

Age: 62. Second oldest of the Tory Normen, after St John-Stevas.
Appearance: Gothic. Possibly based on an early sketch by Charles Addams. Sometimes mistaken for Dracula, though less prominent fangs.
Temperament: Moody. Can be charming, mellow, funny; can be bitter, unforgiving, savage. A loner ('Norman is an island' – John Donne). Asked if he wasn't, deep down, a bit of a softy, said he'd sue.
Occupation: Retired trade unionist. While working as an airline pilot, became a BALPA shop steward and strike leader. Nowadays a company director and abrasive interviewer for Sky Television. Filled in the intervening years with various odd jobs: Employment Secretary, Trade and Industry Secretary, Conservative Party chairman, that sort of thing.
Will historians come to regard him as the father of Essex man? One wouldn't put it past them, though in fact he's a Middle Saxon, from Ponder's End. But his first parliamentary seat was Epping, which is geographically Essex, and his second was Chingford, Essex, until the GLC gobbled it up – and spiritually Essex still. Much of the bullet-headed, no messing, why don't you so-called intellectuals get your hair cut Essex approach is pure Norman.
Got chapter and verse for that, squire? 'I like girls to be girls and chaps to be chaps – I am unashamedly sexist' (February 1986). On immigration, stands at least three and a half square with the *Sun*. Doubted if ethnic minority communities (our term, not his) could pass the 'cricket test': i.e. at Test matches did they cheer Norman Gooch of England, or Norman Khan of Pakistan?
Was he crazy about Thatcher's ankles? No, you're thinking of Norman Clark. But for years he thought the world of the rest of her.
So what went wrong? The lady second-guessed him during the 1987 election campaign when he was party chairman, relying for advice on agencies other than Saatchi & Saatchi and lending an ear to Lord Young. After that, it was never glad, confident Norman again (Browning).
Is that why he left her cabinet after the 1987 election? It may have contributed, but mainly he wanted to spend more time with his wife, Margaret, left paralysed by the bomb in the Grand Hotel, Brighton, in October 1984. Norman was badly injured himself: the effects still linger.
Likes: Self-help, national pride, calling a spade a spade.
Dislikes: Sanctimonious, naive, guilt-ridden, wet, pink orthodoxy. The BBC, which in his view promulgates sanctimonious, naive, etc., etc., values. The untiring attempts of Johnny (or Jacques) Foreigner to sequestrate English traditions and the English way of life: see Norman on Maastricht, passim.
His verdict on John Major? Pass.
Least likely to say: 'Delors is my shepherd.'

Mark Thatcher

Age: 39.
Appearance: Croupier.
Position: Son of Margaret Thatcher and heir to Sir Denis Thatcher Bt. Very rich businessman.
Background: Left Harrow in 1971 after undistinguished academic career. Wanted to be Stirling Moss; instead joined Jardine Matheson as trainee. Left following year to join stockbrokers David, Borkum & Hare. Left after four months. Joined Touche Ross as trainee accountant. Left four years later without qualifying. In 1977 set up Mark Thatcher Racing, which developed cash problems. Joined Australian freight company IPEC, run by friend of father. After mother's election victory, set up Monteagle Marketing (London) Ltd with racing friend.

Soon acting on behalf of Cementation Ltd, which was trying to win £300 million contract to build university in Oman. Mrs Thatcher known to have taken a keen interest in contract.
Subsequent career: Clouded in secrecy. Left for USA in 1984, saying he was 'not appreciated' in Britain. Formed the Grantham Company in Dallas, Texas. Staff forbidden to say what the firm does. Travels first class, with butler in economy. Douglas Hurd agreed to investigate claims he was involved in proposed sale of South African-made arms to Saudi Arabia in breach of UN embargo. Thatcher said to have earned £10 million for one deal with Saudis. Former Reagan official says his name kept turning up in US diplomatic cables relating to arms dealing.
Driving career: Expert at picking up sponsors (Essex Oil, Wendy Wools, Morris Vulcan Toys, Kelly Girl, Toyota, etc.); not so successful at driving. Kept crashing car. Got lost for two weeks in the middle of the Sahara while trying to drive between Paris and Dakar in 1982.
Mummy's boy: Mrs Thatcher reported to believe son can do no wrong. Got him to act as agent for her memoirs. Mark put up backs of everyone in publishing industry. One agent claimed his involvement cost his mother £7–8 million. Also busied himself trying to raise funds for Thatcher Foundation.
Told rich donors in Hong Kong: 'It's time to pay up for Mumsie.'
Who does he answer to? 'I am responsible to three people on this planet. One is my mother, the second is the Almighty, the third is me.'
Defenders: Sir Tim Bell, PR consultant, says: 'He is shy and as a result he is rather aggressive. He has a clipped manner and a lot of people think this is being rude. It is not the case. In fact, he has a sense of humour and introduces himself as Charmless Mark.'
Wife: Diane Burgdorf, gorgeous ex-cheerleader and, according to father, 'just an ordinary millionairess'.
Homes: Neo-Georgian house in Dallas, bought for $600,000 in 1986. Kensington mansion, £2.1 million. Rents £25,000-a-year Swiss penthouse apartment.
Personal wealth: Anything between £10 million and £40 million.
Least likely to say: 'Leave my mother out of this.'

30 November 1992

D. M. Thomas

Age: 57.

Appearance: Like a Hereford bull – florid and horny, with a forelock of white curly hair.

Greatest achievement: In 1981, his third novel, *The White Hotel* – a lurid psychodrama of rape, the Holocaust and naked women – was short-listed for the Booker Prize.

What's he done since? Written six more novels, some poetry and a book of autobiography. Latest novel, *Pictures at an Exhibition*, has just been published by Bloomsbury.

Lurid psychodramas of rape, etc.? I'd say!

What does the D.M. stand for? Donald Michael. Rather than, say, Devilish Misogynist.

In his defence, he says: 'I'm very worried that there is a move towards the unspoken censorship of men's thoughts. We are secretly becoming a very repressive society.'

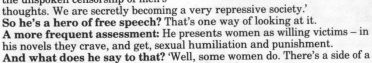

So he's a hero of free speech? That's one way of looking at it.

A more frequent assessment: He presents women as willing victims – in his novels they crave, and get, sexual humiliation and punishment.

And what does he say to that? 'Well, some women do. There's a side of a woman's sexuality that responds to aggression.'

Unlikeliest award: He won the *Guardian* Fantasy Competition in 1978.

Hobbies: Seducing 'big-thighed' students, looking up skirts, etc. (full details in his autobiography, *Memories and Hallucinations*, Gollancz, 1988).

Most shameful boast: That, when he was teaching in Minnesota, he was upbraided by the dean for sleeping with two of his undergraduates; meanwhile, his wife was recuperating from a hysterectomy (ibid.).

Pseuds Corner: On hearing that the US paperback rights to *The White Hotel* had been sold for $200,000 he burst into tears. 'I sobbed from guilt. People died for that!' (ibid.).

Feuds Corner: He was accused in print by Louise Doughty, a young novelist, of an 'excruciating', inept, nudge-wink attempt at seduction under the guise of tuition. He responded with a long, self-justifying account of his experience of Ms Doughty ('I'd really cared'), then said he led her on for 'fun'.

Affectation: Always photographed with a cigarette. Well, it keeps his fingers occupied.

Least likely love match: Andrea Dworkin.

Most likely love match: D. M. Thomas.

Least likely to say: 'How was it for you?'

Emma Thompson

Age: 33.

Appearance: Royal photofit. Anne's mouth, Diana's gait, Windsor jawline and childbearing hips.

Reputation: Thinking man's crumpet.

What it really means: Good looking, but not that good looking.

Achievements before marriage: TV roles in *Tutti Frutti* and *Fortunes of War*. Seemed destined for a lacklustre future as a minor celebrity, with, perhaps, appearances on *Whose Line Is It Anyway?*, *Stop the Week*, a guest slot on *Brookside*.

Bad move: One-woman comedy show in 1988.

Cracked up to be: Bold new post-feminist comedy that did away with macho punchlines.

Critics said: 'Sluggish, self-indulgent and almost totally unfunny.' 'One of the most embarrassing things I have seen on television.'

Good move: Seducing Kenneth Branagh.

Number of times they've been married: Three. As Guy and Harriet Pringle in *Fortunes of War*; as Jimmy and Alison Porter in *Look Back in Anger*; and as themselves at Cliveden.

Postnuptial achievements: Blockbuster film roles in *Dead Again*, *Howards End*, *Henry V*, *Peter's Friends*. Acquired a tan, a sleek new hairdo and a showbiz grin.

Luvvie potential: She said of her panned comedy show: 'It's a little allotment. Above the allotment is a massive, an incredibly beautiful oak tree, and that's Shakespeare.' Carries a copy of Shakespeare's sonnets and Virginia Woolf's *A Room of One's Own* with her wherever she goes. Makes a habit of walking downstairs naked in order to frighten her friend and celebrated celibate Stephen Fry.

Characters she'd be playing if she'd married: (a) Robert De Niro: mob wife with Big Hair; (b) Bruce Willis: mediocre actress who poses naked for *Vanity Fair*; (c) Tom Cruise: pouting babe in a lesbo-erotic thriller.

Obstacles to future success: Too wholesome, too much of a Home Counties bluestocking to be considered in same league as Dench, Jackson or Redgrave.

Why? Not wrecked-looking enough. Her teeth are too good, her skin too healthy, her background too free of emotional trauma to render her interesting enough.

Tip: Live a little.

Ambitions yet to fulfil: Four-page *Hello!* spread chez Branagh.

Projects to consider if it all goes horribly wrong: *Shakespeare! The Musical*. *Good Morning with Ken and Emma*.

Least likely to say: 'God! I wish I'd never married you.'

2 February 1993. Thompson won an Oscar for her performace in *Howard's End*.

Torvill and Dean

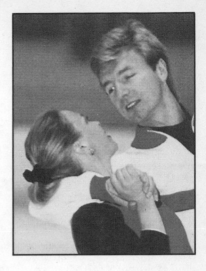

Age: Jayne Torvill's 36, Christopher Dean's 35.

Appearance: Figures on top of a wedding cake.

Occupation: Ice skaters.

Are they anything to do with Tonya Harding? Nothing at all, thankfully.

So why are they in the news? They are about to begin their bid to win the ice dance gold at the Winter Olympics.

Begin their bid? How long does it take? Three days of prime-time viewing, starting with the staggeringly boring compulsory routines and ending with the free dance.

And will they win? We won't know until Monday. In fact, given the complexities of the judging system, we may not even know then. When they triumphed in the European championships in January, everyone was convinced they had come third.

But who can stop our illustrious duo? Various Russians whose names I can never remember.

Do the Brits in Lillehammer need a victory? Let's just say we aren't knee-deep in medals, though we did come 28th in the men's downhill and have high hopes in the four-man bob.

What's the four-man bob? Please, let's do that in four years' time.

There's one thing I don't understand. Didn't they give up competition and turn professional about 10 years ago? What a marvellous memory you have. They bowed out of amateur competition when they won the Olympic title in Sarajevo in 1984, but decided to return following a recent decision to let professionals back into the Games.

I suppose the TV exposure will boost the box office for their exhibition skating? That's a disgraceful suggestion. As they told the *Radio Times* : 'We feel what we're doing is very British – we're doing it for Britain.'

So what will they do after the Olympics? They're planning one final money-spinning tour.

How come they aren't married? The press would love them to be and constantly talk about them as if they were. But marrying other people got in the way.

How to describe them: A fairy-tale couple.

How not to describe them: Borevill and Preen.

Who called them that? They deserve a good horsewhipping: Strangely enough, a writer on the *Guardian*.

Not to be confused with: Orville and Keith Harris, Pearl and Dean.

Most likely to say: 'You grin, I'll bear it.'

Least likely to say: 'I'm not going out there, it's too slippery.'

17 February 1994. T&D were denied a dream end to their Olympic careers, coming third behind the unpronounceable Russians, though of course everyone in Britain considered the result a travesty.

Anthony Trollope

Age: 178.

Appearance: Victorian sage.

Reputation: Growing rapidly: today he is being given the ultimate literary accolade, a memorial stone in Westminster Abbey's Poets' Corner, alongside Chaucer, Milton, Dickens and Wordsworth. Having been written off a generation ago as a third-rater, he has suddenly been promoted to the first rank.

Greatest fan: John Major. He chose *The Small House at Allington* as his desert island book, was involved in the campaign to get Trollope into Poets' Corner and plans to attend this evening's ceremony.

What's the appeal for the PM? Trollope's fictional county of Barsetshire is Mr Major's ideal society: ordered, gentle, supportive; distinct absence of coal mines, no

VAT, not interested in the rest of Europe, in fact barely interested in the neighbouring county.

Any other supporters? Lord Rees-Mogg, founder of the Trollope Society, who said D. H. Lawrence should if necessary be removed from the Abbey to make space.

But what about Trollope? Son of a barrister who went broke; unhappy childhood; went to Harrow – harrowing; mother wrote novels and travel books to pay the bills. Joined the Post Office in 1834 and stayed for 23 years: invented the postbox, set up postal services in Ireland, Egypt and the West Indies. Truly, a man of letters.

Didn't he write the odd novel? Produced his first in 1847, *The Macdermots of Ballycloran*, wrote three in the next 10 years, and then poured out another 43 at the rate of two a year. Wrote two six-volume sequences: *The Chronicles of Barsetshire* and the Palliser novels. Tone grew much darker in the 1870s, culminating in the vision of a morally bankrupt world in *The Way We Live Now*. (Not clear where this stands in the PM's pecking order.) Is thought to have written more words than any other British novelist.

How did he do it? 'It was my custom to write with my watch before me, and to require from myself 250 words every quarter of an hour.' Started writing at 5.30 every morning and wrote during train journeys.

Any other interests? Just a few: ran his own literary journal, the *St Paul's Magazine*; stood as a Liberal in Beverley in 1868 but lost; wrote an account of Caesar's *Commentaries*; produced travel books; hunted three days a week.

Claim to fame: 'I have produced more than twice as much as Carlyle and considerably more than Voltaire.' And, in any case, what did Voltaire ever do for philately?

Least likely to say: 'I'm knackered. I think I'll take the day off.'

Joanna Trollope

Age: 50.
Appearance: Sloane Ranger meets Joyce Grenfell.
Occupation: Writer of bestsellers and laureate of middle England.
Has she written a new one? Happily, no. But an adaptation of her novel *The Rector's Wife* has just started on Channel 4.
Give me the gist: Lovely, brainy, idealistic heroine living in the heart of England is married to a desiccated clergyman; he becomes increasingly withdrawn and dogmatic as his hopes are blighted, and she is drawn towards a dark, tousled, nonconformist . . .
Hang on, that's the Dorothea–Casaubon plot in *Middlemarch*: Well spotted.

Flaubert is in there, too: the Lindsay Duncan character is called Anna Bouverie as a clue for thickies.
So it's wholly drawn from literature, rather than the novelist's own dull and conventional *vie amoureuse*? On the contrary. Once married to a banker who now heads Guinness Mahon, Trollope ran off in her forties with Ian Curteis, a playwright several years her senior.
And now she and Curteis live in an idyllic mill house in a Cotswolds village? Yes, but the poor loves have to rent it, the lease runs out soon and they only switch the heating on when the labradors start shivering.
But she must be loaded. Her last four novels were hugely successful and TV forked out for the rights to all of them? Yes, it's a complete mystery.
This 'Aga saga' jibe – is it fair? Not entirely, as her heroines are usually breaking away from cosy, affluent conformity. But they do tend to inhabit an area bounded by Oxford, Salisbury and Cheltenham, and drive to their romantic trysts in muddy Land Rovers. And Trollope rattles on incessantly in praise of the values of the middle classes, 'the backbone of England'.
So why is she so popular? She says she represents a *fin-de-siècle* 'melancholy thoughtfulness', whereas in the greedy eighties people wanted brazen, raunchy 'escapist blockbusters'.
Like those of her friend and Gloucestershire neighbour Jilly Cooper? Precisely.
Likes: Pets; making the church look nice; baking cakes for the village fête.
Dislikes: Books featuring 'randy apes'; clever critics; chic city-dwelling feminists sent to interview her.
Those Aga saga variants: Gaga saga (Mary Wesley and other oldies). Raga saga (Vikram Seth and other subcontinentals). Lager saga (Nick Hornby and other ' *nouveau* blokes').
Not to be confused with: Anthony Trollope (a distant relative).
Least likely to write: 'Plunging his face into her pubic hair, snuffling as appreciatively as a truffle pig' (© J. Cooper).
Most likely to write: 'She experienced a sensation of glorious blossoming.'

Mike Tyson

Age: 27.

Appearance: Best-looking man on the planet.

Pardon? OK, you tell him.

So he brooks no argument? Iron Mike is not given to Talmudic discussions. He has been able to settle most of his disagreements with the sort of convincing physicality that does not invite a lengthy reply. Away from the bedroom, he is equally persuasive in the boxing ring.

We're skirting around the issue here. Was he not the most feared heavyweight in the world before being banged up two years ago for the rape of a young beauty contestant called Desiree Washington? Yes. But he might be let out of gaol on Monday if he promises to be a good boy and never do it again, as well as offering Miss Washington $1 million by way of compensation.

Will he pay up willingly? Not necessarily. Tyson has always maintained that Desiree did not share with her namesake, George, the Washington penchant for truth.

So, was he guilty? Judge Patricia Gifford didn't believe him when he was sent down, nor did two of the three judges when he appealed last year. Judge Gifford is in the chair again on Monday and Tyson says: 'I'm not holding my breath.'

How's he been spending his time inside? Mike now prefers books to left hooks. He has been learning Chinese and fancies himself as a bit of a philosopher.

Give me a sample. 'That Voltaire was something. They kept putting him in gaol and he kept writing the truth. Unafraid. I love *Candide*.'

Not another beauty contestant, surely? The book, you dolt.

Supposing he gets out on Monday, will he look any different? He's been in the gym every day, according to his friend Chris Eubank, and is close to his fighting weight. He will have one or two adornments, though – a tattoo of Mao on his right arm and Arthur Ashe on his left. 'I love reading about Mao,' he says, 'especially the Long March and all they went through.'

He's found communism then? Don't bank on it. He still wants to get his millions back. His $100 million fortune has been all but eaten up and a bid to regain the world title seems inevitable.

Will he have the calming influence of his former promoter Don King to ease him back into the ring? Tyson told Eubank that he was going to 'start fresh' when he got out – but whether he can break free of King is debatable.

Not to be confused with: Kathy Tyson; Frank Tyson; Franz Thyssen; Tizer.

Favourite Maoism: 'Happiness is a warm thumb in the eye.'

Favourite song: 'Ain't misbehavin' '.

Least likely to say ever again: 'Come up and see me some time.'

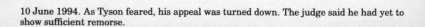

10 June 1994. As Tyson feared, his appeal was turned down. The judge said he had yet to show sufficient remorse.

Gore Vidal

Age: 67.

Appearance: Professional dancer now in twilight years.

Background: Scion of fancy political family; grandfather was Oklahoma's first senator; father was in F.D.R.'s cabinet as aviation administrator; young Gore was youngest American to land a plane (he was 10).

His comment on his background: 'The children of the famous are somewhat different from the children of all the rest, including those of the merely rich.'

Assessment: Has produced vast and fairly readable novels – *Julian, Myra Breckinridge, Burr* – which no one reads. Better known for having scripted *Ben Hur*, for writing essays and for monumental immodesty.

Self-assessment: 'My critics resent everything I represent: sex, wealth and talent.'

The essays: Spends a lot of time balancing epigrams and ostentatiously not splitting infinitives.

Always carries with him: His credit cards, his keys and his learning.

Big theme: The American Empire is in such bad shape that it will not heed Gore's warnings; ergo the American Empire is in really bad shape.

Best phrase: In his celebrated gay novel *The City and the Pillar*, a man's penis is referred to as another man's 'pale quarry'.

What the critics say: 'One had forgotten that English prose could be written like this.'

His biggest enemies: William F. Buckley Jr, and TV evangelist Pat Robertson, who has called him the Antichrist (for his novel *Live from Golgotha*).

Who Gore would like to be in another life: Cassandra; Edith Wharton.

What Gore would like to be in another life: European.

Don't say: 'You're that guy Martin Amis wrote about once . . .'

The Virgin Mary

Age: About 2010.

Appearance: Various. Usually girl-next-door meets Dana. Unless talking about the 167 black madonnas dotted around Europe and the hundreds elsewhere in the world. Then she looks like girl-next-door meets Moira Stuart.

Marital status: Married to Joseph, who did a mean line in bookshelves, and mother of Jesus Christ.

Mother and virgin? So the Bible says. Believers claim it was an immaculate conception.

Can you get that on the NHS? No, although it is free, and a lot more simple than you might imagine. An angel told Mary she had found favour with the Holy Ghost and that was it. She became heavy with child.

Became what? It seems nobody got pregnant in those days. They just put on weight and then had a baby.

Who was this Holy Ghost? God: absentee father, creator of the universe.

Did he fulfil his paternal duties? Well, he never paid maintenance and rarely turned up to see his son if that's what you mean. But then he was quite a difficult person to track down and they didn't have the Child Support Agency then.

What did Joseph make of all this? Joseph was the original New Man. When he first found out, he was a bit miffed. But then an angel came down (useful things, angels), explained what had happened and told him not to worry about it. After that he was fine.

What would Alistair Burt, minister in charge of the Child Support Agency, say? 'As far as I am aware God is not a middle-income earner and so is not on our immediate list of priorities.'

And John Redwood? 'If someone is old enough to father a child he should be old enough to help bring it up.'

Background: Nothing sure is known about Mary's family or where she was born, or what happened to her immediately after Christ's ascension. She lived, it would seem, for her son.

So was she a doting mum? She used to take Jesus on holiday every year to Jerusalem for the feast of Passover, turned up to his first miracle and his crucifixion.

Not to be confused with: Mary Magdalene; Mary Whitehouse; the other Madonna.

Least likely to say: 'No more miracles until you've finished your supper.'

William Waldegrave

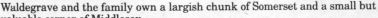

Age: 47.
Appearance: Male escort for the more sophisticated woman.
Position: Chancellor of the Duchy of Lancaster.
What does that mean? He gets to do all the jobs that his colleagues are keen to avoid: introducing the week's Citizen's Charter initiative; explaining why science is underfunded; annoying the Civil Service. Is head of the Office of Public Service and Science (known in Whitehall as OFFPISS).
So is the job important? Opponents don't think so: John Prescott dubbed him Minister for Paper Clips.
Is he well qualified to defend the man in the street? Well, his forebears probably used to own the street. His father is the 12th Earl Waldegrave and the family own a largish chunk of Somerset and a small but valuable corner of Middlesex.
What about his credentials to pioneer open government? Also wobbly. Stands accused of not telling Parliament the ground rules had changed over arms sales to Iraq while he was Minister of State at the Foreign Office. The accusation surfaced at the Scott inquiry on the day he launched his 'open government' White Paper.
Why does he think it was so difficult to maintain the Iraqi arms embargo? 'Screwdrivers are also required to make H-bombs.'
Is he a long-time supporter of open government? Depends what you mean by open government: he wants to change Whitehall's culture rather than introduce a Freedom of Information Act. He says statutory measures are 'not the British way of doing things'.
So what are his qualifications? His presence boosts the cabinet's otherwise lacklustre academic standing. Went to Eton, won scholarship to Oxford, president of the Union, first in Greats, Kennedy fellow at Harvard, fellow of All Souls. Oh, and *Elle* once voted him Britain's sexiest MP.
Did his outstanding academic training bear fruit? In 1977 he wrote *The Binding of Leviathan*, a treatise so dense that, according to Julian Critchley, no Tory had ever been able to finish it.
How do his political skills rate? Gamma minus. Was beaten about the dispatch box by Robin Cook while Secretary of State for Health; made some notable gaffes at the Foreign Office – reminding Israel's leaders of their terrorist predecessors caused a storm; supported the poll tax.
Enthusiasms: Edmund Burke; Aristotle; old cars; tennis; his wife Caroline, who runs the Prue Leith cookery school, and his four young children.
Most likely to say: 'Confidentially . . .'
Least likely to say: 'Just call me Bill.'

21 July 1993. Tipped for the sack in the July 1994 reshuffle but survived to become Secretary of State for Agriculture.

Murray Walker

Age: Youthful 69.
Appearance: Overcooked boiled egg.
Position: BBC's voice of motor racing. Ideal for the job as, rarely pitched at less than a scream, it drowns out the roar of engine noise. Clive James said he always sounded as if his trousers were on fire. The laconic James Hunt has been his commentary partner since 1979, 'the perfect foil for the raving lunatic on his left' according to one pundit.

What friends say about his style: Quick-fire.
What enemies say about his style: Quick, fire.
What James Hunt says about his style: Can I borrow a pair of earplugs?
Background: Father was a top TT rider in the twenties who became a motor sport journalist and commentator. After serving as a wartime tank commander, Walker junior was destined to follow in his tyre tracks. Worked for an ad agency and raced motorbikes in his spare time. Did first commentary in 1949 and has been barking ever since. Has commentated on other sports, including rowing and weightlifting, but high-octane style jarred.
Is he a driven man? Of course he is: 'Most of my reading is things such as *Autosport, Motoring News* and *Motorcycle News*. I am ashamed to say I never read any novels or historical books, or listen to symphonies.' Proudest possession is his BMW 325 Coupé; even his lawn mower has a Ferrari sticker.
King of the cock-up: The Curse of Walker is celebrated each December when the BBC reviews the year in sport. The sequence is always the same: Walker comments that a car is going superbly and seconds later it hits a wall, turns over a dozen times and bursts into flames.
Also king of Colemanballs: A sample: 'Alain Prost is in a commanding second position.' 'There are four different cars filling the first four places.' 'Now Jacques Lafitte is as close to Surer as Surer is to Lafitte.' 'Do my eyes deceive me or is Senna's Lotus sounding a bit rough?'
Doesn't all this mean he's a laughing stock? Not at all: the British love eccentrics, so he has become a national institution. There is a Murray Walker Fan Club, identifiable by T-shirts that read: 'Unless I'm very much mistaken . . . I am very much mistaken.'
Life in the fast lane: Annoyed police by admitting publicly that he drove his BMW at 85mph on motorways. Then had gall to complain that young drivers near his luxury Hampshire home were turning roads into a racetrack.
Life in the fogeyish lane: At the height of Mansell mania, he launched an attack on fans attending the British Grand Prix, lamenting the disappearance of the tweed-jacket brigade and the arrival of flag-waving lager louts.
Least likely to say: 'Could I have a quiet word?'

21 May 1993. James Hunt died of a heart attack in June 1993. Walker remains the linchpin of the BBC's motor racing coverage, now partnered by Jonathan Palmer.

The Warlords

Names: Mohamed Farah Aidid (Somalia, pictured), Ghulam Nabi Noorzai (Afghanistan), General Hersi Morgan (Somalia), Radovan Karadzic (Bosnian Serb), Paulus Vezi (South Africa), General Dudayev (Chechenia), Jaba Ioseliani (Georgia), Ali Dimaporo (Philippines), Lo Hsing-han (Burma), Walid Jumblatt (Beirut, Druze).

Appearance: Rare.

Age: Whatever they say.

Who were the original warlords? The powerful independent military commanders who ruled most of China between 1859 and 1916.

What exactly do warlords do? Use women and children as human shields, take hostages for use as bargaining counters, sign peace agreements and then break them, create internecine strife.

And in their spare time? Thomas Tshabalala, Inkatha chieftain, listens to jazz on CDs.

That Gulbuddin Hekmatyar was a warlord and a half: According to General Abdul Rashid Dostam, no mean warlord himself, he once 'got two Uzbeks and sliced out their noses and eyes and threw them to the lions in the Kabul zoo'.

Essential warlord accessories: Puppet radio station, bodyguards, lair, fiery temper, facial hair (General Dudayev's clipped moustache is said to be modelled on wings of nuclear bomber).

Warlords hate: Helicopter gunships, the UN, white doves.

When is a warlord not a warlord? When he's pro-Western.

Has there ever been a British warlord? The former commander of Britain's troops in Bosnia, Colonel Bob Stewart, has been described as a 'UN warlord'.

What's a warlord's wife called? A battleaxe, according to Colonel Bob's wife.

Is it tough being a battleaxe? Not as tough as being a warlord's son. Tony Franjieh, son of the Beirut warlord Suleiman Franjieh, was killed with 30 family retainers because a rival feared he was being groomed for succession.

Like father like son? Not necessarily. Aidid's son, Hussan Farah, served with the US Marines in Somalia.

Warlord qualifications: Jaba Ioseliani was a professor, Radovan Karadzic was a doctor.

Do say: 'Let slip the Dogs of War.'

Don't say: 'War, what is it good for?'

Least likely to say: 'Make love not war.'

The Duke of Westminster

Full name: Gerald Cavendish Grosvenor.

Nickname: Gussie.

Unsuitable nicknames: Gezza, Wezza, Grozza.

Age: 41.

Profession: Aristocratic landlord.

Appearance: Troubled aristocratic landlord.

Married to: Natalia Phillips.

You mean the daughter of 'Bunny' Phillips, Edwina Mountbatten's lover? The very same.

Home address: Eaton Hall, Cheshire.

Other things he owns: Mayfair, Belgravia, Canada. Most of the Monopoly board except Old Kent Road.

Must be worth a few bob? Between £735 million and £3.5 billion, depending on which estate agent you ask.

Where did the money come from? The fifth baronet, Sir Thomas Grosvenor, who made the prudent decision to marry Mary Davies, heiress to more than 400 acres of smartest London.

Smartest family move: Designating Gerald heir in favour of a clutch of family hopefuls in order to avoid crippling death duties.

Such a rich man could not have a care in the world, could he? *Au contraire.* He is fearfully upset by proposed legislation which would allow leaseholders, including many of his tenants, to buy freeholds to their homes.

How upset? Enough to leave the Conservative Party.

Other controversial things he has done: Declined to swear an oath of allegiance to the Queen when taking up his seat in the House of Lords. Paid thousands of pounds to his workers to help them pay their poll tax.

The Duke on the weighty responsibilities of indecent wealth: 'The easiest thing in the world would be to sell the whole lot up, buy a yacht and sit on it in the Bahamas. But that would not be responsible.'

The Duke on life in the moral quagmire of indecent wealth: 'Given the choice, I would rather not have been born wealthy, but I never think of giving it up. I can't sell. It doesn't belong to me.'

The Duke on the appalling constraints of indecent wealth on the likely career of his son and heir: 'He's been born with the longest silver spoon anyone can have, but he can't go through life sucking on it.'

Things he has in common with Princess Diana: Two O-levels, a sensitive disposition, once knew the Prince of Wales.

Why did his parents veto a career in football? They didn't like the idea of grown men kissing.

Not to be confused with: Cavendish Square; Grosvenor Square; Westminster City Council.

Least likely to say: 'What time's the last tube to Finsbury Park?'

Edith Wharton

Age: Expired at 75 (in 1937).

Profession: Dead writer.

Appearance: Society madame – billowy, lacy dresses concealing a tightly applied corset. Helena Bonham Carter with a graceful walk.

Style: Languorous, involved and full of ironic social observation.

Her corset? Her sentences. Similar to the brain-deadening paragraphs of Henry James, who adored her books.

So why are people talking about her? Martin Scorsese has adapted her novel *The Age of Innocence* for the screen.

Doesn't he make Mafia and boxing movies? True, he has carved out a niche as chronicler of excess testosterone levels in American males (*Mean Streets*, *Taxi Driver*, *Raging Bull*, etc.). He took to the 'tribal ritual' of Wharton's *oeuvre*.

All guns, blood and shiny metal then? More tea parties, French fancies and the odd round of bridge.

And no explicit sex? Well, there's a scene with some flowers . . .

Tell me more: The central character, Newland Archer (played by Daniel Day-Lewis), torn between his naive fiancée and her disreputable cousin, is overtaken by lust in a flower shop, and sends the cousin a bouquet of yellow roses – with a handwritten note.

Shocking! Scandalous. He's breaking all the rules, poor boy. It must have been rough having a bagful of inherited wealth in 19th-century New York – all those matters of taste to attend to between dinner parties.

So it's really a big costume party? Not at all. The Wharton revival began on US campuses. Feminist critics cite her 'brilliant dissections of the construction of subordinate feminity in affluent society'. They've even exhumed scribblings she probably wished were forgotten. Her unfinished novel *The Buccaneers* has just been published with a rudely appended ending and her more obvious anti-Semitic remarks expunged.

She wasn't all sweetness and light then? By no means. She came from a wealthy family but her desire to write immediately put her on the social fringe (her class didn't approve of women showing intelligence).

So she became a nun? Hardly. She left a dull marriage to hook up with bisexual Willam Morton Fulerton, the *Times*'s correspondent in Paris. Fragments of her unpublished erotica even reveal dark incestuous desires.

Will that be filmed? No one has shown any interest yet. But most of the Hollywood film studios have got Wharton projects on line.

Favourite words: Longing, inviolable, inky (as in 'inky draught', which in a rough translation is a cup of tea).

Not to be confused with: Edith Sitwell, a Warburton's brown loaf.

Most likely to say (of Scorsese): 'In appearance his hair seemed matted from the scattered hairs of goats grazing on the Swiss Alps, hiding from view the shadows of despair the critics' displeasure had made on his disportation.'

Least likely to say: 'My new work deals with the sexual desires of a coal miner.'

James Whitaker

Age: 52.

Appearance: A panda on heat.

Nicknames: Answers to sobriquet 'doyen of royal pack' after discovering doyen wasn't an insult. More often known as Fatty, Widow Twanky, the Great Red Tomato.

Background: Minor public schoolboy turned major downmarket hack. Worked for *Daily Mail*, the *Sun* and *Daily Star* before graduating to *Daily Mirror* as the Man Who REALLY Knows the Royals.

So does he know them? Well, he knows their names and can recognise them at a half-mile through binoculars while crouched in Scottish heather next to his faithful cockney snapper, Kent Gavin (Gavs).

Other famous bits of crawling: Through tropical fronds on a West Indian island to capture pictures of pregnant Princess of Wales in swimming costume. On European ski slopes, 1981–93 inclusive. Not bad for a man of 16 stone.

Some claims to fame: First to reveal Lady Diana Spencer would marry the Prince of Wales. First to reveal Princess Diana was living sham marriage.

Truth of claims: False. But he was often a close second.

Major claim to fame: Confidant of Diana for past 13 years.

Truth of claim: Before marriage, when doorstepping Lady Di, he asked her to make up a four at bridge (declined). Bellows regularly to her from behind burly policemen. She sometimes replies: 'Hello, Mr Whitaker.'

Real talent: Self-publicity.

Not to be confused with: Andrew Morton, who broke the real story on Diana, and *Daily Mail*'s Richard Kay, who has spoken at length to her.

Reaction to Morton's book: 'It cannot be true. I Would Have Been Told.'

Original title of latest book: *My Life with Diana.*

Actual writer of book: Christopher Wilson, former Hickey columnist and now at *Today*.

Pack's opinion: Think him pompous and are staggered by his belief in his own myth: 'People in Australia mob me rather than the Princess of Wales.'

Speech pattern: Talks loudly and precisely in headlines and capital letters. Enjoys three-way conversations when interviewing on the telephone; e.g. when talking to Martina Navratilova: 'I Must Put This to You' (to news editor: 'I'm Asking Her Now'). 'Martina, I Have to Put This to You – Are You a Lesbian?' (to whole office: 'She's Put the Phone Down').

Apart from Diana, real loves: Drinking wine, backing horses, buying presents for fiery Polish wife Iwona, investing in the stock market.

Recent attitude to *Mirror* colleagues: 'I Don't Know What They're Complaining About. I've Got a Huge Rise.'

Least likely to say: 'Up the Republic!'

Jimmy White

Age: 32.

Appearance: Pensive bridegroom at shotgun wedding.

Occupation: Perpetual runner-up in world snooker championships; latest challenge is to take on Stephen Hendry in fifth consecutive final.

Nicknames (traditional): The Whirlwind; the Housewives' Choice; Simply the Best; Tooting's Teenage Tearaway.

Nicknames (updated): The Zephyr; the Grannies' Favourite; Good Each-Way Value; Bagshot's Balding Bourgeois.

Is he a reformed character then? Very much so. The glass at his side is no longer filled with four fingers of Stolichnaya vodka; he takes more time over his breaks; and the tales of all-night card games during tournaments and benders lasting a fortnight are fewer. It's a heartening example of a player made mature by repeated failure.

But wasn't he recently sentenced to 120 hours' community service for driving when four times over the alcohol limit? A minor downward blip on a steep upward curve.

And his wife Maureen kicked him out, attacking his 'scumming hangers-on'? OK, two blips. Anyway, the sport has a tradition of hell-raising.

Refresh my memory: Kirk Stevens was a coke fiend; Bill Werbeniuk needed 18 pints of lager per day to steady his cue arm; and White's hero and former doubles partner Alex Higgins was punished for head-butting an official and threatening to shoot fellow player Dennis Taylor. He also once greeted Hendry with the words: 'Hello, I'm the Devil.'

Ah, yes, Hendry. He's unbeatable, isn't he? Depends whether you assume White was permanently scarred by the 1992 final, which coincided with his 30th birthday: leading 14–8, he watched the Scotsman take the next 10 frames and victory. Hendry has a broken arm but that could even be an advantage: the soccer player Danny Blanchflower sometimes wore a sling to psych opponents out.

Rent-a-cliché (© Whispering Ted Lowe): 'Jimmy's problem is that one session where he falls asleep'; 'The best player never to be world champion'; 'Can he ever overcome the psychological block of five losing finals?'

Thought for the Day: 'In which other pastime posing as a sport can a man compete with distinction at the highest level while suffering from a broken arm?' (Patrick Collins, *Mail on Sunday*).

Not to be confused with: Barry White; Billy Wright; Patrick White; Australian White.

Most likely to say: "92? It's completely blocked out, honest.'

Least likely to say: 'Just orange juice for me, Alex, I'm driving.'

2 May 1994. White lost a nail-biting match 18–17, missing a simple black that he said he would 'normally have potted blindfold'. Has vowed to return next year – presumably with a blindfold.

Doctor Who

Age: He's a Time Lord, so birthdays don't count for much.

Television age: 30 on 23 November 1993.

Appearance: Changeable, to say the least. Has taken the earthly form of actors William Hartnell, Patrick Troughton, Peter Cushing, Jon Pertwee, Tom Baker, Peter Davison, Colin Baker and Sylvester McCoy.

Occupation: Saving the world. Scaring kids on Saturday evenings.

Why is he in the news? (1) Steven Spielberg is rumoured to be discussing a new multi-million-pound *Doctor Who* series with BBC1 supremo Alan Yentob. (2) The BBC has made a 30th anniversary episode with five of the old docs.

Where is the *Tardis* travelling for this celebration? In a curious leap through space and time – and TV genres – it arrives in the middle of the *EastEnders* set for a soap and sci-fi drama. It's all to do with the BBC's *Children in Need* appeal.

Is there a whiff of controversy? *Doctor Who* fans have been threatening to exterminate BBC controllers ever since the last episode was made in 1989. Particularly as, since then, BBC Enterprises has made nearly £10 million selling *Doctor Who* videos, cassettes, magazines and pinball tables.

Who will play the Doctor in the Spielberg version? Not decided yet, but the actor must be quirky, charismatic and have the wisdom of the spheres.

That's Tom Cruise and Richard Gere out then? We can but hope. In an ideal world we might be talking about Sean Connery or Leo McKern. The smart money is on David *Baywatch* Hasselhoff.

Can you see the Cybermen in wet lycra cut to the hip? The wet lycra role usually falls to what we earthlings call the Doctor's Young Friend.

What about some new villains to replace the Daleks? I favour the Yentobs, small bearded creatures who, led by a powerful bearded American known only as the Auteur, threaten to flood the world with cute children and special effects. Or the Michael Jacksons – faceless dictators from planet BBC2 who brainwash us with incessant repeats of sixties TV series.

Who was the best Doctor? Dangerous ground here. Orthodoxy would suggest Tom Baker but he married – and divorced – his Young Friend, Lalla Ward, thus ruining the Time Lords' chaste reputation. I'd go for Patrick Troughton: not too camp and with a nice line in recorder playing.

Not to be confused with: Jon Pertwee playing Worzel Gummidge; Peter Davison playing that vet; Dr David Owen playing at being the leader of a political party.

Least likely to say: 'Beam me up Scotty.'

Most likely to say: 'Come my dear, let me show you my *Tardis*.'

William of Orange

Age: 343.

Appearance: Regal, but with bits of paint peeling off his nose.

Occupation: Ruler of the Netherlands, King of England from 1689 to 1702, hero of Protestantism and hammer of the Irish.

This is all terribly interesting but why is he in the news? Is he on a walkabout in Australia or something? Don't be facetious. *The Encyclopaedia of Homosexuality* has claimed him as one of its own.

You mean there was something he wasn't telling his devoted wife Mary? The two-volume 1,500-page tome alleges affairs with fellow Dutchman William Bentinck, handsome young soldier Arnout Joust Van Keppel, whom he made Earl of Albermarle, and numerous officers of the bedchamber.

Did William spend a lot of time in the bedchamber? Not much. He was usually to be found on the field of battle, fighting an almost perpetual war against Louis XIV of France.

Ah, the Fun King: The Sun King, actually.

Who won? It's not quite clear. It was one of those rolling, continent-wide, multi-treaty wars of shifting alliances and shifty allies that were a speciality of the 17th and 18th centuries.

But at least William got England? Yes, thanks to the Glorious Revolution that rid the country of the dogmatic Catholicism of James II.

And the Irish? Their resistance was broken by William at the Battle of the Boyne in 1690.

The glorious 12 July, venerated by Orangemen everywhere? Yes, except the battle took place on 1 July.

And what do the bowler-hatted bastions of morality think of the suggestion that William was gay? They are not amused. The Rev. Ian Paisley, who has campaigned under the slogan 'Save Ulster from Sodomy', calls it 'a slander put about by Romanists'.

Any counter-evidence? The obligatory mistress, Elizabeth Villiers.

Children? No, but remember he was hardly ever there.

Not to be confused with: William the Conqueror; William Rufus (who was certainly homosexual); William the Silent; William the Just.

Don't you mean Just William? Ah, yes.

Most likely to say: Something impenetrable in Dutch.

Least likely to say: 'What are you doing tonight, Louis?'

Most likely to be a relief to: John Major. At least this is one scandal that doesn't concern his government, though the *Daily Mirror* ('Kinky King Was Really a Queen') is looking for a link.

Oh, I forgot to ask, why was he called William of Orange? Perhaps there are some questions better left unanswered.

Barbara Windsor

Age: 56.
Occupation: Actress, star of countless Carry Ons, professional cockney.
Appearance: Peroxide dwarf.
You can't say that: We didn't. Sue Knight did.
Who's she? Ronnie Knight's wife.
Who's Ronnie Knight? I can see this is going to take a bit of explaining. Ronnie is Barbara's former husband. They split up a decade ago after 21 years of marriage when Ronnie fled to Spain to evade arrest on a £6 million robbery charge. He then married Sue but has now come home, driven, according to Babs, by his obsessional love for her. Sue has reached for the vitriol and the affair has naturally been dubbed the Knight of the Wronged Wives.

And was it passion that was driving him? No, it was burly representatives of the *Sun*, who have brought Knight back from his Spanish poolside to face the music.
Wow. How did the *Sun* manage that? Cunning strategy, feats of derring-do, bravery over and above the call of duty? The waving of a magic chequebook may have been a factor: Mr Knight is reported to have received £40,000-plus for rights to his surrender story.
Was it worth it? On the face of it, no. Sun, sea and sangria have been replaced by slopping out: he is now on remand in Brixton Prison.
What about Babs? She must be mortified: Absolutely. 'This has brought all the old memories flooding back. I can barely sleep.'
So she'll be there at visiting time? Not necessarily. 'There is no way I would ever want to live with that man again. He is living in cloud-cuckoo land.'
These Windsors are always getting into marital difficulties: Babs is not thought to be one of *the* Windsors. In fact, her background is about as far removed from Buck House as you can get.
You mean tough but lovable East Enders, pearly queens, pub sing-songs, good times, bad times: You're getting the idea. She was born in Shoreditch, the daughter of a market trader. Went on the stage at 13; did a song-and-dance stint in Soho; had a fling with Charlie Kray ('The most gentlemanly man I've ever met'); was a protégée of Joan Littlewood, and appeared in everything from Bart to Brecht before finding fame and fortune in *Carry On Spying* in 1964.
And what was the secret of her success? I'd been dreading that question. Let's just say she was very upfront.
You mean she has enormous tits? How vulgar. We'll be getting letters from Jonathan Miller. She does admit her boobs are 'a trademark', though.
Not to be confused with: Diana Dors, Dolly Parton, Windsor Castle.
Most likely to say: 'Ron, wot you doin' 'ere? I though you done a runner.'
Least likely to say: '*Bienvenida*, Ronnie.'

Michael Winner

Age: 57.
Appearance: Too many dinners.
Latest campaign: Better dinners!
Favourite journey: The walk to the dining table.
A dinner too far: 'Heart Op for Frisky Old Mr Death Wish' announced in the *News of the World*.
Death Wish 1: Too many cigars.
Death Wish 2: Too much food.
Death Wish 3: No exercise. 'I've been a bloody fool,' Winner reflected. But in the *Sunday Times*, as the scourge of restaurateurs, he was back on the snaffle, describing a quest for extra egg on his pizza.
His struggle: Son of millionaire father and gambling mother who depleted his fortune by losing £3 million at the Cannes casino. At 13, he was syndicating a column,

'Michael Winner's Show Talk', to 35 newspapers. At 16, he was asked to leave a Quaker school. He'd been paying another boy to clean his room. After Cambridge, Winner got into films, shooting his first feature, *This Is Belgium*, in East Grinstead. The rest is history.

Oh, no, it isn't. OK, then he grew up and made over 30 films, becoming, according to the new Olympus camera adverts, 'the most successful living British film director'.

Eh? You know – *Scorpio, I'll Never Forget What's'isname, Won Ton Ton the Dog That Saved Hollywood, Lawman, Death Wish, Scream for Help*, etc.

Strange but True 1: Winner has a low sperm count, stole money at school (now refunded), has nine toilets and successfully sued the *Sunday Correspondent* for calling him 'kinky'.

Strange but True 2: Passionately abhors violent crime (founding the Police Trust, supporting Guardian Angels) – and passionately defends violent films.

A rare flop: His capacious Y-fronts, which failed to impress kiss 'n' tell actress Simone Hyams, despite costing £34 from Lanvin.

Hobbies: Writing to newspapers, making table mats, being difficult.

Scream for Help: Winner advises diners to attract waiters by smacking the tabletop, shouting ''Ere!', or waving napkins high in the air.

Does this work? He has just been banned from a country hotel. The owner said: 'I've never met a more rude, arrogant son of a bitch. I'll never have him back.'

Most likely to say: 'It's a remake of *The Fly*, set in a bowl of soup.'

Least likely to say: 'It's a remake of *The Quince Tree Sun*, but without all the violence.'

Terry Wogan

Age: 54.

Appearance: Small-time villain from *The Sweeney* now in retirement on Costa del Crime.

But what is that growth on the top of his head? Unquestionably all his own hair – after all, he paid for it himself. But it certainly looks like a 'weave'.

Broadcasting style: Cloying whimsicality mixed with chirpy self-deprecation, his pantomime Irishman act includes the phrases 'Jeez' and 'yer man' but stops just short of 'begorra' and 'to be sure'.

Latest venture: Has just released (for charity) a *Best of Wogan* compilation album of songs performed on his now defunct BBC chat show.

Credentials as judge of popular music: His greatest success was 'The Floral Song', and also released 'Me and the Elephant', a lesser hit.

Background: Grew up in Limerick the son of a grocery store manager, but his claims of a Jesuitical upbringing must be questioned. Any self-respecting Jesuit would have knocked all the nonsense out of him very swiftly. Worked as bank clerk before going into Irish TV, then joined BBC. Lives in £2 million house in Berkshire with wife Helen; three children.

Current job: Back in his old Radio 2 morning slot.

Why was his chat show axed? You never saw it then?

No: Suffice it to say that Andrew Lloyd Webber appeared nine times, and Cliff Richard eight, and its ratings were regularly beaten by *Praise Be*.

Finest interview: George Best on his richest form. Terry seemed astonished that Bestie appeared a little the worse for wear having been fulsomely entertained in the hospitality room.

Worst interview: Madonna, with whom Wogan was so star-struck that he made Jonathan Ross's effort, itself in the first rank of sycophancy, look like Jeremy Paxman with piles.

Other high spots: Wogan to Anne Bancroft: 'Why do you hate this interview so much? Is it me?' Bancroft (not joking): 'Probably.'

Salary: Reputed to have plummeted from £400,000 to a poverty-line £120,000.

Interests: Tennis, golf, self-congratulatory charity work.

But is he in the vanguard of feminist thinking? Not quite. 'Just take Selina Scott and Joanna Lumley. Both dynamite, aren't they? Great legs.'

A rare attempt at wit from Prince Philip: 'The only difference between Terry Wogan and the M1 is that you can turn off the M1.'

What people say about Wogan: 'He always does the Eurovision so brilliantly.'

What Wogan says about Wogan: 'I'm the greatest con man in television. Everyone thinks I'm brilliant. In fact I'm nothing of the sort.'

Woodrow Wyatt

Age: 74.
Appearance: Cross between Rumpole and Denis Thatcher.
Position: Chairman of the Tote. 'Voice of Reason' in the *News of the World*.
Background: Son of prep school proprietor, who took instant dislike to his offspring. Rebellion against father took form of joining Labour Party at Oxford. Became MP at 27 after decent war. Gadfly political career spoiled by ease with which he made enemies and by propensity for philandering. Lost seat in 1970, but had already developed second, more successful career as writer and broadcaster. Cruised the world for *Panorama* and became household name. Started small newspaper chain and once confessed he would really have liked to have been Rupert Murdoch.

Damascene conversion: Wrote 1977 article in *Daily Express* damning Labour and announcing he would vote Conservative in future. Since then has written virulently right-wing columns and became trusted friend and adviser of Mrs Thatcher.

Voice of Reason: Wyatt has been obsessed by thoughts of Reds in the unions and at the BBC for as long as anyone can remember. Devoted his latest Lords speech on the subject to attack on Liz Forgan. Said she was 'a fearsome lady' not fit to be in charge of political programmes though 'she might do well on gardening programmes'. Believes Jeremy Paxman is a sinister threat to society. Constantly plugs Sky TV in his column. Says anyone who thinks he does this because he works for Rupert Murdoch 'has to be nuts'.

Love life: Prodigious, at least by his own account. Has been married four times (though only confesses to two in *Who's Who*). His autobiography charts numerous affairs, including with a 17-year-old Muslim girl 'like a soft, ripe peach'. Says: 'Man's biological function is to impregnate the highest possible number of females.'

Family: Had a son, Pericles, in 1963. Arranged for him to be given to childless relation soon after birth. When son was 4 Wyatt remarried and decided to have son back. Daughter, Petronella, is a fragrant hack on the *Sunday Telegraph*, where she is darling of the Worsthorne College set.

Why does he wear a bow tie? Because he spills his food, and shirts are easier to clean than normal ties.

So is he a complete buffoon? Not at all. Frank Johnson has described him as the age's 'single most influential person'. His influence lies in access to powerful people. Powerful people doubtless attracted by his close friendship with Mrs Thatcher.

Friends say: 'You couldn't like him. But you can be fond of him.'

Enemies say: 'The trouble with Woodrow is that most people find him obnoxious and he cannot understand why' (Joe Haines).

Least likely to say: 'I don't have an opinion on that subject.'

Boris Yeltsin

Age: 62.
Appearance: A heavy in a James Bond film.
Position: President of Russia.
Nicknames: Tsar Boris, the second Gorbachev, Boris the Brave, Brinkman Boris.
Background: Born the son of peasants in Butko, a village in the province of Sverdlovsk. Bright pupil and star volleyball player. Attended Urals Technical Institute. Worked as an engineer in the construction industry. Joined Communist Party in 1961; steady rise to head party in Moscow by 1985. Attacks on apparatchiks weakened his position, forcing him to resign in 1987. Won seat in Congress of People's Deputies in 1989, became President of the Russian Parliament a year later, and the first directly elected President of Russia in June 1991.
Friends say: He saved Russian democracy by standing on a tank, and has done much to reduce the number of nuclear missiles.
Enemies say: He is two-faced, authoritarian, vacillating and has sold out to Western ideas. Frequent assassination attempts.
What the man on the Minsk omnibus thinks: As long as there is bread in the shops, I don't care who's in charge.
Worst moment: Humiliation by Gorbachev ('He murdered me with words') when he lost the leadership of Moscow Communist Party.
Finest moment: Humiliating Gorbachev in Parliament as the world watched on television.
Enthusiasms: Vodka (he was seen being carried on to a plane), cooking, volleyball, Western aid. The goods and chattels he inherited from Gorbachev. A dacha owned by Stalin. Referenda.
Health: Disappears for reasons of ill-health (vodka?) without giving any notice. Has had a heart attack.
Missing parts: Two fingers on left hand that he lost playing with a grenade as a boy.
Enemies: Ruslan Khasbulatov, Alexander Rutskoi, hyper-inflation.
Friends: Parts of the army, reformist Russians, the West.
Most likely to say: 'Après moi, le déluge.'
Least likely to say: 'No thanks, I'm driving.'

Tim Yeo

Age: 48.

Occupation: Environment minister, and Tory MP for Suffolk South since 1983.

Appearance: His pot-belly sticks out from a list of undistinguished features.

Family man? Sure. Married for 23 years with grown-up children.

Why is he in the news? He has admitted fathering an illegitimate child, born in July 1993 to Julia Stent, a solicitor and Conservative councillor in Hackney whom he met nine months previously at the Tory conference.

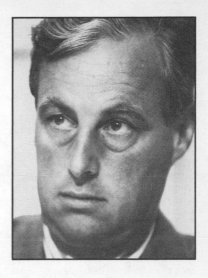

What was he doing at that conference? Organising his own unofficial one-to-one fringe meeting, by the sound of it. And not listening properly to what was being said on the platform about family values.

And officially? At the time he was, as Parliamentary Under Secretary of State for Health, one of Virginia Bottomley's underlings. Social work, including the issues of children and community care, were part of his brief.

So he should be an expert on one-parent families? Certainly. The *News of the World* says he had this to say to his local branch of Relate: 'It is in everyone's interests to reduce broken families and the number of single parents. I have seen from my own constituency the consequences of marital breakdown.'

What about his own background? No hint that he would go so rashly astray in middle life. His father was a doctor; he was educated at Charterhouse and Cambridge.

Will the Tory Party forgive him? Hard to say. He's not valued by Major in the same way that Parkinson was by Thatcher; nor does he have Parky's local popularity.

Will his boss in the Environment Department forgive him? That's the high-minded John Gummer, not given to compromise on matters of personal morality. Ironically, he might have got more sympathy from his former boss, Mrs Bottomley, who was herself briefly a single parent.

Will the Child Support Agency be getting on his case? Apparently not. He is paying maintenance and Miss Stent has issued a statement in which she says: 'I am in full-time employment and neither I nor my daughter are a burden on the state.'

Least likely next appointment: Minister for Family Values.

Not to be confused with: Popular greeting in black street slang.

Haven't you got any better quips than that about him? Get real – Peter Carter-Ruck is his solicitor.

27 December 1993. Yeo attempted to tough out the scandal but 10 days later bowed to pressure and resigned his ministerial post.

The Duke of York

A.k.a.: Andrew Albert Christian Edward. Not to be confused with Edward Antony Richard Louis (younger brother).

Nicknames: Randy Andy; the Petulant Prince.

Status: Fourth in line to throne; father of two; divorcé-to-be.

Looks like: Essex Man who sells Rollers in a West End car showroom.

Latest role: Starring part as royal PR person in *Windsor's Burning*. Got rave reviews from media for his informed, cooperative performance.

Most immortal line: 'Her Majesty is devastated.'

Last big role: Started as co-star in *The Fergie Saga*. Recently relegated to walk-off part in same series.

Next big role: If the royals follow up their success in *It's a Knockout*, he'll lead the Windsor Gladiators.

Character: Followed his father to Gordonstoun and into the navy without becoming as objectionable as Prince Philip. Likes a joke, usually his own. Said to be oafish, unbookish, bit of a leg man. Also potentially rather nice – sweet, even. But hung up on class. Unquestionably brave as helicopter pilot in the Falklands War. And at the weekend joined a human chain of lackeys to get heirlooms out of danger. Also kept the Queen informed from the fire-front 'until the battery in my portable phone packed up'.

Luckiest break: Being born to HM and Phil when everyone thought they were sticking to single beds.

Latest lucky break: 11.37 last Friday morning. Was first royal to spot smoke pouring out of private chapel in Windsor Castle.

Unluckiest breaks: Koo Stark and Sarah Ferguson.

What his mum said about him at the weekend: 'Thank God for Andrew. He is there and in charge.'

What his mother-in-law (Mrs Susan Barrantes) is alleged to have said about him: 'Andrew is a good-looking boy and has a heart of gold – to the point where he would be without any money himself to help someone. But he has not got any character. Absolutely none.'

What he really needs: His own ship and a good woman.

Most impertinent public question: When ITN's royal correspondent breached protocol in April and asked him: 'Any chance of a reconciliation, sir?' Hack hustled away by police.

Most embarrassing public moment: When press photographers persuaded a bystander to put on a Fergie mask and walk up to him when he was visiting Merseyside.

What he'll never say: 'I need a telephoto lens to take some family snaps. What do you recommend?' (To an assistant in a photographic shop.)

Vladimir Zhirinovsky

Age: 47.
Appearance: Disturbing/disturbed.
Crazy name, crazy guy? Indeed.
Known to many as Volodya
Zhirinazi, his patronymic is,
embarrassingly, Wolfovich.
Why embarrassingly? He is a
rampant pro-Russian nationalist, as
anti-Semitic as he is anti-everyone
else, and Wolfovich sounds like a
Jewish name. Born in Kazakhstan,
Zhirinovsky once explained: 'My
mother was Russian, my father was
a lawyer.'
Occupation: Leader of Russia's
Liberal Democratic Party, which has
just done remarkably well in the
Russian elections.
So is he a liberal then? Not
exactly. For instance, he believes
that Russia's 20 million Muslims
should migrate to Asia, since they
are spreading diphtheria via rotten fruit, and that summary executions
should be adopted to stem crime.
A democrat? Sadly not. One of his favourite slogans is 'Less democracy!
More economy!'
An economist? No, an ex-lawyer, but his popularity rests largely on the fact
that most Russians are dissatisfied with Gorbachev's and Yeltsin's harsh
economic reforms which Zhirinovsky says he would reverse. Both vodka and
brassiere prices, he claims, would fall if he were in power.
He likes the idea of power? Loves it. He is publicity mad, constantly
holding press conference breakfasts in the Iraqi embassy in Moscow,
sometimes on New York time to make live transmission easier.
So, he's pro-Iraqi? Strangely, considering his passionate xenophobia, yes.
He dispatched 10 soldiers to Iraq to fight the American aggressor and has
great respect for Saddam Hussein.
Not much of a one for the West then? Not much of a one for anyone. He
thinks Western aid is part of the hated economic colonisation. Britain should
'watch out', the Baltics should be made part of Russia again, and the
republics 'will beg us to take them back'.
Japan? 'I would nuke them.'
Is there anything good about him? He does raise the issues that your
average Russian cares about – the ghastly economic situation and the 'rape'
(gang rape is his favourite metaphor) of Russia by the West. Oh, and he likes
Yeltsin's constitution.
Not to be confused with: Alessandra Mussolini.
Most likely to say: Death to America, Israel, Turkey, Estonia, etc., etc. . . .
Least likely to say: Love thy neighbour.